BORDEAUX / BURGUNDY

*The publisher gratefully acknowledges
the generous contribution to this book provided
by the Literature in Translation Endowment Fund
of the University of California Press Foundation, which is
supported by a major gift from Joan Palevsky.*

· · · · ·

*Publié avec le concours du Ministère français
chargé de la culture, Centre National du Livre.*

*Published with the assistance of the French Ministry
of Culture's National Center for the Book.*

BORDEAUX / BURGUNDY

A Vintage Rivalry

Jean-Robert Pitte

Translated by M. B. DeBevoise

UNIVERSITY OF CALIFORNIA PRESS

Berkeley   Los Angeles   London

University of California Press, one of the most distinguished
university presses in the United States, enriches lives around the
world by advancing scholarship in the humanities, social sciences,
and natural sciences. Its activities are supported by the UC Press
Foundation and by philanthropic contributions from individuals
and institutions. For more information, visit www.ucpress.edu.

University of California Press
Berkeley and Los Angeles, California

University of California Press, Ltd.
London, England

Library of Congress Cataloging-in-Publication Data

Pitte, Jean-Robert
  [Bordeaux/Bourgogne. English]
  Bordeaux/Burgundy : a vintage rivalry / Jean-Robert Pitte ;
translated by M.B. DeBevoise.
      p.   cm.
  Translated from French.
  Originally published: Paris : Éditions Hachette Littératures,
2005.
  Includes bibliographical references and index.
  ISBN: 978-0-520-24940-0 (cloth : alk. paper)
  1. Wine and wine making—France—Bordeaux—History.
2. Wine and wine making—France—Burgundy—History.
3. Viticulture—France—Bordeaux. 4. Viticulture—France—
Burgundy. I. Title.
TP553.P5713 2008
641.2′209447144—dc22   2007034023

Manufactured in the United States of America

17 16 15 14 13 12 11 10 09 08
10 9 8 7 6 5 4 3 2 1

"Your Honor," an old marquise of the Faubourg Saint-Germain once asked, from her end of the table to the other, "which do you prefer, a wine from Bordeaux or from Burgundy?"

"Madame," the magistrate who was thus questioned answered in a druidic tone, "that is a trial in which I so thoroughly enjoy weighing the evidence that I always put off my verdict until the next week."

Jean-Anthelme Brillat-Savarin,
The Physiology of Taste (Varieties XXI)

CONTENTS

MAPS

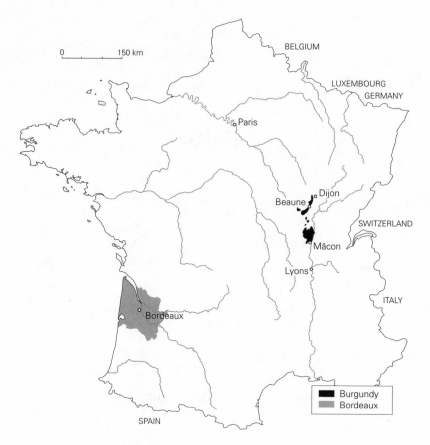

Map 1. Bordeaux and Burgundy.

PREFACE TO
THE AMERICAN EDITION

It is to the cause of reconciliation among the fraternal enemies of the lands of the Saône and the Yonne, on the one hand, and those of the Garonne, the Dordogne, and the Gironde, on the other, that these pages aspire to make a contribution. They owe much to the innumerable viticulturalists and wine professionals whom I have met in both regions since 1966, the date of my first memorable harvests at Chorey-lès-Beaune, and to all the tastings that I have shared with them. These pages draw a part of their inspiration as well from roots planted for a time on the slope of Villars-Fontaine, a beautiful and promising corner of the Hautes-Côtes-de-Nuits that I discovered one day in June 1986 thanks to André Noblet, cellar master at Domaine de la Romanée-Conti, on the eve of his premature passing. André had a gift for bringing together like-minded people. His talent survives.

Unlike Bernard Frank, I fell in with Burgundy when I was quite young, and so my side seemed to have been chosen from the outset. But I have learned since to put some Bordeaux in my wine (to reverse Frank's memorable phrase), and I am all the better for it! From the bottom of my heart I thank my teachers, colleagues, and students of geography, who have helped me to learn more about the wines of Bordeaux, Burgundy, and other regions in France, on which they are—or, alas, were—authorities: Sylvaine Boulanger, Marie-Pierre Cerveau, Henri Enjalbert, Rolande Gadille, Gérald-Jack Gilbank, François Guichard, Françoise Grivot (Sister Marie-Françoise, OCD, Carmel de Beaune), Jean-Claude Hinnewinkel, Alain and Christian Huetz de Lemps, François Legouy, Sophie Lignon-Darmaillac, René Pijassou, Michel Réjalot, Philippe Roudié, and Raphael Schirmer, among others. Their work has honored the memory of Roger Dion, who remains their master and mine, while challenging or qualifying some of his arguments. I have learned much from reading these authors, from tramping about the vineyards in their company, from chatting and drinking with them in good humor. May they be so kind as to forgive me if I dissent from one or another of their conclusions. Mine, like theirs, can only be provisional: thus the rule of scientific research. The aim of this brief volume is in no way to provoke or to settle scores. It seeks as far as possible, and without undue illusion, to sharpen the critical spirit.

Trying to penetrate the mysteries of two wine civilizations as different from each other, and yet as similar, as Bordeaux and Burgundy involves the same difficulty as trying to understand England and France. This is not wholly accidental, of course. Fortunately for Europe no less than for French viticulture, the centennial celebration in 2004 of the Entente Cordiale did little to erase the differences between the two countries, which in some ways resemble squabbles between two brothers—the result sometimes of real disagreement, sometimes of affectionate rivalry. Bordeaux and Burgundy are indisputably two opposite civilizations, two distinct ways of feeling. And yet, for all of this, they are united in their ambition to produce the best wines in the world. For what does the plainspoken native of the Burgundy countryside have in common with the sophisticated city dweller of Bordeaux if not a shared passion for excellence?

Bordeaux and Burgundy diverge in any number of ways. Not only do grape varieties differ between the two regions, but the practice of blending wines of the same vintage (or the refusal to do this) distinguishes their growers and merchants, who have in any case never sought to appeal to the same customers: Bordeaux has always made wines for export to the British Isles and northern Europe; Burgundy for a continental clientele of differing tastes and backgrounds. And yet there are similarities as well. Vineyards in each of the two regions have benefited over the centuries from influential patrons and prestigious commissions. The effect of this has been to encourage their owners to bring out the best qualities of their land (as also in Champagne, but to a much smaller extent in the other wine-producing regions of France). Alas, both Bordeaux and Burgundy have from time to time in the course of their history betrayed the confidence that has been placed in them. In recent decades, however, both have elected to reserve a significant part of their production for high-quality wines, keeping the needs of the land in mind—France's only choice, looking to the future, if it hopes to go on exporting its wines to the rest of the world.

This is the whole point of preserving the agricultural traditions of local wines, what are often called *vins de terroir* (though sometimes, it must be admitted, they are not very good), as opposed to the production of standardized wines by industrial methods, *vins technologiques* (which nonetheless can be very good indeed). When a wine is made from living soil, from vines cultivated with minimal reliance on chemical agents, with a view to achieving the smallest possible yield, using perfectly ripe grapes and techniques of vinification that are both strict and gentle, the grape variety disappears from view, leaving only the land, which in the case of Bordeaux and Burgundy is incomparably fine. For the educated and attentive wine lover, the pleasures are immense.

France invented local wines. It must not abandon them now simply because poor prophets have insisted that the multiplicity of its controlled appellations, by blurring the image of these wines in the public mind, is harmful to commerce, and that this system must therefore be renounced in favor of a small number of more easily produced and marketed brands. Burgundy's system of microappellations and microvintages is complex, everyone agrees; but this is not a defect, because it opens up a marvelous universe of nuances that a lifetime is scarcely enough to analyze—much less appreciate! Nor is the world of five thousand châteaux in Bordeaux, a few hundred of which are devoted to excellence, easy for consumers to understand. Even so, France has every reason to remain attached to so many different styles. They are, of course, a legacy of the past, a patrimony, in fact; but they have the additional and immense advantage, thanks to the talents of their makers, of being alive, of developing from year to year.

In the meantime, still fiercely attached to the peculiarities of their culture, jealously protective of the surpassingly rich assets that nature has bestowed upon each of their regions, and blinded by the rival passions that prevent them from seeing how many things they have in common, Bordelais and Burgundians continue to show little more than disdain for each other. If only they would take the time to examine these passions, and try to understand them, one may hope that one day they will come to respect each other, and to get along for once rather than forever go on squabbling.

CHAPTER 1
WEIGHING THE EVIDENCE

The famous anecdote of the Faubourg Saint-Germain told by Brillat-Savarin, which I have used as an epigraph, reveals an educated and eclectic connoisseur who varies his wines to suit the food he eats, the weather, and his mood. Brillat-Savarin himself, another amiable judge, delighted in having been born in Belley, at the gates of the ancient capital of the Gauls, a land superbly irrigated by all the fine red wines of France: "Lyons is a town of good living: its location makes it rich equally in the wines of Bordeaux and Hermitage and Burgundy."[1] He does not say that these wines were frequently mixed in the secrecy of the *négociant*'s warehouse, a practice that was already venerable in his time and that one hopes has now, at the beginning of the twenty-first century, finally ceased.

Many poets, bacchic or other, have sung of their fondness for Bordeaux and Burgundy. Thus André Chénier, on the eve of the Revolution:

> On the blessed banks of Beaune and Aï,
> In rich Aquitaine, and the lofty Pyrenees,
> From their groaning presses flow streams
> Of delicious wines ripened on their slopes.[2]

Even if Thomas Jefferson passionately loved the great wines of Bordeaux, he also had a high regard for those of Burgundy, which we know he thoroughly enjoyed on passing through the Côte d'Or in March 1787.[3] In the early nineteenth century, the chansonnier Marc Antoine Désaugiers traveled as far without leaving home:

> Friends, it is in preferring
> The bottle to the carafe
> That the most ignorant man
> Becomes a good geographer.[4]

> Beaune, land so highly praised,
> Chablis, Mâcon, Bordeaux, Grave,
> With what exquisite pleasure
> I visit you in my cellar![5]

And thus, a bit later, the bard of good food and wine, Charles Monselet:

> It is one o'clock in the afternoon
> When all the fine wines meet at a feast,
> The fraternal hour when Lafite appears
> In the company of Chambertin.

> No more quarrels now
> Among these valiant friends;
> No more ill feelings
> Between Gascons and Burgundians . . .

> They have shed their cleverness
> Without forsaking their style.
> —After you, monsieur de Lur-Saluces!
> —After *you,* my dear Montrachet.

> Pommard looks benignly upon
> Suave, gentle Brane-Mouton.
> To Latour no one says, "Beware!"
> Not even the fiery Corton?[6]

It is probably among food and wine critics that one is likeliest today to meet the descendants of these unprejudiced and warm-hearted drinkers. In *La Revue du Vin de France* and in many other wine guides available today in France and abroad, the wines of Bordeaux and Burgundy enjoy a notice that is more or less proportional to their share of the market, and the authors of the articles devoted to them show no sign of preference, either declared or concealed, for one or the other. One can only applaud this state of affairs.

In 1963 the Burgundian cellar master and wine taster Pierre Poupon adopted a very civil tone: "I am not jealous of the wines of Bordeaux. These are difficult wines for our Burgundian palates; we have to spend a long time with them, with an open mind, before being able to detect their great virtues. But they are so different from ours that I manage to like them only when I stop trying to compare them."[7] And the Parisian journalist Bernard Frank cheerfully confessed, "I had probably never drunk a single glass of wine when I chose my camp once and for all: Bordeaux rather than Burgundy. Once and for all! But one lives and learns. Since then I have learned to put some Burgundy in my wine. . . . The palate must give way to the mind."[8] A fine phrase, this last one, which illuminates a whole geography of wine, a geography founded upon the marriage of pragmatism and the senses.

It is true that in Bordeaux the aristocrats of the vine sometimes condescend to serve one or another of the great white wines of Burgundy at the splendid feasts they hold in their townhouses on the Pavé des Chartrons or in their châteaux. Bernard Ginestet describes a prodigious luncheon given not so very long ago at Mouton by Baron Philippe de Rothschild, one of the most discriminating gourmets and connoisseurs of the Médoc:

> With the fried filets of sole, sauce tartare, a Montrachet was served, Marquis de Laguiche 1952; a marvelous wine, pale golden yellow in color, flecked with green tints. It captivated the entire table, which was unanimous in its praise.
>
> "You spoil us, dear friend Philippe," declared Édouard Minton. "There is hardly anywhere in all of Bordeaux, except in your home, that one can drink white Burgundies of such quality. This one is truly magnificent. We don't have such wines."
>
> "Glad you like it, my dear Édouard. For a long while now I have

exchanged two or three cases of Mouton every year for some Montrachet from my friend Philibert. Do you know how large his vineyard is?
Hardly more than two hectares! I serve this wine only to those who are
worthy of it. But I find it agreeable to let my taste buds wander through
other lands."[9]

The scene and the dialogue are no doubt unusual (and probably
slightly retouched by Ginestet for effect), but nonetheless they are quite
plausible, for they feature Philippe de Rothschild, the peasant who lived
in silk pajamas, as he liked to say, and who translated Shakespeare in
bed—a man as far removed from commonplaces as he was from ordinary wines. Anybody else in Bordeaux would have served a white
Haut-Brion or a Carbonnieux—indeed a dry Doisy-Daëne or a "Y"
d'Yquem—on such an occasion.

It is probable, too, that Philibert de Laguiche, thanks to the fruit
of these exchanges, sometimes arranged surprising marriages for his
guests in Burgundy. Let us imagine the scene. In his Château de
Chaumont, in the Saône-et-Loire, the marquis is entertaining Robert
Drouhin, the director of the venerable house of Joseph Drouhin in
Beaune. Drouhin has the privilege of cultivating 2,625 hectares, as well
as making and selling the hundred or so hectoliters of Montrachet produced by the Laguiche family, which for three centuries has possessed
the largest parcel (out of a total area of almost 8 hectares) of this appellation. The menu includes a *lièvre à la royale,* the hare having been marinated for a long time and slowly simmered in the lees of the wine to be
served with the dish, which for any self-respecting Burgundian would
be a *grand cru,* either Gevrey or Vosne. The guests are surprised to find
themselves presented instead with a very dark wine in a carafe (the
practice in Burgundy is to serve wine in bottles). A nectar whose provenance they cannot guess sends them into ecstasies. "Our red wines from
the Côte de Beaune are too delicate to stand up to wild rabbit," Philibert
de Laguiche observes. "Rather than resort to the nobility of the Côte de
Nuits, I thought that the structure and smoothness of a 1945 Mouton

would go well with the powerful and sensual aromas of the noblest game of our fields." One might invert the tale and imagine a Volnay escorting an *agneau de Pauillac* roasted over vine stock and shoots, the lamb being accompanied by a few boletus mushrooms sautéed in the Bordelaise manner; or, more daringly, a fully mature Sauternes with an Époisses almost past its time, followed by—indeed, served with—a slice of warm gingerbread from Mulot et Petitjean in Dijon. A fireworks display for the nose!

A VERY FRENCH QUARREL

Exchanges of this sort are unfortunately exceptional in both the Gironde and the Côte d'Or.[10] Seldom do they do each other such favors. Ask the natives of these two universally renowned wine-producing regions about each other, or read what they have written, and you will not find the slightest sign of sympathy or fellow feeling. They are not from the same world—a fact they miss no occasion to proclaim loudly and clearly. Not content to ignore each other, hardly tasting each other's wines, they delight in denigrating each other more or less fiercely.

The Bordelais are annoyed by the subtle smells of the great pinots, by their color, which is often less bold than the reds of the Gironde, and by the fact that these wines nonetheless manage to overwhelm the head and the senses with lighthearted ease. They are a bit jealous, too, of the best chardonnays, tinged with the flavor of honey like their sweet, strong white wines, yet at once dry, full-bodied, and round. But above all they are irritated by the division of minuscule appellations into a multitude of parcels belonging to many owners: to the Bordelais mind, such a practice is incomprehensible and unjustifiable.[11] Jean-Paul Kauffmann, who, though he is not originally from the Gironde, sang the praises of its wines for years as the editor-in-chief of *L'Amateur de Bordeaux,* comes straight to the point: "The system of classification of Burgundies is a work of art, but, like all works of art, it contains an element of mystery. Its beauty is a real puzzle. . . . Burgundy, with more than a hundred different appellations, is as complex as the duchy of the same name in the time of Charles the Bold. With fifty-one hectares, the Clos Vougeot consists of some ninety parcels divided among eighty different owners. Nothing lasting can be built on such subtleties."[12]

Let it be said, too, that the Bordelais find it hard to get along with these crafty, food-loving peasants, whose hands are calloused and deformed by manual labor, their heads habitually covered by an old cap; who roll their *r*s and who are given to telling crude jokes when they get together, drinking to excess like their ancestors, the bearded Gauls and ancient Burgundians. None of this prevents them from having access to large piles of money, in the form of real estate and business profits both, which they spend on expensive foreign cars like so many vulgar nouveaux riches.

Some years ago, the television host Bernard Pivot devoted his Christmas show to the subject of good eating and fine wine. One of his guests, the Bordelais Jean Lacouture, expressed a rather favorable opinion of one glass he was given to taste. On learning that it was a fine Burgundy, Lacouture replied, "Burgundy, really? I had no idea. It's excellent, but just the same I prefer wine." Some years later he acknowledged having issued this backhanded compliment, saying that he still did not understand Burgundies and could fully appreciate only Bordeaux.[13] It is true that poor Jean Lacouture is much to be pitied, suffering as he does from a dramatic impairment of the faculty of taste known as anosmia, or insensitivity to smells—a fatal impediment in the case of Burgundy![14]

In saying as much, however, Lacouture was only following in the steps of François Mauriac, perhaps without knowing it. Father Maurice Lelong recounts a delightful anecdote told to him by the superior general of the Dominicans, Father Martino Stanislao Gillet. Gillet was living in Dijon and hoped to be elected to the Académie Française. Mauriac, accompanied by another academician, paid him a visit. The candidate took his guests to Aux Trois Faisans and ordered, altogether correctly, a bottle of Burgundy. At this point, Lelong relates, one of the Immortals, congenitally devoted to a certain vineyard of the Gironde, doubtfully pursed his lower lip. There was a long silence, the kind that occurs when a faux pas has been committed. The eyes of the guest searched the eyes of the host, who now found himself in a state of most painful anxiety:

"It's wine," said the most reverend father, who told this to me with a certain bitter amusement.

"I shouldn't have thought so," replied M. François Mauriac, with the inimitable tone of false naivete for which he was famous.[15]

The epilogue to this story will not come as a surprise: Father Gillet never became a member of the Academy. Mauriac, for his part, naturally placed Bordeaux, his Bordeaux, at the pinnacle: "For me, the superiority of Bordeaux comes from its naturalness: it is born of my earth, of my sun, and of the attentive love that my people devote to it. . . . The primary virtue of Bordeaux is honesty."[16] Extraordinary—to think that honesty has always reigned along the Quai des Chartrons!

Philippe Sollers, another Bordelais, has expressed himself still more explicitly on this point, and far less good-naturedly:

True wine exists only in Bordeaux. I would like to make it clear that wine which is not from Bordeaux is a false wine. . . . Of course, there is Burgundy! But it's too full-blooded; it doesn't have the circulation, the sifting of the various states of matter that you find in the wines of Bordeaux. It isn't by chance that one says "beef bourguignon," for the wine accompanying it is indistinguishable from the sauce. I know that the French much like this sort of thing, but then again, I don't much like the French.

Not content to leave matters there, Sollers went on to indulge a taste for doubtful historical commentary that would have brought him a defamation suit in the courts of Dijon: "It is no use to recall the immemorial struggle between Armagnacs and Burgundians—this is a fundamental reality of French history. There is a France of ports and a continental France, a France of the periphery and a France of the land, a

France of trade and a central, centric France, which conjures up for me the various episodes of the closing of the nation—the incessant reproduction of the peasant spirit of collaboration with foreign powers, German or Russian—the supreme tragedy of which in France is Pétainism."[17] Sollers reverted to this theme a few years later: "I loathe Burgundy, it is a wine of sauce and blood. . . . It is necessary just the same that people be made aware of the fact, and recognize that Burgundy is not wine, it is a drink used for making sauces. The more Burgundy one consumes, the more one has the terrible sensation of drinking something bloody, not to mention the dreadful heaviness of the land that one senses in it as well. For me, then, anyone who likes Burgundy (and Beaujolais) is, let's face it, a hick."[18]

One of the emblematic monuments of Bordeaux, as everyone knows, is the Porte de Bourgogne, thus named by the Marquis de Tourny, the royal intendant of the province in the mid-eighteenth century, in honor of the Duke of Burgundy. A local merchant recently had the genial idea of using an image of it on the label of one of his generic Bordeaux Supérieur wines, which he intended to call Les Portes de Bordeaux. After all, it would have been unthinkable to market a wine from Bordeaux under the name La Porte de Bourgogne; and yet this would have been an honest gesture, elegant and droll at the same time.

Last but not least, there is the example of the great geographer René Pijassou, who concludes his magnificent treatise on the viticulture of the Médoc—the result of fourteen years of meticulous research in the archives and among the vineyard owners—by paying tribute to the "greatest center of the civilization of vine and wine, that which produced the great vineyards of the Médoc."[19] Even so, like Philippe de Rothschild and other true wine lovers, Pijassou himself is not averse to serving good Burgundies at his table (white Burgundies, of course). Did Mauriac have such "honest" elegance?

The domaine owners of Burgundy, for their part, fail to understand the red wines of Bordeaux, which give themselves up to the nostrils and taste buds with such difficulty until they have reached maturity, especially if cabernet sauvignon is predominant. The sweet white wines of Bordeaux sicken Burgundians, and in any case they do not know what to drink them with. The notion that one might produce the same wine on domaines of several dozen hectares belonging to a single owner has been totally foreign to them since the Clos Vougeot was dismantled in the nineteenth century. They distrust the Bordelais practice of skillful blending, so contrary to their devotion to single grape varieties, small-scale production, and small parcels.[20] Most of all, they dislike the pretensions of the lords of the great Bordelais estates and the wine merchants and brokers of the Chartrons, with their light southern accents (and English intonations), their bow ties, their tweeds (old, but impeccably tailored), and their handmade English shoes (worn, but well polished). Many years ago the Parisian poet Raoul Ponchon, a man who seldom, if ever, touched water, and who inherited the capital's ancient predilection for the wine of Burgundy, dashed off a few lines that no Burgundian today would disavow:

Oh! never to have been trailed
By a lackey serving me Bordeaux;
I make no bones about it,
It's Burgundy I prefer above all.[21]

Jean-François Bazin, a former president of his region and bard of Burgundian viticulture, recalls that during his childhood Bordeaux was practically never mentioned in the family home of Gevrey-Chambertin. No bottles of Bordeaux appeared on the table: "We abandoned it willingly to its medicinal vocation and to its sad fate as the 'wine of the sick,' contenting ourselves with [drinking] the 'wine of the healthy.'"[22] People made fun of the shape of the Bordeaux bottle, stretching their necks and hunching their shoulders. A more serious cause for complaint was the stingy Bordelais custom of allowing guests to taste only a little wine from the barrel: "When you visit a cellar [here] at least you are offered something to drink. Unlike in Bordeaux."[23] Jean Laplanche, a professor of psychoanalysis and formerly the owner of Château de Pommard, had a cruel experience of this practice not long ago, in 1989. "Since then," he says, "whenever I receive visitors from Bordeaux in my cellar, I give them a glass of the newest wine in casks, and then I announce: 'The *visite bordelaise* is over. Now begins the *visite bourguignonne*'"— and, with it, the opening of a dozen bottles, some of them quite old, going back through all the great years.[24] Ah, what sweet vengeance!

With a great roar of laughter, Laplanche admits that he now enjoys a glass of Bordeaux once it has matured, but that in the past he had always found that it resembled the ink he knew as a schoolboy.[25] As an eminent member of the Confrérie des Chevaliers du Tastevin, and despite two official and reciprocal visits, he notes that the members of his brotherhood have never managed to establish close, friendly relations with their counterparts in the Bordelais *confréries*. Laplanche adds that on the wine lists of restaurants in Burgundy one always finds at least two Bordeaux wines—a small gesture, to be sure, but better than nothing, since the like of it, he says, is never found in the Gironde with Burgundies.[26]

It must be admitted that exchanges of courtesies of this sort, whose value is inevitably a matter of opinion, testify to the existence of a geographic barrier between two impenetrable worlds. With the death of Jean Calvet in Beaune and the recent failure of negotiations between Château Smith-Haut-Lafite and Château de Pommard, financial investment in one region by a house from another is hardly ever contemplated anymore.[27] Yet the requisite capital is lacking in neither Burgundy nor Bordeaux. It is invested instead in Languedoc or abroad.

To hope to be able to heal the rift, and one day to move beyond it, we need to understand its origins, and therefore to examine not only the whole cultural and economic history of the two regions, but also the people who manage the vineyards, their customers, and, incidentally, various aspects of the natural environment. To use the term *incidentally* in this context may seem an affront to the viticulturalists and the many professional experts who assist them in their work—soil scientists, agronomists, biologists, chemists, oenologists, lawyers, bankers, and geographers, all of whom have devoted years of research to explaining the nuances of winemaking. Yet after listening to Philippe Sollers, one cannot reasonably suppose that a few hours of sunshine and a bit more or less gravel will suffice to bridge the gap.

Roger Dion, in his masterly *Histoire de la vigne et du vin en France des origines au XIXe siècle* (1959), which remains a revolutionary piece of scholarship even today, was right to insist on the importance of the consumer: what connoisseurs want, producers achieve by bending the land to their will. If the wines of Bordeaux and Burgundy do not resemble each other, this is largely because of their distinctive histories, notwithstanding the indisputable differences between the soils and climates that gave birth to them. Conversely, it is a very clever person who can tell what separates certain *vins technologiques* made in California from ones made in Australia, even though these places are some twelve thousand miles apart and their physical environments still more distinct from each other than those of Bordeaux and Burgundy. The reason these wines are so similar, of course, is that their customers are the same (right down to their culturally cloned taste buds), the methods of cultivation and vinification are the same, and the multinational firms that market them are the same. This may sound a bit like the caricature drawn by Jonathan Nossiter in his film *Mondovino* (2004), whose principal target is the American giant Mondavi. But Nossiter forgets that small is not always beautiful: there are large, impersonal multinationals that make fine wines, and there are small, friendly firms that produce plonk.

Bordeaux and Burgundy do not really resemble each other, either to the nose or in the mouth, but this is because, when they are honest, they are at heart geographical wines—*vins de terroir,* if you like. They are the product of different human temperaments, which have created and developed different wine-growing environments in different political, economic, and cultural contexts. My purpose in writing this book is not to widen the gulf between them (Bordeaux/Burgundy is one of those oppositions that the French are so fond of, like right/left, pro-European/

Eurosceptic, inherited wealth/self-made fortune, believer/unbeliever, Catholic/Protestant, city/country, sea/mountain, soccer/rugby, PC/Mac, Larousse/Robert, and so on),[28] but rather to remind my readers that there are only good wines and bad wines; that among the good ones there must be enough to please all tastes; and that the more one drinks them, if they are at all well made, the more one's life is enriched.

CHAPTER 2
MARKETS AND CONSUMERS

If there is one thing that annoys people as much in Bordeaux as in Burgundy, it is the suggestion that soil and climate do not exclusively determine the quality of wines. For the estate owners, the merchants, and the many other professionals who work with them, the physical landscape is an inviolable fact that suffices by itself to explain why great wines are produced in the Gironde and the Côte d'Or. Any challenge to this belief is seen as a sacrilege, one that can only be committed by people who know nothing about wine or else by jealous natives of other regions whose controlled appellations are less prestigious than those of Bordeaux and Burgundy.

One of the most talented proprietors in the Médoc, Bruno Prats, who was responsible for some of the greatest vintages of Cos d'Estournel and is now retired, remarked a few years ago, "Why is it precisely in the region of Bordeaux, one may well wonder, that the 'finest wines in the world,' as Richelieu used to say, are found? . . . Only one reply can be given: natural elements combine with one another there in perfect harmony."[1] Some years ago, the new owner of one of the vast châteaus of the Graves became utterly exasperated upon hearing me make a number of iconoclastic remarks about *terroir* in the course of a lecture at Cambridge University, in England: "You will understand, sir, that I

cannot subscribe to your views, having liquidated all my assets to purchase this estate and place my fortune beneath my feet." His anxiety was
understandable, for the audience included the masters of wine of the
great colleges of the university, all of them potential buyers.

The urge to defend a tradition whose clearest manifestation is a piece
of real estate, the value of which may be no less colossal than the income
from the wines that are made on it, is natural enough. But it denies a
reality that the actual practice of vine growing and winemaking confirms more clearly each day on all continents: the land can be improved.
Indeed, it has been exploited to such a degree by artificial methods over
the centuries that one can no longer truly speak of nature at all. As scan-
dalous as it may seem, the essential component of the land consists of
taste buds, pleasures, and purchasing power—in a word, the consumer.

This is exactly what Roger Dion, the foremost authority on the history and geography of winemaking in France, succeeded in showing a
half century ago. "The role of the land in the making of a *grand cru*,"
Dion wrote, "scarcely goes beyond that of the material used in making
a work of art."[2] But in speaking so provocatively he was only confirm-
ing a very old idea, one that goes back to a famous passage in Olivier de
Serres's *Théâtre d'agriculture,* published in 1601: "If you are not in a
position to sell your wine, what will you do with a great vineyard?" The
expression "great vineyard" applies here as much to the extent of plantation as to the quality of production. Underlying the economic factor is
a cultural motivation, namely, the pleasure of drinking wine, if possible
a good wine. Dion's argument seems sounder today than ever. But it is
not yet by any means a universal opinion.

SEDUCTIONS AND ILLUSIONS OF THE PHYSICAL LANDSCAPE

It is plain why such ideas should be resisted, for the financial stakes of
French viticulture are considerable. In devaluing the role of the physical landscape, one calls into question a great many privileges arising

from blind faith in the authority of famous names and traditional classifications (of 1855 and later). But in fact the charm operates only on a clientele that believes that certain parcels of land were endowed with superior characteristics and that wines can be judged by their labels. Many owners, whether they are from Bordeaux, Burgundy, or elsewhere, continue to entertain this illusion as well. Consider the opinion of Jacques de Lanversin, an academic and winemaker in Provence: "I very sincerely believe that the credit attributable to the *vigneron* alone does not represent more than 10% of the overall credit to be assigned for creating an excellent wine."[3] To try to quantify the effort involved in making a product that mixes nature and culture as thoroughly as wine does is loony enough, but to reduce it to 10 percent is an obvious ploy, a transparent attempt to evade the real issue. Can anyone seriously imagine a great violinist declaring that her interpretation of a Beethoven concerto owes 10 percent to her talent and 90 percent to her Stradivarius? Would Michelangelo have claimed that his *Pietà* or *David* owed by far the better part of its beauty to the exceptional quality of the blocks of Carrara marble he used?

Promotional bodies, financed by winemakers and merchants, are more than happy to take the same line, however. In the early 1990s, when the Bureau Interprofessionel des Vins de Bourgogne (BIVB) created a massive publicity campaign around the slogan "Burgundies, from land blessed by the gods," the glass of wine in the photograph accompanying the text of the advertisement was surmounted by a golden halo![4] In a dozen-page insert that appeared in various magazines in 1993, the BIVB fancifully retraced the history of winemaking in Burgundy, without even mentioning that the decision to plant the pinot grape as the sole varietal for fine red wines went back to Philip the Bold in the fourteenth century. In this view of the world, trained experts are mere ectoplasms who do no more than protect and collect the manna of the vine: "15 September, somewhere in Burgundy. In a few days, the grape harvest. The die is cast after four seasons of shared labor in which the grape variety, land, and climate come together to make the best of the wines blessed by the gods. So many gifts from the heaven protected by the system of classed appellations." One finds "the gods" mentioned nineteen times in this potted history, "God" four times, "Jesus Christ" once, "heaven" three times, "benediction" three times, and "creative gift," "eternal," "eternity," "reverence," "divine inspiration," "miracle," "Holy of Holies," and "Christianity" once each. Good Lord! In putting religion to use for commercial purposes, this way of flogging wine hardly differs from advertisements for certain pseudo-monastic cheeses, apart from the missing Rabelaisian wink of the eye. How could the sponsors of the BIVB have allowed the name of their organization to be invoked only four times, "man" twice, and "owner" once? Evidently the recognition of natural privilege, and with it of landed wealth, is well worth a few sacrifices!

The concurrent campaign of the Conseil Interprofessionel du Vin de Bordeaux (CIVB) was subtler, boasting simultaneously of the quality of the region's gravelly soil and the discrimination of its wines' consumers. In 1992 the Médoc was favored with the slogan "The land that is the envy of the whole world," illustrated by a globe of compacted soil in which an abundance of quartz pebbles is plainly visible. This theme was restated in various ways in the years that followed, with many châteaus subsequently using it in their own advertisements. Already in 1984, a pamphlet issued by Château Giscours had declared, "Nature has outrageously favored this corner of the world. . . . The land that is ours to work, and the humility the laws of nature oblige us to feel, together form the soul of the wine of Château Giscours."[5] In 1993 the slogan "The land that is the envy of the world" was applied to *crus bourgeois*. The gravel was now assembled not in the form of a globe, but in that of a château, which is to say in a way that paid homage to the scale of the investment made by the great owners of the Bordeaux region, and to their art of making wine and of living.

Less spectacular, but nearer to reality, are the images that the CIVB now uses to illustrate these doubtful claims, of Baccarat glasses (from the "Perfection" line) half filled with red or white wine and dressed at the top of the stem with a garnet-red or yellow bow tie. The text no longer leaves any place for the illusion of a miraculous soil: "Bordeaux: the color of good taste." The homage here is clearly being bestowed both on the educated *amateurs* who know how to choose wines and on the enlightened proprietors who know how to bring out the best in the land. The bow tie is perhaps superfluous, but it is not wholly out of fashion in the Gironde, and in any case evokes more the social milieu of producers than of consumers (a little like the traditional Breton women's headdress reproduced on packets of Pont-Aven crêpes). Still more recently, the producers' association of the Médoc ran an advertisement in a quite different style meant not only to flatter the snobbery of buyers who judge wines by their label, but also to charm connoisseurs of genuinely good wine, who will not suffer being taken for fools. The photo shows a young semi-anonymous cellar master looking directly at the camera, wearing a pullover and a big smile and holding a glass of red wine in his hand, with the caption "Portrait of a *vigneron*. Médoc cellar master Damien L. is proud of the finesse of his new vintage." Another ad shows a young wine merchant named Édouard, hair neatly combed, wearing a white shirt with cuff links that is open at the neck down to the third button in the style of Bernard-Henri Lévy—a cleverly calculated attitude of casualness that nonetheless does not cast doubt upon the seriousness of an honest professional. Although the clientele for Bordeaux is more diversified now than it once was, as advertising agencies have not failed to perceive, it remains attached to smart Gironde fashion.

I do not mean to downplay the role of the environments in which the wines of Bordeaux and Burgundy are born, nor to suggest that they resemble each other. The best wines in both places are made with respect for the physical landscape, which implies a desire to maximize the wines' potential while minimizing their defects, just as parents and teachers try to do in educating children. This requires a great deal of effort and, in the case of wine, a great deal of labor, material, and therefore capital. Investment on this scale is imaginable only if there is some hope of making a profit. Hence the importance of inquiring into the clientele for different wines and, therefore, following the lead of Roger Dion, standing the usual argument on its head. As Jean Kressman rightly observed, "There is more history than geography in a bottle of wine."[6]

TWO LATE GALLO-ROMAN VINEYARDS

When Gaul became part of the Roman Empire, in the middle of the first century B.C., it did not produce wine. Its elite had appreciated wine for centuries, however, and it was one of the major products purchased or bartered from Phoenician, Greek, and Roman merchants. So great was the Gauls' passion for wine that they drank it undiluted by water, easily became drunk, and even traded slaves for amphorae, so that when a rich man managed to obtain a store of wine he no longer had a servant to pour it for him.[7] In fact, slaves constituted the principal export of the Gauls. All the excavated sites dating from pre-Roman Gaul have yielded innumerable shards of amphorae of Mediterranean origin, the oldest of which go back several centuries before the Christian era. It is known that under Augustus sizable quantities of wine from the vicinity of Narbonne were carried over the Naurouze Pass (linking Languedoc with the Aquitaine basin), which met up again with the Garonne and then descended to the port of Bordeaux, where a part of each shipment was loaded onto ships going to the British Isles.[8] A comparable volume of traffic passed through Burgundy, in the Saône Valley. In the early twentieth century two months' dredging of the riverbed at Chalon brought up some 24,000 small pieces of wine jugs.[9] More were found later. A part of the cargoes of wine must have been unloaded in this port, and then transported via the Autun basin to the Loire and Yonne, and from there sent westward as far as the Paris basin. The rest continued on its way, by river and by land, to the lands of northeastern Gaul. Along the way the cities of the Aedui and the Lingones were provided with fresh supplies, as the masses of shards found at Bibracte testify. Both Bordeaux and Burgundy were therefore centers of the wine trade well before they were planted with vines, their second vocation being closely linked to the first.

Prior to its arrival in these regions, the vine first established itself in two outposts far removed from its home in the Greco-Roman world of the Mediterranean: in Gaillac, in the lower valley of the Tarn, and in Côte Rôtie and Hermitage, on the banks of the Rhône south of Lyons.[10] This suggests that traders were looking for a way to bring production nearer to consumers, which would have required an adaptation of grape varieties and techniques of viticulture. It is possible that *Vitis allobrogica* (mentioned in Roman sources as early as the first century A.D.) was either a wild vine native to the Rhône Valley or that it was the product of spontaneous crossings with varietals of Mediterranean origin, a process that later might have occurred farther north.

It is practically certain that the vine was not yet planted in Bordeaux by the beginning of the first century A.D. Roger Dion argues that the geographer Strabo, who described the city and its environs at the end of Augustus's reign, would not have failed to mention it, so sensitive was he to its presence in the landscape.[11] Once Caesar's conquest of Gaul was complete, the Bituriges-Vivisci turned first toward Catalonia in search of provisions, and then to the south of Spain, Italy, and the Aegean Sea, as the amphorae found in excavations recently carried out in Bordeaux demonstrate.[12] Finally, in about 40 A.D., they set out to plant a vineyard in order to satisfy local demand without having to import wines from towns farther upstream along the Garonne or, still less profitably, from the Mediterranean.[13] This was probably the first commercial disappointment for the vine growers around Gaillac, prefiguring subsequent misfortunes in the Middle Ages and in modern times.

Traces of a vineyard with well-aligned vine stocks dating from the first half of the first century have been uncovered in the Saint-Christoly quarter of Bordeaux. At this point in the archaeological record, foreign amphorae are replaced by vessels made in Aquitaine—irrefutable proof of local production that was confirmed contemporaneously by

Columella and Pliny the Elder, who wrote around 75 A.D. The Bituriges seem to have imported a grape variety from Epirus, in northwest Greece,[14] capable of resisting the humidity and wind; this was the *basilica,* renamed *biturica,* which all the evidence points to as the ancestor of the Carmenet family.[15] The reputation of the wine made from it established itself very quickly and spread throughout the empire. The amphorae used to package it are the ancestors of the modern Bordeaux bottle; the sole difference is that they were as potbellied as Mediterranean amphorae were spindly, unlike their glass descendants, which, in the twentieth century, came to be distinctively slimmer than the rounded bottles common everywhere else in France. In the second century, amphorae themselves were abandoned in favor of barrels, as we know from textual sources (the barrels themselves, held together with bands of pliable oak rather than iron, rotted over time, leaving no archaeological trace). These were to enjoy a monopoly as containers of fine wines until the present day. The extent of local vineyards was vast. Part of the land of each of the villas owned by Ausonius in the region of Burdigala in the fourth century, for example, was planted with vines.

In Burgundy, the appearance of viticulture seems to date from the same period, to judge from the bas-reliefs in the museum at Sens, in particular one representing the vine grower's tools, and from the shards of locally manufactured amphorae.[16] Recent archaeological discoveries support the view that the cultivation of vines went back to the end of the first or the beginning of the second century A.D.[17] The Villa Selongey, reconstructed at the end of the second or the beginning of the third century, then destroyed around 250, was incontestably a wine-producing estate. A large number of grape seeds have been discovered at Chalon. The presence of viticulture in the first century, at Neublans in the Jura, on the edges of the Côte d'Or and the Saône-et-Loire, has recently been attested by palynological studies as well. All of this suggests that the many regionally manufactured amphorae discovered at sites from the same period were used as containers for local wine and not solely for wine imported by boat in huge terra-cotta vessels known as *dolia* and then decanted.

But it does not suffice to prove that there existed an early commercial vineyard. Roger Dion advances a very strong argument against the likelihood of such a state of affairs in Burgundy. In the second century of the common era, he points out, the corporation of *negotiatores vinarii,* which shipped wines from the Rhône Valley and the Mediterranean northward along the Saône, was still very powerful in Lyons.[18] Indeed, it is not implausible to suppose that the imperial administration favored these shippers by restricting wine production north of Lyons, despite the size of the demand there.

There is no doubt, however, that viticulture was developing in the third century. A message of thanks addressed by the inhabitants of Autun to Emperor Constantine in 312 mentions the existence of a vineyard of good quality in the Pagus Arebrignus, which corresponds exactly to the Côte d'Or. The vineyard, however, had been run down by the intertwining of roots:

> These vines, admired only by those who ignore their true state, are so exhausted by age that they hardly feel the attention that we give them anymore. Their roots, whose age we no longer know, have formed, by intertwining their thousand foldings, a mass that prevents trenches from being dug to the desired depth, so that, for want of sufficient covering, the layered stock is exposed to the rains, which drown them, and to the rays of the sun, which burn them. And we do not have the advantage here, common in Aquitaine and in other provinces, of anywhere being able to find the space necessary to create new vines, hemmed in as we are between the uninterrupted stony ground of the hills and the hollows where frost is to be feared.[19]

This interlacing of roots in the soil was due to the ancestral practice of provining (or layering), a method for reproducing a vine stock that consists of burying a branch in the ground while leaving its buds exposed to the air above; once it has established roots, the plant is separated from the "mother vine" and constitutes a freestanding vine. Repeating this procedure several times was enough to cause vine stocks to become extremely congested in only a few decades. Before the phylloxera of the late nineteenth century, there were twenty thousand feet of stock per hectare in Burgundy, with some three hundred feet per hectare being layered each year.[20]

Dion stresses that the regional economy of Burgundy prior to the Roman conquest was centered on Bibracte (afterward Autun), Alesia, and Langres, towns *(oppida)* located in hilly regions with plateaus that were favorable to the techniques of cereal agriculture of the period. The marshy rift valley of the Saône, with its faulted, sloping, and stony borders, held no interest for the Gauls. With the advent of Roman rule this land was drained, and major roads were opened up linking Lyons with the Rhineland, enlarging the economic prospects of the Saône plain. The Lyons–Trier road was so well built that it is still visible today, although its original purpose has long been lost over most of the route. On both sides the forest was cleared and villas constructed, vestiges of which can yet be found in the heart of the woodlands that grew back during the early Middle Ages.

Later, probably during the first half of the third century, with the advance of the vine toward the north, the economic potential of the escarpment that bounds the plain to the west began to make itself felt, definitively altering the settlement patterns of the region. The foot of this slope was now more attractive than the ancient towns of the region, even if their control was long to persist, in particular through the landed possessions of their bishops and chapters. The fascination with this narrow strip of land was undiminished throughout the centuries that followed, and during the Revolution the Côte d'Or became the name of the department of which it occupies only a tiny part. Thus it was that Dijon came to supplant Langres, just as Mâcon superseded Autun farther south.

Again, one must follow Roger Dion in resisting interpretations of the letter sent to Constantine in 312 as proof of the great antiquity of viticulture in the region, in preference to Gaston Roupnel, who is inclined to assign an earlier date for the origin of agrarian activity than the evidence warrants.[21] The invasions of 250–80 that destroyed a large part of Gaul probably occurred after the planting of vineyards, whose reputation for quality was quickly established, but not by many years. Dion's hypothesis remains appealing. Under the Antonine emperors (96–192), Lyons was too powerful for Rome to try to undermine its merchants by authorizing the planting of vineyards farther north. Under the Severans (193–235), however, Lyons's importance declined in relation to Trier, suggesting that the Treviri, along with the Aedui and other tribes, may then have been permitted to plant vineyards. In that case, viticulture in Burgundy must be dated from this period, prior to the troubles of the following decades and the broader authorization to plant vineyards throughout Gaul issued by Probus in 280. Yet this edict, a happy event in the history of winemaking, nonetheless had the consequence of placing the vineyards of Bordeaux and Burgundy in a difficult position, for it allowed the northernmost provinces of the empire to satisfy the barbarian demand for wine themselves.[22]

PRELATES AND PRINCES IN MEDIEVAL BURGUNDY

In Burgundy, as everywhere in Europe, it was the Church that maintained the tradition of viticulture during the early Middle Ages. Only vestiges of the ancient vineyards remained, as the use of wine was limited to the celebration of the divine office and the entertainment of clerical guests. And as everywhere in Gaul, ravaged by the invasion of Germanic tribes, and later in the kingdoms to which these invasions gave rise, the bishops of Bordeaux and Burgundy and their chapters carried on with their viticultural mission, gradually initiating the occupiers into this delicate art. Saint Germanus, born in 378 at Auxerre to a family that possessed several renowned vineyards, probably maintained

the tradition upon becoming bishop of his native town.[23] The production of wine was so important that some bishops did not hesitate to
move the titular episcopal see to lands more favorable to cultivation of
the vine. Saint Gregory, for example, bishop of Langres in the sixth
century, took up residence much more willingly at Dijon *(castrum di-
vionense)* than next to his cathedral.[24] Today Langres is still one of the
coldest towns in the plains of France, and the vineyard that grew up in
its vicinity a few years ago produces no more than a pleasant, rather
rough, traditional wine. Gregory of Tours was surprised: "I do not
know why it is not Dijon that has the title of *civitas*. Yet there are
around it springs of a rare quality, and, toward the west, slopes that are
very fertile and covered with vines from which the inhabitants make a
Falernian wine of such distinction that they disdain the wine of
Ascalon."[25] Although Dijon was not to rival Langres until much later,
becoming an episcopal see only in 1731, the princes of the Church had
long laid claim to this town and its environs, which were so congenial to
vine growing. The bishops of Bordeaux, for their part, resided in the
heart of their city but owned two estates at Lormont, on the right bank
of the Garonne, whose vineyards were very carefully tended.[26]

The first of the great abbeys was Cluny, founded in 910 at a time of
relative peace in Western Europe. The importance attached to viticulture there was commensurate with the monastery's spiritual, artistic,
agronomic, and economic purposes. Cîteaux was established in 1098,
and with it the Cistercian order, which required of its monks that they
withdraw from the world and build their sanctuaries in the wilderness.
The mother abbey was situated near the Saône, just off the old Roman
road, probably still in use at the time, and the Chalon–Dijon road that
was soon to replace it. Moreover, vine-covered slopes were visible from
the clearing of the monastery. The decision to erect it along one of the
major axes of circulation in Europe, near a wine-producing territory
that had been renowned since antiquity, was clearly a way of declaring
that, notwithstanding the monks' obligations of strict observance, the
abbey did not intend to renounce the duty of hospitality without which

it could neither flourish spiritually nor attract the favors and gifts of the powerful. A love of work accounts in large part for the subsequent development of an order whose demanding rule organized the life of its members around the two poles of *orare* and *laborare*.

It was thus that the Clos de Vougeot came into existence, on land of only average quality because it was clayey in its lower extent, but lying on a part of the Côte nearest the abbey, perhaps a dozen kilometers away. Around 1110, first the powerful family of Vergy (a nearby château in the Hautes-Côtes) and its allies, and then the monks of Saint-Germain-de-Prés, gave to Cîteaux, or sold to it for a symbolic sum, a certain number of parcels situated at the foot of the Côte, to the south of the source of the Vouge River (from which the Clos took its name). The monks planted vines there, constructed a cellar (which still exists) between 1116 and 1160, and later received or purchased additional parcels that enabled them to create one of the first walled vineyards, which they enlarged over the course of the succeeding centuries until it reached its final size. Called a *cellarium* at the end of the twelfth century, this monastic grange, which was to become the most prestigious and renowned of Cîteaux's properties, was referred to as a *clausum* in a text of 1212 and then, in 1228, as a *magnum clausum cisterciense apud vogetum.*[27]

A *clausum* (from which the French word *clos* is derived) was a vine-yard protected by walls, which had the purpose first of marking off a seigneurial property, lay or ecclesiastic, and of protecting the plantation from stray cattle left to roam after the harvest was taken in.[28] In Burgundy the walls had other uses as well. They provided a reason for clearing a slope such as the Côte d'Or of the many large stones created by the erosion of at least two layers of hard limestone in a fault scarp. The exfoliation of this limestone in thin flakes made it possible to build high walls by laying the fragments on top of one another, sometimes crudely pointing them with lime mortar. Moreover, the walls had the microclimatic virtues of cutting the wind and accumulating the heat of sunny spring and summer days, which was then partially released at night, softening the effects of frost and assisting the ripening of the grapes.

At the Clos de Vougeot, the monks of Cîteaux applied techniques that had been steadily improved from one year to the next. They decided to abandon the old Roman practice of complantation, which involved mixing fruit trees (peach, cherry, walnut, and so on) with vines, and even letting the vines wrap themselves around the trunks and branches of these trees. This practice does not do much harm on the sunny shores of the Mediterranean, but in Burgundy it produces too much shade for the grapes, retarding their maturation. Additionally, the trees absorb mineral matter from the soil that is therefore denied to the vines, a phenomenon that the Cistercians of the Middle Ages may have noticed, though its causes were not understood until much later. In 1366 the duke of Burgundy, Philip the Bold, ordered that "the walnut trees and other trees of the *clos* of Chenôve, harmful to the vine[s] of this *clos,* be pulled out and taken away."[29] Complantation was still very widespread in Burgundy in the eighteenth century, though absent by that time in the Clos de Vougeot; until recently it was still to be found in vineyards of lesser reputation in the region (at Villars-Fontaine in the Hautes-Côtes, for example, the last vine planted among apple and pear trees was pulled out only in the mid-1990s). Other improvements followed at the Clos de Vougeot, notably with respect to vine varieties and the exclusive reliance upon the pinot family of grapes, as on the ducal estates.

Other great civil and ecclesiastical institutions established walled vineyards in Burgundy, typically on the part of the Côte between Dijon and Chalon: Clos du Roi, Clos du Duc, and Clos du Chapitre at Chenôve; another Clos du Roi on the slope of Corton and at Beaune; Clos de Bèze (a dependency of the abbey of the same name) and Clos Saint-Jacques at Gevrey-Chambertin; Clos de la Roche, Clos des Lambrays, Clos Saint-Denis, and Clos de Tart (of the abbey) at Morey-Saint-Denis; Clos des Langres (of the chapter of the cathedral) at Corgoloin; and many others that do not bear the name Clos, though they are no less vineyards for that, such as Romanée at Vosne, created by the abbey of Saint-Vivant, a dependency of Cluny.[30] The major proprietors possessed several such vineyards, among them the Hôtel-Dieu de Beaune (a civil hospice that later became a hospital), which from the fifteenth century onward held title to one of the principal *domaines* in Burgundy.

In mapping the ownership of these vineyards, one traces the geographical area over which Burgundy wine was consumed during the Middle Ages by the abbeys of Burgundy and the Île-de-France; by the bishops of Langres and Autun and their chapters; by the king of France, who resided in Paris and the Île-de-France; and by the dukes of Burgundy, whose domain extended as far as the North Sea, and the lords of their court.[31] Other occasional consumers included the popes and their cardinals in Rome and Avignon, as well as the recipients of gifts of wine, dispersed throughout Europe.

All of these vineyards, above all Vougeot, made very good wines. Excellent viticultural technique came to be combined with meticulous methods of vinification, evidence of which survives in the impressive presses of the Duke of Burgundy (still to be seen at Chenôve today) and those of the Cistercians in the vat hall of the Clos de Vougeot. The medieval Burgundians produced the *grands crus* of the period, which is to say wines that were of high quality despite being drunk very young. The majority of these today have become *premiers* or *grands crus*—obvious proof of a judicious choice of land by shrewd owners, but still more of the cumulative effect of careful management of this land over the intervening centuries. There are, of course, some exceptions (medieval vineyards that today are classed as "village" appellations), but these are fairly rare and found mainly in the communes nearest to Dijon, Chenôve, and Marsannay, dedicated in recent times to the production of ordinary wines for the working-class population of the region's capital.

Henri Enjalbert's concern with demonstrating that fine wines were an invention of the châteaus of Bordeaux during the eighteenth century leads him to declare:

> The notion of *"clos"* must be insisted upon. It was to give way later to *"climats,"* which today are identified with *terroir,* and therefore *cru.* . . . Excellent results were thus obtained; merchants learned of them and

came from Paris, Avignon, and elsewhere to make their purchases there. [But] it should not be supposed that a Burgundian vineyard producing fine wines was therefore already established. Near Dijon there are formerly renowned *clos* located on land that today is poorly regarded; conversely, *"climats"* that are famous today, around Nuits, for example, had no notable *clos* during the Middle Ages.[32]

Surely there is a certain contradiction between recognizing that the wine of the monastic vineyards was considered to be so good that it was shipped as far away as Avignon, Paris, and even the heartlands of Bordeaux's maritime trade and Flanders, and asserting that Burgundian vineyards did not produce fine wines? To the contrary, the selection of pinot grapes in these vineyards proves that they did.

The influence of proprietors who appreciated good wine upon the emergence of high-quality production made itself felt in the first instance through selection of the best grape varieties. Until the phylloxera epidemic of the late nineteenth century, plantations throughout Europe and Asia were characterized by immense variation in vine types, which were generally mixed together within estates and within the parcels into which these estates were subdivided.[33] This is still the case today in many vineyards, including some of the most renowned ones, such as Châteauneuf-du-Pape (thirteen authorized varieties) and the region of Bordeaux (five red varieties and at least three white). In Burgundy, not the least of the achievements of monastic vineyards in the Middle Ages was to recognize the excellence of the pinot variety in comparison to all the others, especially gamay, in making good red wine (or "ruby" wine, as it was then called). The duke of Burgundy, Philip the Bold, took a great interest in the quality of his wines, allowing his name to be associated with the turn toward pinot; indeed, Roger Dion has suggested that he may have been personally responsible for establishing the reputation of the grape, of which no mention prior to 1375 is known.[34] What is certain is that the duke so liked pinot that, in the famous ruling of 31 July 1395, he came to the defense of the "best and most precious and suitable wines of the kingdom, consumed by the pope, the king, and several other lords." He ordered the uprooting, while also forbidding the planting, of the "very bad and unlawful plant of the gamay, from which plant comes a very great abundance of wine . . . , which wine is of such a nature that it is very much harmful to human creature[s] . . . for it is full of very great and horrible bitterness." Accordingly, he called upon his subjects to "extirpate it, destroy and annihilate it, on pain of [a fine of] sixty sous coined at Tours per *ouvrée de vigne* [a measurement of area equivalent to a man-day of labor]."[35] Even so, gamay remained appealing on account of its hardiness and high yields. Philip the Good reiterated the ban in 1441, as did the king of France, Charles VIII, in 1486, Burgundy in the meantime having been restored to the French crown. The ruling of 1395 stipulated a further injunction against fertilizing the soil with animal excrement, ordering that a fine be assessed upon anyone who persisted in "hauling manure and refuse into the vineyards where the good plants are found." Finally, the public proclamation of the date on which harvesting was to begin *(ban de vendanges),* and the concern for the maturity and health of the grapes themselves that this implies, testifies to a mastery of the cycles of vine growing and winemaking. Bacteriological questions aside, it is plain that medieval *vignerons* knew perfectly well which methods made it possible to obtain wines with novel and concentrated flavors.

To claim, as Henri Enjalbert does, that the *grands crus* were invented by the winemakers of Bordeaux in the seventeenth and eighteenth centuries amounts to denying the prior existence of a hierarchy of quality outside this region. Such a ranking certainly existed throughout Europe not only in the Middle Ages, but in antiquity as well.[36] Then, as now, it rested on the technical knowledge of vine growers, the high standards of estate owners, and the refined tastes and purchasing power of buyers. Roger Dion has made a compelling argument in favor of the role played by the long-term accumulation of incremental improvements in viticultural methods, noting that the majority of present-day *grands crus* in Burgundy are located on the territory of the former bishopric of Autun,

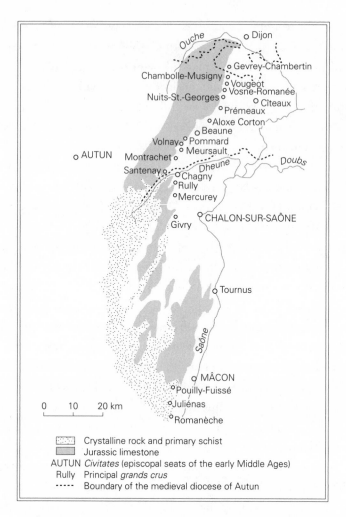

Map 2. Concentration of *grand cru* vineyards on the Côte
d'Or within the boundaries of the former diocese of Autun.
Source: Dion, *Histoire de la vigne et du vin en France des
origines au XIXe siècle,* p. 47.

which coincided with that of the seat of the Aedui, one of the earliest tribes converted to Roman civilization, and therefore to the love of good wine (see map 2).[37] The notion that the settlement of Autun was a consequence of the town's viticultural potential is implausible on its face, since it was first populated well before the appearance of the vine there. From the end of the Middle Ages the wine of Beaune was among the most talked-about wines in continental Europe outside the lands bordering the Atlantic. Thus Erasmus of Rotterdam wrote to Marc Laurin, "O blessed Burgundy ... , province well worthy of being called the mother of men, she who possesses such milk in her veins."[38] The affection for the wine of Burgundy that is still felt today in the Walloon region of Belgium, for example, is a cultural vestige of the ancient political configuration of the grand duchy of the Western kingdom. Still, the importance of the medieval vineyard of the Côte d'Or must not be exaggerated; it was less far-reaching than that of lower Burgundy (Auxerre, Chablis, Tonnerre, Sens), Champagne, and the Île-de-France.[39] Even so, its reputation was immense. The court of the popes in Avignon was enamored of Burgundy wines. They were used for the coronation of kings at Rheims.

The wines of the Yonne, then said to be from Auxerre,[40] arrived in huge quantities in Paris. They sold so well that growers no longer even cultivated cereal crops or raised cattle, as we know from a Franciscan monk, the Italian Salimbene de Adam, who wrote during his stay in Auxerre in 1248, "The men of this land do not sow, nor harvest, nor store [grain] in granaries, but they send their wine to Paris, and there they sell it honorably and from it they take all their nourishment and the clothes with which they cover themselves." This same text reveals a boundary in the geography of drink in the thirteenth century that remains a bit mysterious: "In the province of France—I speak of the province of the Minorites [a mendicant order founded by Saint Francis]—there are eight districts [*custodies*], of which four drink beer and four wine. Note also that there are three lands that in France yield wine in abundance, La Rochelle, Beaune, and Auxerre."[41] The list of *custodies* of the province of

France in 1248 has not been preserved, but we do know that in 1343 there were nine: Paris, Rheims, Champagne, Normandy, Artois, Lorraine, Liège, Flanders, and Vermandois. It is possible that Artois (the present-day department of Pas de Calais), Flanders, and Vermandois (now the region of Picardy) drank beer, but more than this we cannot say.

THE EXTRAVAGANT PRIVILEGE OF BORDEAUX

The situation in medieval Bordeaux was different.[42] Bordeaux looked northward to a vast market, accessible by sea, that included Flanders and, above all, the British Isles. But the port of Bordeaux was not alone in collecting wines for ocean shipment. At the beginning of the twelfth century it had already largely been supplanted by the port of Châtelaillon in Charente, and then, after 1130, by the newly founded port of La Rochelle. By the late twelfth and early thirteenth centuries, the province of Aunis and the islands of Ré and Oléron were covered with the largest commercial vineyards in Europe. Bordeaux also exported wine, but in lesser quantity. Its position gradually became more prominent in the decades that followed as a consequence of Duchess Eleanor of Aquitaine's separation from the king of France, Louis VII, and her remarriage in 1152 to Henry Plantagenet, heir to the crown of England, who became king two years later under the name Henry II. Aunis and the province of Saintonge continued to export their wines, along with the whole of Aquitaine, through Bordeaux. In the first quarter of the thirteenth century, Bordeaux was a port of transshipment for wines from the entire valley of the Garonne and its tributaries, as far away as Bergerac, Cahors, Gaillac, and Pamiers (see map 3).[43] Nothing qualitatively distinguished the vineyards of the lower part of this riparian region from those of the upper part, or those of the Garonne and Dordogne basins from those along the Charente River (to the north) or the Adour River (to the south). John Lackland, who became king of England in 1199, was still in 1207 buying his wine at Moissac and Cahors and also, of course, in Anjou (the lands of his ancestors), but not

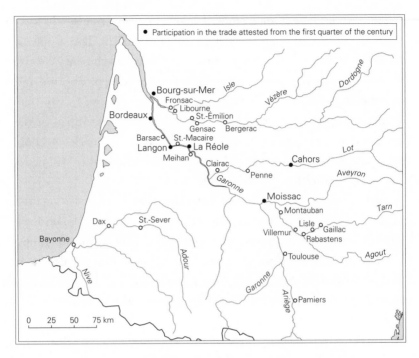

Map 3. Towns and cities of Aquitaine recorded in the thirteenth
century as exporting wine to England. Source: Dion, *Histoire
de la vigne et du vin en France des origines au XIXe siècle,* p. 381.

at Bordeaux, which again was only a port of transshipment. Unlike in
Burgundy, with its walled vineyards, the great estates had not yet been
invented in the region of Bordeaux. I use the word *invented* here deliberately, in its dual sense of "discovered" and "created."

A turning point occurred in 1214. Acceding to the pressing demands
of the Bordelais, King John of England granted them an exemption
from payment of the customary tax on exported goods. In order to
counter the strong pressure being exerted on Aquitaine by Philip
Augustus, king of France, John needed to unite the great families of the
capital of the duchy. Ten years later, the people of La Rochelle, feeling
themselves neglected by the English crown, which now bought more

and more of its wine from the merchants of Bordeaux, transferred their allegiance to Philip Augustus's successor, Louis VIII. The people of Bordeaux forthrightly declared which camp they had chosen: "We are, for our part, resolved to resist the enemies of the king of England and to preserve our loyalty to him. By all means possible we fortify Bordeaux. . . . All these expenses, all these losses, we suffer them in the opinion that the public good requires it. It is necessary to defend Bordeaux, the town of our lord the king of England, whom we will never fail to serve faithfully, as long as we shall live."[44]

Such devotion merited consideration and compensation. By 1241 the people of Bordeaux had achieved everything they possibly could have hoped for. In that year they won a major commercial victory, obtaining from the king of England recognition of an extravagant privilege that they had claimed for themselves in 1224: the right to sell their wines abroad first, before those arriving from upriver estates. Now the wines of the *haut pays* could reach the port only after the feast day of Saint Martin (11 November). By this date the better part of the English market had been supplied, so that wines arriving afterward no longer found buyers. In lean years, however, the merchants of Bordeaux enjoyed full discretion to satisfy foreign demand by supplementing their production with the vintages of inland producers. It must also be kept in mind that wines during this period were drunk young, for they did not keep well and rapidly lost their value as the months passed. Wines that had been aged in casks for a year were simply sold off at reduced prices in order to make room for the new vintage.

This commercial guarantee amounted to the first certificate of quality issued in the Gironde. It also marked the entry of wines from everywhere else in the southwest into a long period of eclipse with respect to both quantity and quality of production, from which they were to emerge only in 1776. Even so, they never fully recovered from the blow dealt them by the edict of 1241, and none of them has yet regularly attained the level of the *grands crus* (though this may change). For more than five centuries, by contrast, the winemakers of Bordeaux had the leisure to plant vines in their country estates *(bourdieux)* and to improve the wines these yielded, secure in their monopoly of foreign markets in England and throughout northern Europe. One may have some idea of the prosperity of the city of Bordeaux and its surrounding countryside during this period by considering that in the year 1308–9, for example, 100,000 barrels of wine (some 900,000 hectoliters) were loaded in the port onto ships sailing for England.[45] Everyone—the archbishop, the chapter, local lords, even the king of England himself—who owned poor land that was unfit for plowing, either because it was gravelly or marshy, planted vines and granted leases for working them. These parcels were principally on the immediate periphery of Bordeaux, the region that currently bears the Graves appellation, to which were added the harvest of the Libournais and, if need be, wines from the *haut pays.* In the Middle Ages very little of the Médoc was planted, in part because it was forbidden to load wine onto a ship downstream from Bordeaux.[46] It is estimated that the English drank annually some twenty liters of wine per person, considerably more than today,[47] and that this was mainly wine from Gascony, though Rhenish wine was now beginning to make its way across the channel. Shakespeare, in *Henry IV,* has Falstaff drink an entire fleet's worth of Bordeaux wine, the equivalent of what Gargantua consumed in Chinon wine.

The wines of Bordeaux also benefited from tax exemptions once they had reached their country of destination. The favorable treatment provided for by the Count of Flanders' decree in 1337, for example, was confirmed a little later when Flanders had been incorporated into the duchy of Burgundy. Philip the Bold sought to assure the prosperity of the merchants of his port cities, even though this ran counter to his plans for the commercial expansion of the wines of Beaune. Even today more Bordeaux than Burgundy is drunk in the Flemish port cities, while the opposite is true in the interior of Belgium.

It may seem surprising that the privilege granted to Bordeaux in 1241 was upheld following the return of Aquitaine to the French crown in 1453, in view of the manifest injustice this represented toward inland producers already disadvantaged by the need to send their wine downriver to Bordeaux by barge, there to be loaded onto oceangoing vessels. At the request of Cahors, Gaillac, Albi, Agen, and other towns, Charles VII did in fact abolish the privilege in 1453, but the following year, out of fear of betrayal by Bordeaux in the event of a resumption of hostilities, he reinstated it, even pushing back the date of the authorized arrival of wines from the hinterlands to 30 November. Seven years later, in 1461, Louis XI pushed it back still further, to 25 December, an arrangement that all his successors were to maintain. In 1773 the president of the parliament of Bordeaux, M. de Gascq, told the governor of Guyenne, Marshal de Richelieu, in no uncertain terms, "Be assured that the parliament will sooner abolish itself than suffer the descent of wines from upriver."[48] Beginning in the sixteenth century, Bordeaux's monopoly was further protected by the requirement that, in order to be sold at Bordeaux, wines had to be stored in barrels of a certain capacity and style. Shipments not meeting this standard were turned away. In this way the merchants of Bergerac, who enjoyed a privilege of their own, were discouraged, along with their counterparts in the Dordogne and the Garonne, from pursuing the export trade,[49] all of them devoting a part of their vineyards to other uses (the cultivation of plums at Agen, for example). More fundamentally, these shipping restrictions were responsible for a lasting inequality between the prosperous countryside of the Gironde and the *haut pays,* which remained poor for centuries afterward. Nature, it need hardly be emphasized, had very little to do with bringing about this state of affairs.

Such contrasts existed in Burgundy, as we have seen, but there they were mainly the consequence of a form of positive discrimination that favored the Côte d'Or, which fell within the sphere of influence of Autun and Dijon. In Bordeaux they were the result of a clear and sustained determination to thwart external competition. Once again one can only agree with Roger Dion when he speaks of "an institution marked . . . by all the signs of excess and iniquity," while acknowledging the talent of the winemakers and merchants of Bordeaux, who managed for so long to perpetuate this system "with the greatest skill," as Turgot said on bringing it to an end in 1776.[50] Great skill, indeed, for it was not enough to protect one's commercial interest; one had also to be able to produce good wine—something at which Bordeaux excelled—in order to meet the demand of a discerning clientele in northern Europe.

THE CALL OF THE NORTH

However great may have been the commercial skill of the merchants of Burgundy and Bordeaux in the Middle Ages, and however great the ability of their growers and vintners, neither region had complete control of its wines on their journey to consumers abroad. Once sent on their way along the Seine and the Saône, and once loaded on English and Flemish ships, their wines were in the hands of foreign merchants. Nor did these merchants have complete control over the wine that they delivered to their clients; they were able only to choose it, to establish a scale of prices based on its quality, and to monitor its progress until it reached its final destination—a prince, a bourgeois notable, another merchant, a tavern owner. For economic reasons it was natural to seek to master the supply chain from beginning to end. Two solutions were possible: either producers and merchants from Burgundy and Bordeaux could settle in the cities where their wine was sold in order to maximize their profits, or foreign shipowners and merchants could come to live in the wine-producing centers and establish themselves in local commerce and viticulture. Both these things occurred in the seventeenth century, but to an incomparably greater extent in Bordeaux than in Burgundy. From this point onward the paths of the two regions diverged, with differences in social and economic circumstance having a greater effect than differences in their geographic situation. The physical environment mattered, but producers, and especially their customers and the merchants who supplied these customers, mattered still more. It is a rule of economic life that the consumer is king, and that producers must adapt to demand; but this rule is not one that wine pro-

fessionals, who take it for granted that they matter most of all (while at
the same time insisting on the blessings and constraints of the physical
landscape), are generally inclined to acknowledge.

The Bordelais have never been great seafarers. They called upon
sailors from the Basque country, Brittany, and Saintonge to undertake
the voyage to the Antilles or the cod shoals of Newfoundland. Foreigners retained control of the transport of wine. The first traders to set foot
in Bordeaux were Dutch.[51] Beginning in the sixteenth century, these
remarkable merchants and navigators supplied themselves with wine
on the shores of France, and from 1617 onward with brandy, a vital
restorative for sailors who passed long months on the sea and in the
tropics.[52] They even ventured into the *haut pays* in search of wine, hoping in this way to find a means of circumventing the regulations of
Bordeaux. Finally, they began to acquire French nationality, at the rate
of two or three families per year, and set to work draining the wetlands
of the Médoc, as they did with many other coastal marshes in France.
The wines that they bought in Gascony they then repackaged in the
ports of Amsterdam and Rotterdam. These were typically adulterated
through the addition of sugar, alcohol, and occasionally various spices.[53]
It was the Dutch who encouraged growers to produce white wines containing more residual sugar and alcohol, making them easier to transport and preserve. This was the origin of the great sweet wines that
were to be perfected in the following centuries—a clear example of climatological conditions and oenological techniques converging to meet
the needs of merchants, who took it upon themselves to educate their
customers, who in turn rapidly acquired a taste for the new product.

Jean de Ridder was one of the first Dutch settlers in Bordeaux, arriving in 1638. That same year he obtained his *lettres de bourgeoisie,* despite
the opposition of certain families of Bordeaux merchants, who viewed
this entitlement as an unwarranted intrusion upon their privileges. In
1641 he married the daughter of the pastor Daniel de Ferrand, thus
entering into respectable Bordeaux society through the side door of its
Protestant minority. Others followed: Daniel Oyens, Guillaume Wijs,

Jean de Bary Willemszoon.[54] In 1654, his membership in the bourgeoisie having been officially recognized, Oyens married the daughter of the German-born Protestant merchant Jacques Savage, and then in 1669 he arranged the marriage of his daughter to the son of Jean de Ridder. The habit of intermarriage took hold, with the result that separate communities emerged in the wine trade. The Catholic Gascon aristocracy, for its part, was allied to the world of the northern merchants by ties of business rather than blood. This pronounced pattern of social and professional segregation—a source of fascination on both sides, as we shall see—is one of the most distinctive features of the culture of Bordeaux.

The British presence was extensive as well. Following the example of the Dutch, trading families from the British Isles opened branch offices along the Garonne. The city proper and the Port de la Lune, already very crowded, were closed to them, but the wetlands downstream from the Château Trompette were available for settlement. These lands belonged to the Chartreux, monks of the Carthusian order founded by Saint Bruno in the eleventh century. Thus came into existence the Quai des Chartrons, which, once the marshes were drained and the banks of the river reinforced, became one of the most important ports of the wine trade in the world for two and a half centuries, on the same level as Paris, Oporto, Seville, London, Bristol, and later Sète. The British merchants lived in apartments that faced directly onto the wharves, with their warehouses extending to the rear, or else on the very elegant Pavé des Chartrons, today called the Cours Xavier-Arnozan.

The first families associated with this residential quarter were the Colcks, Bartons, Johnstons, Lawtons, and Lynches.[55] The history of the settlement in Chartrons of Thomas Barton and Abraham Lawton, Protestants from Cork in Ireland, is well known thanks to the archives conserved by their descendants. German families, such as the Bethmanns of Frankfurt-am-Main, the Schylers of Hamburg, and the Cruses from Holstein, took up residence there as well.[56] All were Protestant (though some later converted to Catholicism) and married into one another's families, forming an endogamous community that gradually gained control over a large part of the brokerage, trading, and transport of wine to the cities of northern Europe, where it was resold to relatives or trusted agents. Once their mortgages on property in Chartrons had been paid off and their fortunes made, they turned their attention to the countryside, looking to acquire existing wine estates or land that was favorable to viticulture. Thus it was that Château Langoa became the pride of the Bartons. Soon these families were as powerful in the countryside as the magistrates of the appeals court *(parlement)* of Bordeaux. Less well connected in northern European trading circles, this parliamentary aristocracy managed to preserve a part of its landed wealth in the Bordelais and the Antilles, but gradually lost its monopoly on the wine trade to the immigrant families of the Chartrons district.

A notable exception to this pattern of migration was the settlement in London of an old parliamentary family from Bordeaux, the Pontacs, but their example seems scarcely to have been imitated. In 1663 the wine of Haut-Brion ("Ho Bryan," as Samuel Pepys famously called it in the 10 April entry in his diary of that year)[57] was sold at the Royal Oake Taverne in London, where it was very highly regarded by connoisseurs. In 1666 Arnaud de Pontac, the *président à mortier* of the parliament of Bordeaux and owner of the Château Haut-Brion at Pessac, sent his son François-Auguste to London to open a tavern, Pontack's Head, in Abchurch Street in the heart of the City. It was a fashionable establishment, at once a deluxe grocery, caterer, and forerunner of what later in Paris were to be called "restaurants."[58] The luminaries of London society—among them John Locke,[59] Daniel Defoe, Jonathan Swift, and Saint-Évremond[60]—came and delighted in drinking the wine from the Pontac family's estate in Bordeaux. Haut-Brion owes its excellence still today as much to the bold initiative of an old aristocratic French family that in the seventeenth century managed to combine political skill and business sense with the ability to make fine wine as to the fine mound of deep gravel that nourishes its vineyard. Other great aristocrats, typically parliamentarians as well, possessed great estates on which they were to plant vines and make fine wines in the eighteenth century, foremost among them the Ségurs at Lafite and Latour, but also the Pichons and the Rauzans in Pauillac and the Aulèdes in Margaux. In 1755, three-quarters of the income from real property of seventy-eight parliamentary families whose records were examined came from the sale of their wines. Their viticultural holdings are estimated at 3,300 hectares, of which half were in the Médoc and the Graves, a significant share of a total area devoted to viticulture in the Bordeaux region estimated at 100,000 hectares.[61] Notwithstanding the admirable care they showed in choosing and managing their domaines, however, only the Pontac family had the idea of delivering its goods directly to the customer.

Merchants in Bordeaux played a decisive role in the revolution in the quality of vine growing and winemaking that occurred in the eighteenth century, a development that is now well documented.[62] Until then they were hampered in the exercise of their profession by the fragile and unstable character of the wines themselves, which therefore had to be sold and consumed in the months immediately following their production. Quite early the Dutch, soon followed by the English, showed an interest in sweet fortified wines, assuring the success of Oporto, Jerez, and Madeira, among other coastal Mediterranean vineyards. Nevertheless, many connoisseurs continued to value the body and roundness of dry red wines.

THE COMPLICITY OF PARIS AND BURGUNDY

The vineyards of Burgundy, lacking the stimulus provided by resident foreign merchants and the insistent demands of an immense market in northern Europe, were smaller in extent than those of Bordeaux. In part this was due, too, to the disadvantage of a more difficult climate, especially during the "little ice age" of the eighteenth century. In the sixteenth century, the wines of the Côte d'Or still benefited from the reputation they enjoyed in the time of the grand dukes of the Western kingdom, particularly in Flanders, as Erasmus testifies.[63] Thanks to Louis XIV's physician, Fagon, they won a place of honor for themselves at the court of Versailles after a hard-fought struggle. The king's favorite wine, from Champagne, was suspected of upsetting his nerves and of giving him gout. Fagon noted in his diary in 1694:

> Toward the end of these throes of gout, whose pain and discomfort persuaded the king better than all the reasons I had often had the honor of recalling to him in hopes of obliging him to give up the wine of Champagne and to drink old Burgundy wine, he resolved to conquer the injury it caused to his taste and to try to see if he could accustom himself to it. I heard this announcement with great joy, and I did not in the least doubt that he was absolutely resigned to it, knowing with what resolve his heroic courage made him persevere in courses of action that he thought the best and on which he had decided himself without allowing himself to be disturbed by difficulties.[64]

Fagon went on to remark that "the smoothness of the good wines of Burgundy, caused by the power of the vital spirits, gives them a taste by which the tongue is gently caressed, as soothing for the nerves as it is tasteless to the mouth."[65] Note the reference not only to the smoothness of these wines but also to their lack of flavor. Louis XIV, of course, like all civilized drinkers since antiquity and long after his own time as well, diluted his wine with water.[66] However much the king may have preferred the still wines of Champagne, he nonetheless complied with his doctor's wishes and thereafter drank only Burgundy. There is no indication that he really liked it better, or that his gout disappeared as a consequence, which is unlikely in view of his diet. And yet polite society in Paris followed the royal example without hesitation. Bossuet, a native of Dijon who retained his Burgundian palate, relished Volnay.[67]

The memory of this beneficial prescription remained vivid in the region, but since Fagon's diary was not published until 1862, authors rearranged the facts in the interval to suit their own purposes. A document composed in July 1794 (18 Messidor of Year II of the revolutionary calendar), at the time of the sale of property seized by the state, described this decisive choice in very romanticized terms:

Louis XIV, having been treated for a fistula, was reduced to a deplorable and disturbing state of weakness. The physicians gathered to find a way to revive his strength. They were of the opinion that the most effective way was to choose the most excellent old wines of the Côte de Nuits and [the Côte] de Beaune. Some [of these wines] were purchased, the patient availed himself of them, and his health was promptly restored. That of Romanée indisputably worked the greatest wonders.[68]

Fagon, in any case, although he was born in Paris and had not a drop of Burgundian blood in his veins, soon passed for a native son, with a street being named after him in Nuits-Saint-Georges. The royal commands had an immediate effect: demand soared and the market price of Burgundy wines doubled. What motivated Fagon to take up the cause of these wines with such fervor? Quite simply, a desire to take the opposite line from his predecessors, champions of the wines of Champagne (red, pale pink, and white, though not sparkling).

We know that as early as 1652 a physician from Beaune, Daniel Arbinet, had argued in favor of the eminently healthful properties of Burgundy wine; physicians from Champagne naturally argued the contrary position. The quarrel lasted well into the eighteenth century, when the international triumph of sparkling champagne finally caused it to die out. Red Burgundy wine no longer had anything to fear, for red wine was hardly produced anymore in Champagne, and the production of sparkling red wine in Burgundy was to remain limited in the nineteenth and early twentieth centuries;[69] as for the sparkling white wine (crémant) made in Burgundy today, it presents no challenge to champagne's market dominance, if only for reasons of price.

The passage from Fagon's diary reveals another aspect of Burgundian oenology in the late seventeenth century that has been little noticed: he recommends that his royal patient drink *old* wine from the Côte de Nuits. Though Burgundy wines of this period probably did not resemble the ones that were to be produced later, still they ranked among the best then available in Europe, and refined methods of production ensured that they now kept longer than before and, more importantly, improved with age.[70] Fagon's prescription notwithstanding, the king and his courtiers were sufficiently discerning to recognize the superior wines of their day, and wealthy enough to afford them. The judgment of Henri Enjalbert, that the wines of Burgundy at the beginning of the eighteenth century were "new, pure in taste and quite honest, but in no way great wines, such as Burgundy was to produce at the end of the eighteenth century," therefore cannot be accepted without qualification, any more than his verdict with regard to the wines of the medieval vineyards; it can apply only to run-of-the-mill wines.[71] The revolution had already taken place in the *clos,* above all in Nuits-Saint-Georges.[72] It is also clear that if the wines of Bordeaux had been markedly better than those of Burgundy under the reign of Louis XIV, which Enjalbert does not claim, this would have been known, and it would have been a simple matter to create a commercial route from Bordeaux to Paris via the Atlantic, Rouen, and the Seine Valley. The reality is that a few wines from the Côte d'Or, along with a few from the Graves and the Médoc, were among the best ones then available on the European market, and already enjoyed some of the benefits of aging. They were not yet highly concentrated wines suited to long keeping, but both regions were already experimenting with methods for achieving this result.

As in Bordeaux and everywhere else in France, the great parliamentary families of Burgundy invested in land, preferably vineyards.[73] In 1618, André Frémyot, the president of the Chambre des Comptes, bought the Clos de la Violette at Chenôve, a property of the king. He was followed by a councillor named Morizot, who acquired the Clos Saint-Jacques at Gevrey; by Jomard, who acquired the Clos de Bèze, also at Gevrey, until then the property of the chapter of Langres; by Bouhier, chief magistrate of the *parlement,* who in 1662 bought for Cîteaux the Clos de la Perrière at Fixin; and by d'Esmonin, who bought Charlemagne for the chapter of Saulieu. Other noble families from outside the region also settled there.

The most celebrated acquisition was that of the Domaine de la

Romanée by the Prince of Conti.[74] Originally this exceptional *clos* belonged to the abbey of Saint-Vivant, located at the foot of the Château of Vergy, a few miles away. The monks leased it on a long-term basis (up to ninety-nine years) to various dignitaries of Dijon beginning in the late sixteenth century. In 1631 the vineyard passed by marriage to Philippe de Croonembourg, a native of Flanders who was lord of Saint-Genois in Burgundy; it remained for four generations in the same family and then, on 18 July 1760, André de Croonembourg sold it to Louis François de Bourbon, Prince of Conti, lord of Nuits and Argilly, who paid 80,000 francs (plus another 12,400 francs under the table) for forty *ouvrées* (less than 1.8 hectares).[75] To appreciate how exceptional this parcel of land (or *climat*) was, one must keep in mind that the Clos de Bèze at Gevrey—incontestably a *grand cru,* covering 428 square meters (about one-twelfth of a hectare)—had been sold ten years earlier for a sum almost ten times less per *ouvrée* (250 francs, as against 2,310 francs in the case of La Romanée). This extraordinary transaction proves that connoisseurs could already tell the difference between the wines and that this ranking of quality justified all manner of extravagance. During the last years prior to the sale, the Croonembourgs sold their wine *en feuillettes* (half casks of 114 liters), and its price was six or seven times higher than that of wine from the Clos de Vougeot, just as today the straw wines of the Jura and the ice wines of Germany are sold in half bottles for a small fortune. The purchase at this unprecedented price of the part of La Romanée that was to become Romanée-Conti caused such a stir that a legend grew up around it.[76] Richard Olney and Jean-François Bazin have finally disposed of the myth of a fierce struggle between the prince and the Marquise de Pompadour (who admittedly had little love for him) invented by the inhabitants of Vosne in order to enhance still more the prestige of their greatest vineyard.[77] The extravagance of the sum paid by the Prince of Conti is also explained by the fact that it included the debts that Philippe de Croonembourg had bequeathed to his son André, who pocketed only the under-the-table portion of the sale price.[78]

The prince accepted André de Croonembourg's proposition in exchange for the exclusive privilege of being able to serve the most precious wine of Burgundy at his sumptuous table, both in the Palais du Temple in Paris and at the Château de l'Isle-Adam in Val d'Oise. In view of the scale of production (hardly more than two thousand to three thousand bottles per year, and sometimes much less),[79] the Prince of Conti never sold any of it, not even to his royal cousin, who had in any case allowed himself to be carried away—la Pompadour surely did have a hand in this—by the pleasures of champagne bubbles. The entire vintage was reserved for the refined indulgence of the great minds who dined with the prince at the Temple and at L'Isle-Adam. The fact that dining etiquette in these twin centers of Enlightenment sociability was very strongly influenced by the Anglomania of the prince's mistress, the Comtesse de Boufflers, suggests that Romanée-Conti at this time was (and perhaps still is today, considering that only a small number of very wealthy people can afford it) drunk in the same spirit as the *grands crus* of Bordeaux in London.

The whole Dijon bourgeoisie subsequently followed the lead of the parliamentary magistrates, buying *clos* and building splendid manors in the villages and towns of the Côte. These residences constitute a good part of the classical architecture of Beaune and Nuits, and of villages such as Gevrey, Vosne, and Aloxe. A few châteaus were constructed in the region as well, equipped with vast cellars such as those of Meursault and Pommard, for example, but there was nothing on the scale one finds among the estate proprietors of Bordeaux, who have not ceased building for four centuries. It is true that most domaines in Bordeaux are considerably larger, with greater quantities of wine to be stored and more customers to be captivated. The old Burgundian custom was to pretend that the show was sold out, as it were, reserving a domaine's wine for the consumption of its owners and a few favored friends, in the manner of the abbey of Cîteaux and the Prince of Conti. Even today, as we will see, many domaines do not accept new clients, and the details of their production are confidential. Under these circumstances there is no need for propriety.

Trade likewise made its appearance in Burgundy in the eighteenth century, only here it was in the hands of families from the region rather than buyers from the north.[80] The merchant house of Champy opened for business in 1720, Lavirotte in 1725, Bouchard in 1731, Labaume in 1734, Poulet in 1747, and Verry-Chanson in 1750. As in Bordeaux, some merchants also invested in vineyards and became owners: Claude Jobert at Gevrey, for example, who worked the Clos de Bèze and many other renowned vineyards, and Claude Marey at Nuits, founder of the famous dynasty that was to become Marey-Monge. All these merchants sold their wine in Paris, in the north of France, in Wallonia, and in Germany, where some houses built up fabled clienteles.

The eighteenth century was a very auspicious time for both Bordeaux and Burgundy. Acquisition of land by powerful families and the growing density of parcels planted with vines, together with the investment that accompanied them, gave rise to perceptible progress in viticulture and the quality of wines. The prosperity was general, enriching winemakers and society as a whole. The properties under cultivation were not the same, and increasingly the wine that came from them differed between the two regions, but the causes of progress were the same: the demands of connoisseurs raised both viticulture and vinification to new heights. As in the Middle Ages, the boundaries between the respective areas of consumption remained clear, with Bordeaux wines going to countries accessible by sea in northern Europe, and Burgundy wines to Paris and to lands accessible by road or river.[81] Their consumers were distinguished, too, by the cultural significance that they attached to wine. This distinctive geography of consumption was to have a powerful effect on the wines themselves.

THE SIMULTANEOUS INVENTION
OF LONG-KEEPING WINES

The two regions, each supported by substantial numbers of wealthy customers, jointly underwent a technical revolution in the eighteenth century that was to lead to the production of wines benefiting from longer maceration of the skins of the grapes in their juice *(cuvaison)*. These wines were therefore more deeply colored, richer in natural alcohol, better suited to aging, and more likely to improve as a consequence of aging. Despite the relative isolation of Bordeaux and Burgundy from each other, this revolution occurred more or less at the same time in both places as a result of recent advances in the agronomic and biological sciences.

Wines that blend power and finesse can be achieved only by very deliberate efforts on the part of winemakers. Their work costs money, and therefore is performed only in response to a demanding and wealthy clientele. Henri Enjalbert somewhat chauvinistically tries to show that Bordeaux discovered the secret of fine wines well before everyone else, going as far as to claim that "it was only very gradually, during the nineteenth century, that the slopes characterized by flows of chalky, stony soil were identified with the vineyard of the Burgundian Côte."[82] This is to neglect the Clos de Bèze (which, beginning in 1049, the canons of Langres had eagerly sought to buy from the abbey that owned it, succeeding only in 1219), the Clos de Vougeot and the Cloux de Vosne, and Montrachet (esteemed since the Middle Ages for its white wine, "the most curious and the most delicate" in France, as the Abbé Arnoux said in 1728).[83] The trial of 1760 involving Claude Jobert, owner of the Clos de Bèze, and the chapter of Langres, title to whose land Jobert held in copyhold—an arrangement that obliged him to deliver annually to the chapter's canons ten casks of good wine from the vineyard—unambiguously shows that the canons, educated connoisseurs that they were, could tell the difference between the select *tête de cuvée* that they were entitled to receive and the mediocre lots that were actually sent. The canons clearly specified what they expected: "No one does not know that in making a selection from the ripest grapes, and in separating the fruits of the old plants from the ones that the new plants give, a first *cuvée* is made that will be very superior in quality to the second. Such is the method of those who wish to provide themselves with the most exquisite wines from the best year possible."[84]

Enjalbert is quite right, on the other hand, in explaining the slowness with which the wines of the Côte d'Or made their presence felt on the Paris market by reference to the little ice age, the effects of which were particularly pronounced in 1709,[85] and to the habit that arose from this of looking to Hermitage, and even farther south to the Côtes de Rhône, for alternative sources of supply.[86] In temperate years, however, the white wines of Auxerre and Chablis, nearer and easier to ship by river routes, managed to carve out a sizable part of the Parisian market for themselves. Above all, Enjalbert emphasizes that "the taste peculiar to [Burgundy's] principal clientele, that of Dijon and Lyons, Montbéliard, and Lorraine . . . , gave preference to young wines, of agreeable taste and moderate price, which therefore did not encourage the pursuit of finesse through aging."[87] This analysis agrees with that of Roger Dion in assigning to consumers the major role in the emergence of quality. Once Louis XIV and his court, and then the Prince of Conti, desired to drink fine, full-bodied Burgundy, the revolution took place. During this period Bordeaux enjoyed no decisive advantage with respect to the volume of production, except where the difference was already substantial. By the middle of the eighteenth century, there existed very great Bordeaux wines (the famous "new French clarets" favored by the English, first mentioned in 1703) and very great Burgundies of equal quality, even if the former were available in greater quantities than the latter.[88] The technological developments that created them, a response to the demand of a sophisticated clientele, were practically the same.

The selection of grape varieties had already been well underway since the Middle Ages in the best vineyards of the Côte d'Or, where pinot noir and chardonnay yielded the finest wines, whereas other properties in the region still used many grape varieties, among which gamay was dominant. Wines made from this productive grape were intended for working-class consumers. The mixing of grape varieties within individual vineyards (one vestige of this practice survives today in the form of Bourgogne Passetoutgrains) derived from the search for a way to guarantee a constant level of production from year to year in the face of crop losses due to bad weather. Gradually, in the course of the nineteenth century, the turn toward monocultural production took shape within individual *climats,* whose wines did not always manage to achieve their fullest potential in the event that an out-of-favor varietal was chosen.[89] I shall come back to this point later.

In Bordeaux, by contrast, the situation is different: several prestigious grape varieties still compete with one another today, in proportions that vary from one area of the region to another and from one estate to another: cabernet sauvignon, cabernet franc, merlot, petit verdot, and cot (malbec) among the reds, and sémillon, sauvignon, muscadelle, ugni blanc, and colombard among the whites. The skill of the proprietors and their vineyard managers consists in choosing the right combination, and in some cases the particular grape variety, that will make it possible not only to realize the virtues of the soil and the microclimate as fully as possible, but also to satisfy consumers' tastes.

In the seventeenth century a serious question arose, as much in Burgundy as in Bordeaux,[90] having to do with the blending of local wines with ones from other regions, notably Hermitage and Côtes-du-Rhône (and, in the case of Bordeaux, with *haut pays* wines made from Alicante and Benicarlo). The practice was common and, like its prohibition, was long to remain so. In 1756, for example, the *parlement* of Bordeaux strictly forbade all blending of local wines with others.[91] This is readily explained, for the magistrates were all owners of vineyards and producers of good wines, and therefore wished to maintain their privilege. Such blendings were typically carried out in the warehouses on the Quai des Chartrons, even after the merchants had themselves become owners of châteaus, for they marketed a wide range of wines, from *grands crus* to table wines. I shall consider this situation in greater detail later.

Making a *grand vin,* which is to say the finest wine produced by a

château, requires enlisting nature's assistance by choosing those loca-
tions that are most favorable to the sinking of the vines' roots and the
ripening of their fruit. Soil and climate can, of course, be improved, but
it is certainly an advantage if initial conditions are good. The first step
is therefore to identify well-drained soils that force the vine to strike
deep into the ground in search of nourishment in the form of water,
mineral salts, and organic matter. The ripening of the fruit is much
more of a problem in Burgundy, where the growing season is shorter
than in Bordeaux. Assuming adequate drainage, a slope in Burgundy
with the right gradient and exposure to sunlight can approximate the
growing conditions of more southerly regions. The soundness of the
judgment of vineyard owners in choosing the best *terroirs* was first manifested, as we have seen, in the Middle Ages in Burgundy, and subsequently in the seventeenth and especially the eighteenth centuries, this
time in both Burgundy and Bordeaux. Enjalbert insists, again altogether correctly, that a process of trial and error had to be undergone
before the exact relationship between good wine and good land could
be determined, arguing that "this 'realization' could only have come
about as a result of experiment, in other words, once the desired quality had been obtained."[92] It was an exciting and time-consuming business, greatly accelerated today by modern advances in agronomic and
oenological knowledge, and it is now taking place throughout the
world, in old vineyards of secondary renown in France and elsewhere
in Europe, in new lands conquered by the vine in North America, and
in wine-producing countries of the southern hemisphere. This process
of trial and error illustrates the absence of any geographic inevitability
or determinism—the equivalent for space of what some used to call,
with regard to time, the "direction of history"—in the development of
viticulture. It fully confirms the interpretation proposed by Roger Dion,
and calls to mind Jean Bodin's adage that there is no wealth other than
human wealth.

In both Burgundy and Bordeaux the seventeenth and eighteenth
centuries were marked by notable changes in the art of making wine.

As far as viticulture was concerned, it is probable that little or nothing changed before the phylloxera invasion of the mid-nineteenth century, except with regard to the not insignificant issue of the maturity of the grapes when harvested. In the case of white or rosé (light red or pale pink) wines, it was important to preserve enough acidity so that they could travel and keep at least until the next harvest, and therefore to select a certain quantity of unripe grapes for their juice. Thus Abbé Tainturier wrote in 1763, "We need some cooked, roasted, and green [grapes]; these last are even necessary, they improve in the vat through fermentation with the others, they are what gives freshness to the wine.... It is not a matter of having to decide whether complete maturity is needed or [grapes that are still] a little green. Experience has [already] taught us that complete maturity renders wines heavy, sluggish, and ropy, flowing like oil."[93] The defect of oiliness that Abbé Tainturier describes was in fact due to a lack of hygiene and reliance upon used barrels. At the time he wrote, the better domaines (religious, aristocratic, and bourgeois) had already learned to avoid it. They also harvested at just the right moment, when the grapes were sufficiently ripe to yield wines with rather high alcohol content that were therefore better able to extract the color and tannins of the grape skins, resulting in a more full-bodied and longer-keeping vintage.[94] Abbé Tainturier's advice, then, was plainly directed to small peasant proprietors who produced generic wines. In these wines the right amount of acidity could only assist their preservation, especially if they were stored in used casks, whose cleanliness was doubtful. The habit of adding verjuice was to persist on the Côte throughout the nineteenth century, and in the Hautes-Côtes until the 1990s. Today Burgundian makers of white wine are inclined instead to rejoice in the presence at harvest of a few grapes affected by the noble rot, for it gives some "fat," or fullness, to the wine. In the case of reds, by contrast, they avoid harvesting grapes affected by rot or adding any verjuice. Strict standards of hygiene are observed almost everywhere today, so unpleasant surprises on this account are few.

The great revolution of the eighteenth century in the realm of hygiene, involving the use of sulfur, came from Holland. A sulfur wick was burned in a rinsed cask in order to disinfect it—that is, to kill bacteria—before it was filled with wine from a racked barrel. Even if the wine loses a little color at this stage, it is quickly recovered, and the wine keeps for a long time. René Pijassou discovered the first mention of this procedure in a document composed in English dating from 1765, conserved in the archives of Nathaniel Johnston et Fils, the Chartrons firm founded by a family of Irish merchants.[95] There this wick is called a Dutch match, revealing the origin of the procedure. The Dutch also appear to have tried to protect against secondary fermentations and deleterious oxidations, for they were great connoisseurs of fragile sweet wines, which they imported in quantity. The sulfur wick technique spread rapidly in the late eighteenth century, not only in Bordeaux, but also throughout Europe, including Burgundy. There are purists today who seek to dispense with the use of sulfur in the process of vinification and subsequent cellar work *(élevage)*. This can be done successfully only under perfectly sanitary conditions; but because the risk of infection can never be entirely eliminated, the majority of winemakers around the world today continue to rely on it, both on the vine, in the form of a copper sulfate known as Bordeaux mixture, and in the cellar, even if much less sulfur is used now than two or three decades ago.

Other improvements in the techniques employed in the cellar following fermentation—topping up, racking, *fouettage* (the whipping up of a fining agent such as egg white), fining,[96] and, of course, the addition of spirits (the basis of what was called *travail à l'anglaise*)—made it possible to keep wines in cask for up to three years before they were bottled.[97] Additionally, the use of new barrels became more widespread for *grands vins,* increasing the sale price. All these technological advances came from the merchants of the Quai des Chartrons; it was only later that they were adopted by the châteaus of the region.

The packaging of wines was important as well. Glass bottles date back to antiquity, although glass in its earliest form could not be blown to form large vessels.[98] The bottles that were produced first in ancient Egypt, and thereafter throughout the Mediterranean basin, were small and used mainly for perfumes and various kinds of cosmetics. Large bottles were made in the Middle Ages and during the Renaissance, particularly in Venice, but their walls were so thin that they could not be transported over long distances, and they were used instead for the presentation of wines on prestigious banquet tables. Most were so fragile that they were cased in straw or wicker and covered with leather. Moreover, their bottoms were typically rounded, since they retained the shape of the bubble detached from the glassmaker's blowpipe, a rudimentary technique that was preserved in Tuscany for straw-sheathed flasks of Chianti until quite recently.

It was the English, Flemish, and Dutch who perfected the art of bottle making, a necessity for merchants who bought wines in casks and needed to sell them on a retail basis. Refinements in the composition of glass, together with the use of coal as fuel for furnaces, made it possible to produce glass bottles that were both thicker and darker. Bottles manufactured in northern Europe during the seventeenth century originally had a half-onion shape, but already it was known how to make a recessed bottom using a punty so that the bottle could stand up. Gradually, in the late seventeenth and early eighteenth centuries, the use of molds permitted bottles to be made in the shape of an inverted truncated cone (so that they could be more easily removed from the mold after blowing) and in ever-closer approximations of a cylinder, allowing them to be laid down for storage. Another source of innovation in bottling technology was the success of sparkling champagne. In the absence of bottles and, of course, the ability to seal them as hermetically as possible, the precious carbon dioxide that resulted from the second fermentation in the spring following harvest could not be conserved. It was therefore rather a chicken-and-egg situation: effervescent champagne was not possible without solid bottles, but without champagne there was little need for solid bottles. Both Bordeaux and Burgundy stood to benefit from the fashion for champagne, however, and merchants, like consumers, very quickly recognized the great advantage of bottling. The black color of the glass and the sealing of bottles with Spanish or Portuguese cork allowed still red and white wines to be kept in excellent condition and, when they were well made, to improve over the years, acquiring much richer and more nuanced colors, bouquets, and flavors than young wines.

In response to demand, merchants in both Bordeaux and Burgundy contracted with local manufacturers in order to be able to ship their best wines already bottled and with more extensive guarantees of safekeeping than previously had been possible. The first glassworks to produce bottles of black glass, using English coal, opened in Bordeaux around 1723–25, in Sainte-Foy-la-Grande in 1735, and in Libourne in 1750.[99] In Burgundy, the family of Clermont-Tonnerre opened the first glassworks at Épinac-les-Mines in 1752.[100] Beginning in 1728, however, one could buy old Chambertin in London, shipped in bottles and twice as expensive as other wines, a reflection also of its exquisite quality. We have the testimony of Abbé Claude Arnoux, then an exile in the English capital: "I drank some six years after the year that produced it, which fell cloudy and thick into the glass, and which cleared up at once before our eyes, and which then by the motion of its spirits took on the clearest and most vivid color."[101]

It is plain, then, that there are many more similarities than differences in the history of the origins of winemaking in the two regions. One of the principal divergences, which I have already emphasized more than once, has to do with the destination of their wines. The wines of Bordeaux traveled by sea to lands lying on the English Channel and the North Sea; the wines of Burgundy traveled along rivers and roads as far as Paris, northeastern France, present-day Belgium and Luxembourg, and northwest Germany. Cultural differences among these various customers accentuated the differences among the wines themselves, all the more since foreign merchants had settled in Bordeaux and left a strong mark on both the vineyards and the wines of the region, whereas the Burgundy trade remained mainly in the hands of local and Parisian houses. Of course, even if this geohistorical approach grants primacy to the role of a wine's clientele, it can hardly ignore the part played by the physical landscape and the ways in which it was recognized, tamed, and modified in order finally to be able to make fine wines, which is to say wines that pleased their consumers and flattered their taste.

CHAPTER 3
THE PHYSICAL ENVIRONMENT

No matter that the physical environments in which the wines of Bordeaux and Burgundy were born scarcely resemble each other; they nonetheless have certain characteristics in common, the same ones that all vineyards of quality have shared since antiquity. The vine, that unruly creeper of arid Mediterranean lands, produces fine grapes that yield good wines as long as it has its feet in dry earth and its head in the sun. The less water the soil retains, the deeper the vine sinks its roots in search of the precious liquid and the more fully it mobilizes the mineral matter that comes to be concentrated in the grape. In Bordeaux it is hot enough for the vine's fruits to ripen even on flat land; but not in Burgundy, where exposure to the sun and therefore the steepness of the slope assume great importance, as they do everywhere to the north of a line running from Valence to Nantes. In both regions the presence of gravel, which favors drainage, is an essential factor in the qualitative differentiation of *terroirs*. Of course, the fine clayey and marly matter that coats the larger pebbles also plays a positive role, endowing wines with richness and roundness. Yet the interaction of these elements is hardly straightforward: the vines of Château Latour are planted in the thickest gravel in all of Bordeaux, whereas scarcely a pebble is to be found at Château Pétrus.

The physical component of the landscape must therefore be approached with the greatest caution, all the more since owners (as well as many scholars who have studied the question) readily assume that the established hierarchy of classed wines is intrinsic to an immutable, definitive geography, and that nothing can ever be done about it. In reality it is all a question of scale and of the commercial prospects for development. Official rankings, following rules that have been in force since the creation of the Institut National des Appellations d'Origine (INAO) in 1935, are based on "local, fair, and constant" practices. Constancy, an unjust and in any case debatable criterion, assumes the antiquity of a wine's reputation, which is far from being explained solely by the "natural" virtues of the land from which it comes.

UNDERWORKED *TERROIRS* IN BURGUNDY

In the vicinity of the famous vineyards of both Bordeaux and Burgundy, one finds land that is favorable to the production of fine wines but that, owing to its situation with respect to markets of consumption, has not yet been developed to its full potential, and so remains undiscovered.

In Burgundy one thinks of the slopes north of Dijon, where viticulture has traditionally yielded mediocre results and where the vines destroyed by phylloxera have not been replanted. In the Haute-Saône, for example, the few surviving vineyards that now are trying to rise up again from their ashes (Champlitte, for example) produce agreeable wines, but nothing comparable to what comes from the Côte d'Or or the neighboring districts of the Jura.[1] This is all the more surprising since, still farther to the north, the southern part of the Champagne region has enjoyed a remarkable upturn in the last fifty years. Certain champagnes from the Aube, made by the growers themselves, are more than honorable. The rosé from the village of Les Riceys enjoys an impressive reputation that has made it one of the most expensive still pink wines in France, and indeed in the world. So prestigious is the image of champagne that considerable pressure has been exerted, probably not altogether properly at first, to extend the area of the AOC; thanks to the combined efforts of merchants and growers, the gap that once separated these wines from those of the Côte des Blancs and the Montagne de Reims has now been almost completely closed. The vineyards of Verzenay, for example, like those of the north-facing slopes on the left bank of the Marne, are rated at 100 percent.[2] The pinot noir grapes harvested there yield wines of a fine fullness, which goes to show that exposure does not account for everything, especially when, in order to protect vineyards from biting spring frosts, managers take the precaution of spraying them with water so that the buds are covered by a protective shell of ice.

To the south the contrast is less dramatic but striking nonetheless. The slopes of the Côte Chalonnaise and the Mâconnais district of Burgundy have excellent soils that are the product of various sedimentary layers. Well exposed to the east and the south, in addition to being more southerly, these slopes are less vulnerable to spring frosts. The red and white wines produced there from the same grape varieties as in the Côte d'Or, pinot noir and chardonnay, are honorable, and occasionally excellent, but none reaches the level of reputation of the *grands crus* of the Côte de Nuits or the Côte de Beaune. This is not due to a lack of talent for making wine. The main reason has to do with yields, which (with the approval of the INAO) everywhere exceed sixty hectoliters per hectare.[3] Concentrated wines cannot be produced under such conditions.[4] If yields were lower, obviously the sale prices of these wines would be higher. In that case, growers claim, their wines would find no buyers, for their clientele is not prepared to pay more than a certain price for a bottle of Rully or Mâcon-Viré. Thus, it is supposed, the real (or presumed) customer is served. As a result, the price of vineyards here is markedly lower than in the Côte d'Or, which helps keep the wines at a reasonable price, far lower than that of wines from more prestigious appellations to the north. Even Georges Blanc, chef-owner of a Michelin three-star restaurant in Vonnas, in the Ain, sees neither the possibility nor the advantage of escaping the logic of this state of affairs at his Domaine d'Azenay, where he produces a perfectly acceptable but unmemorable Mâcon, and one that at seventy hectoliters per hectare is more expensive than most of its competitors.

The best proof that there is nothing inevitable about the undervaluation of Mâcon is that some viticulturalists have nonetheless dared to defy tradition and succeeded in producing fine wines. Regarding Domaine Guffens-Heynen at Vergisson, for example, one finds this judgment in Bettane and Desseauve's well-respected guide:

> We hardly know of any vineyard that is better cultivated than this tiny prestigious domaine situated on the magnificent slopes of Vergisson and Pierreclos, which at last redeems all those of its kind. . . . Maine Guffens . . . supplies her husband with grapes that are bursting with juice and aroma, ideally balanced, that he vinifies with inspired intuition, the old-fashioned way, with the aid of his little upright hand-operated press and his top-quality barrels. Their sparkling collaboration produces wines that, for their richness and elegance, are probably the most unforgettable of the Mâconnais region.[5]

Meticulous attention of this sort, with yields not exceeding forty hectoliters per hectare, obviously comes at a cost to the consumer. The wines of this domaine sell for about €15, about twice the average price. The exceptional wines produced by Jean Thévenet at Clessé, with the same yields, go for €20 a bottle. J.-A. Ferret at Fuissé sells his Pouillys, produced at twenty hectoliters per hectare, at about the same price, a very honest rate of exchange that warrants the following comment from Bettane and Desseauve: "The Perrières and Ménétrières have the most distinctive character, with notes of roasted hazelnut that recall the best Corton-Charlemagnes, while the Clos and especially the Tournant-de-Pouilly give more delicate and purer bouquets, very near to the supreme elegance of a Chevalier-Montrachet."[6]

Much the same thing might be said about the properties and the wines of the Côte Chalonnaise. The Rullys made by Jacqueson and the

Givrys from Jablot and Clos Salomon are further proof that great pinots can be wrested from the soil of Burgundy for less than a dozen euros a bottle.[7] The methods applied by Aubert and Paméla de Villaine on their estate in Bouzeron, much of it planted with the worthy aligoté grape, are comparably rigorous to those employed at Vosne-Romanée. The yields hover around forty hectoliters per hectare, or about half the usual figure, with surprising results. Bettane and Desseauve put their finger on the essential reason: "To be honest, there is nothing at all humble about the *terroir* of Bouzeron, because it gives the aligoté grape a force of expression and a harmony unknown elsewhere in Burgundy, with real possibilities for aging. The reds of La Digoine are more exceptional still, for the elegance of their bouquet and the sensations they produce in the mouth, thereby showing the promise of properties whose potential too often fails to be sufficiently exploited."[8] In the vicious circles of vinous mediocrity and the virtuous circles of excellence, the decisive factor is none other than the work of the winemaker.

For a long time land in the Hautes-Côtes of Beaune and Nuits was similarly underworked. In the eyes of the owners and growers of the Côte d'Or, these properties, which have the misfortune of lying some one hundred meters above them, merited only the scornful name Arrière-Côte (Rear Slope), a phrase still condescendingly used by Rolande Gadille in her 1967 work on the vineyards of Burgundy, written at a time when these half-ruined villages practiced a dull polyculture, cassis being one of the only profitable crops.[9] And yet in 1935, a teacher posted to Meloisey named Étienne Kayser recommended planting pinot noir rather than gamay, rightly accusing the latter of having kept the area mired in mediocrity and identifying it as the reason for the refusal of the INAO to approve a specific appellation. The merit of his advice was eventually recognized, and the appellations Bourgogne Hautes-Côtes-de-Beaune and Bourgogne Hautes-Côtes-de-Nuits were awarded in 1961. Today viticulturalists such as Claire Naudin, Gilles Jayer, Bernard Hudelot, and Gilbert and Philippe Germain, by dint of disciplined effort and an intimate knowledge of their slopes, have succeeded in producing Burgundies that regularly reach the level of those of the "Basse Côte."[10] This should in no way come as a surprise, since fault systems above Beaune and Nuits have endowed the upper slopes with the same soils as the prestigious appellations below. Thus, for example, in the named plots of land owned by the Rouard and Jiromée families of Villars-Fontaine (the latter parcels having been sculpted into narrow terraces using a mechanical excavator), one finds the same exposed south-facing white marl as at Corton-Charlemagne. Nor is it surprising that the chardonnay grape should give stunning results there: meaty wines, long in the mouth, mixing notes of honey, lemon, and toasted bread. They are thought expensive for the Hautes-Côtes, but very fairly priced indeed by comparison with the unaffordable white *grands crus* cultivated below. It is worth noting that the quality producers of the Hautes-Côtes represent practically a first generation of winemakers, since their parents were typically cereal growers and animal breeders rather than vine growers, and since the wines produced here were long made from gamay, aligoté, and a number of appalling hybrid grapes.

One of the best viticulturalists of the upper slopes, Bernard Hudelot, foresees a promising future for the wines of this appellation. The exceptional character of the 2003 vintage, the year of the great heat wave in France, and the quality of the preceding years, also due to the unusually high temperatures of recent summers, fill him with hope: "Never in the past have the Hautes-Côtes-de-Nuits regularly yielded wines as high in alcohol, with dark and deep colors. This 'new quality' of wines, quite comparable to what one finds in the *premiers crus* and *grands crus,* has been repeated for eight years in a row. The continuation of this warming trend in the future would have the consequence, in the short term, of shifting to the north and to higher altitudes the 'great wine *terroirs*' that are particularly favorable to pinot noir."[11] Hudelot is not alone in anticipating changes to the viticultural methods presently practiced in the Côte d'Or. Martin Prieur, at Meursault, still does everything he can in accordance with local tradition to maximize the exposure of the chardonnay grapes of his domaine to the sun, lifting up vine shoots and drastically pruning them. But he warns that Mediterranean methods would have to be introduced if summers in the future remain as hot as they are today and the harvests remain as early. In that event, pruning would have to be curtailed and the foliage pulled down toward the ground to make sure that overripening of the grapes does not cause their level of acidity, and therefore the wine's capacity for aging, to fall too sharply.[12] A continuation of climatic warming would in any case have the great advantage of eliminating chaptalization (the addition of sugar to the grape juice or must in the course of fermentation to increase alcoholic strength), a practice that has been used and abused in all northern vineyards.[13]

The underexploitation of potential is also found in the Beaujolais. Falling within the orbit of Lyons, with its large market of working-class consumers (going back to the silk workers of the nineteenth century), this region was oriented from a very early time to the production of cheap, thirst-quenching wines. Gamay, a hearty and productive grape well suited to local soils and, in particular, to the granite bedrock was a natural choice, and today it remains the basis for a wine that has become the third river of Lyons.[14] The national, and then international, vogue for Beaujolais nouveau was a magnificent stroke of advertising that assured the appellation healthy profits, but momentum has now been lost.[15] And yet even in an area so devoted to high-volume production that some producers take pride in adorning their labels with the phrase *pisse-dru* (piss-thick), others are turning away in the direction of finesse and concentration. Marcel Lapierre, in Villié-Morgon, is one of the pioneers of this tendency, which is likely to grow.[16] Another owner-grower in Villié-Morgon, Louis-Claude Desvignes, produces exceptional bottles that Bettane and Desseauve claim are "perfectly capable of competing with the best Cortons." It is true that, like Moulin-à-Vents, Morgons sometimes rival the pinots of the Côte d'Or; but to go from rivaling a Corton to being confused with a Corton is a big step. Even so, that step is now apparently being attempted, again in defiance of the sacrosanct doctrine of *terroir* and grape variety.

Chablis illustrates yet another recent development in Burgundy. For a long while the wines of the Yonne were shipped by river to Paris, where they were valued for their roundness, a quality that was a bit more pronounced in these wines than in those of the Île-de-France. After the Second World War, America became enamored of Chablis, so much so that the same name came to be used for certain California wines. Later the Japanese followed the Americans in their enthusiasm. Production of Chablis experienced a sharp increase, yet prices continued to rise—at the same rate, alas, as yields, which had the effect of diluting the wines. A few gifted viticulturists nonetheless proved once again that it is possible to make elegant, concentrated wines in large quantity. Bernard and Jean-Marie Raveneau are among them, along with René and Vincent Dauvissat; but they are a minority, which cannot be considered acceptable in such a prized and expensive appellation. In the competitive context of the global wine market, every overvaluation is dangerous and is paid for dearly. This is never the case with undervaluations, on which connoisseurs congratulate themselves and which make it possible to arrive at a fair price and, sooner or later, a just reputation.

UNDERPERFORMING *TERROIRS* OF THE SOUTHWEST

Similar undervaluations and happy surprises are found in the neighborhood of Bordeaux, whose accumulated prestige for centuries defeated the vague attempts outside its immediate sphere of influence to improve the quality of production. Exceptional wines, even ones made from disparaged grape varieties, are now being produced in appellations considered second-rate at best.

This is true, for example, of the wines of Cahors, usually considered murky and rough, which are chiefly made from the Auxerrois grape (elsewhere called cot or malbec) and which for a long time were just good enough to survive the journey to Russia, where they were used by Orthodox priests to celebrate mass.[17] In recent years a few serious viticulturalists have sought to resurrect this appellation, with the result that a number of fine wines have been conjured out of a flood of mediocrity. Those of the Verhaegue brothers at Vire-sur-Lot, for example, "are black like ink, very dense, with a silky, concentrated texture, full-bodied, with aromas combining intense fruitiness with ample woodiness." The wines of Alain-Dominique Perrin, at Château Lagrezette, are "full, attractive, fat, without the usual hardness of traditional Cahors wines."[18] More than a quarter century ago, the merchant Georges Vigouroux achieved a tour de force by creating from nothing a property devoted to the production of fine wine, the Château de Haute-Serre, on the limestone plateau overlooking Cahors, which until then had supported only poor pastureland for sheep, exposing the soil with a scaling hammer to break up the almost denuded stone of the plateau. Like all the great European vineyards, only with a delay of a few centuries, the wines of Cahors benefited from the solicitude of princes. The marriage of Henri de Montpezat, descended from an old Cahors family, to the future Queen Margrethe II of Denmark in 1967 gave it renewed fame, all the more so since the couple—once again in keeping with ancient tradition—proceeded to purchase the château and vineyard of Caïx, which supplied the royal table of Copenhagen.

For hundreds of years the vineyard owners of Bergerac, Monbazillac, and the surrounding area had to content themselves with the custom of the bishop and bourgeoisie of Périgueux, while conducting a minor export trade in sweet white wines with the Netherlands. When at last they managed to break free of the market of their native Périgord, they filled the niche in the national market for the Sunday wines consumed by a middle-class clientele satisfied with a distant imitation of the great red and sweet white wines of Bordeaux. There was evidently no pedological or climatological obstacle to producing better wines, since the sun shines in Périgord almost as constantly as it does in Bordeaux and the banks of the Dordogne offer a variety of developed soils that likewise lie upon gravelly, sandy terraces and layers of red earth covering fragments of limestone.[19] Here again a few winemakers have successfully thrown themselves into the search for quality—quite an undertaking, actually, since it meant having to devise local variants of techniques used in Bordeaux for two or three centuries and having to identify a clientele willing to pay for quality, as much as €80 for a 50-centiliter bottle of Monbazillac, roughly the price of a Sauternes *grand cru*.[20] In the event, customers were found, and highly flattering reviews gave a further boost to promotion ("As for the sublime Cuvée Madame," enthused Bettane and Desseauve about the Monbazillac from Château Tirecul La Gravière, "it takes its place year after year among the great sweet wines of the world"). Here as elsewhere, the makers of these upstart wines are not infrequently newcomers, without inherited land or indeed, in some cases, any past viticultural experience; but they are full of imagination and passion, and therefore free of local prejudices and the cult of entrenched traditional practices. They have all accepted the hazards of the trade, from the first trial-and-error experiments to the ultimate rewards of oenological and commercial success. Thus, for example, two enterprising English investors, Richard Doughty and Patricia Atkinson, bought land at Saussignac, where prices are far lower than in the area around Sauternes; each has succeeded in creating very fine sweet wines.[21] In accordance with local tradition, the appellation sets the maximum authorized level of residual sugar at eighteen grams per liter. The wines of these pioneering domaines turned out to be much richer, however, making it necessary each year to obtain a special dispensation, as in the case of Jean Thévenet's late harvests at Quintaine in the Mâconnais, where an exemption from the customary rule has also been granted. There is reason to believe that similar results will also be achieved by heirs to older methods of viticulture who seek to bring about a change in practice. Economic success can only encourage bold innovation.

The same narrowing of the gap in quality that one observes between the wines of Bordeaux and their less prestigious neighbors can now be found in every region of the country. In the southwest itself one thinks of the Côtes de Frontonnais, north of Toulouse, where the négrette grape, mocked for its uncouthness in the Médoc, delivers more than honorable results provided that it is planted on fertile terraces, that its yields are sharply limited, and that the fermentation process is competently managed, as in the case, for example, of Château Baudare at Labastide Saint-Pierre or François Daubert's property at Fronton. As with the Auxerrois grape in Cahors, the recent history of the négrette demonstrates that the established hierarchy of grape varieties, unquestioned from the Middle Ages until the 1970s, can be challenged by force of talent. One critic speaks of "enchanting aromas of violet, strawberry, and licorice."[22] Some Alsatian vineyards produce exceptional sylvaners; muscadet, made from the melon de Bourgogne grape, reaches its height in certain domaines of the Nantes region; the mondeuse grape is capable of producing fine lots of wine in the hands of the best viticulturalists of Savoy. Nor should one omit to mention the splendid successes from the part of the southwest that produces Jurançon, based on the gros manseng and petit manseng varieties; from the Madiran and Pacherenc du Vic Bilh appellations, whose wines are made from the tannat, courbu, and arrufiac varieties; and from Gaillac, with its multitude of old grape varieties, as well as from Irouléguy in the Basque country and the Côtes de Marmandais near Bordeaux.[23] Impressive advances have also been made in the *haut pays,* at Marcilhac, Estaing, Entraygues, and Fel. The hereditary lords of the Bordelais would do well to inquire more closely into all these worthy wines, which have managed to improve without putting on airs. They ought even to take a look at what is happening in certain appellations considered secondary within their own sphere of influence, and to regard the old classifications, untouchable though they may be for the moment, with a degree of circumspection. Sadly, however, many of these proprietors are handicapped by the privileges of their birth. They are not used to questioning themselves, and feel not the least bit of doubt in the face of challenges to their assumed superiority.

THE INVENTION OF *GRANDS TERROIRS*

To invent is to discover something new, often in a fortuitous fashion, or as a result of trial and error. But it may also involve creating something new out of purposefully assembled materials, technologies, and ideas, as a consequence of logical reasoning or a series of linked intuitions. The historical emergence of wine *terroirs* falls within both these senses of the term.

The great vineyards of Bordeaux and Burgundy have been set above others by viticulturalists for quite a long time. This was true in the Middle Ages in Burgundy, as we have seen, with the fame of the Clos de Vougeot, Montrachet, and the Romanées, a hierarchy that came to be established still more forcefully in the eighteenth century. In Bordeaux, it was not until the seventeenth century that Haut-Brion distinguished itself from the other wines of the region and its remarkable character was recognized in London, at Pontack's Head, whose co-owner, François-Auguste de Pontac, sold his vintages to the city's most knowledgeable connoisseurs (Swift, Defoe, and Locke among them). Then the Médoc achieved renown with the recognition of the exceptional quality of Lafite, Latour, and Margaux, and, in the Sauternes district, Yquem. Through experiment and tasting, the owners and vintners of these properties realized that their wines far surpassed those of neighboring vineyards. Little by little they paid greater attention to cultivation, vinification, and cellar work, then sold their wines for higher prices, which in turn allowed them to invest more in their estates and to entrust the work to the best professionals available, thus increasing their competitive advantage still further.[24]

This is the virtuous circle of high-quality viticulture, the logic of which applies to all human activities, as much in agriculture and industry as in the service sector, but also in the intellectual and artistic domains, and indeed in the education of children, whose chances of social success are a function of the environment into which they are born.[25] Then there are vineyards that have long produced mediocre wine and that continue to do so today, as in La Mancha in central Spain, for example, and in the lowlands of the Hérault and the Camargue in France. In the two latter cases, the environment scarcely admits of any other possibility, but nearby there are superb slopes where quality viticulture is now enjoying a boom. Producers who used to make ordinary table wine have successfully reorganized their operations, proving once again that there is no inevitability at work here.

In the view of most experts, however, the fundamental constraints on winemaking are associated with natural endowments, and almost all fine wines come from *terroirs* that in their original state were particularly favorable to the ripening of grapes harvested on judiciously selected vines. This is the burden of the work of Rolande Gadille on the Côte d'Or and René Pijassou on the Médoc, following the line taken by the INAO since the 1930s. Gadille concludes the second part of her book ("Foundations of High-Quality Production: Physical Potentiality and Revelatory Human Interventions") with a discussion of the respective merits of viticulturalists and what she calls the geo-pedological and microclimatic complex:

> To be sure, no one can deny that our high-quality vineyards are a human creation. . . . And yet all this energy, all this vigilance remains captive to the conditions of the environment, practically powerless to break through the limits assigned by the ecological complex. Within these boundaries, human ingenuity has finally contented itself with implementing the best techniques, but it has not been able, on the Burgundian Côte, to effectively remedy the handicap of natural conditions stamped with the seal of discontinuity in time and in space.[26]

Gadille came from a family of vine growers that had lived in intimate contact with the pedo-climatic environment for generations. Embarking upon her inquiry just as Roger Dion completed his masterwork, she began by insisting upon the need to describe "the ecological and human conditions that permitted such success in the making of wines in the very particular form of a vine-growing area composed of properties that are as thoroughly divided up as they are hierarchically organized."[27]

Gadille therefore emphasized the system of ranking properties in the Côte d'Or, neglecting not only its place within Burgundy as a whole, but also the larger region of northeastern France, France as a whole, Europe, and the world. To favor one level of analysis over others is exactly what a geographer, whose discipline might be called the gymnastics of scale, must never do. It distorts the evidence and, in this case, creates a bias toward deterministic explanations that cannot help but satisfy the proprietors of the great vineyards, all the more as such explanations furnish the means for justifying their continued economic advantage. In the 1960s, growers in the small appellations hardly dreamed of rebelling against what they still imagined to be an unalterable state of affairs, still less of seeing equally good methods of production employed on their own properties. Brokers and merchants, owners' associations, professional bodies, and administrative agencies all insisted upon the immutability of this hierarchy and perpetuated it in their tariffs, rulings, and writings. Whether they were cynical or sincere is neither here nor there; and whether or not their behavior pleased the most socially prominent *vignerons,* the fact remains that the old certainties have been shattered in the years since. The inequality of winemaking opportunities is no longer a dogma.

From such assumptions, not to say prejudices, Gadille developed sophisticated and powerful methods of analysis that allowed her to obtain the results she desired. Thus the higher albedo (or light reflection coefficient) of the marl of the Corton slope, together with its southern exposure, explains the feats of the chardonnay grape in Charlemagne, despite the altitude there.[28] So, too, the *grands crus* are the product of permeable soils that are agronomically rich in assimilable mineral elements, as in Chambertin or Pommard-Rugiens. Gadille goes so far as to construct a topo-pedological index that serves to confirm the eternal verities supporting Raymond Dumay's claim that "Bordeaux is made in the sun, champagne in the cellar, and Burgundy in the soil."[29] Thomas

Jefferson had wittily reported the same explanation in 1787: "At Meursault only white wine is made, for there are too many pebbles for red. And this is the sort of circumstance on which the fate of man may depend."[30] At that time, unlike during the Middle Ages, white wines were sold much more cheaply than red, with the exception of Montrachet.[31] As a result, the inhabitants of Pommard ate good white bread made from wheat, whereas those in Meursault were forced to make do with dark rye bread.

René Pijassou took the same approach a few years later in Bordeaux. Although he did not come from a wine-producing background, his work owed as much to the training he received from his teacher Henri Enjalbert, who had been fascinated by pedology since writing his doctoral thesis on the soils of Aquitaine,[32] as to the warm welcome he received from the outset of his research from the owners of the great châteaus of the Médoc and the merchants of Bordeaux, who were eager to see their claim to superiority definitively established. Matters were clear for Pijassou. Everything came from "this amazing 'alluvial palimpsest' constituted by the *terroirs* of Médoc, which support the greatest vineyards of France."[33] One has to have actually seen Henri Enjalbert and René Pijassou among the vines of the great properties of Margaux and Pauillac, jubilantly collecting the famous gravel found there and explaining the precise provenance of this or that pebble— Mont Lozère, Aigoual, the Millevaches plateau, or the peak of Aneto, Couserans, or Cerdagne—in order to understand their obsession with the soil and their urge to find in it reasons to justify the happiness of those fortunate enough to own such pebbles.

After fifteen years of meticulous research, Pijassou arrived at conclusions that he formulated in terms similar to those used by Gadille, privileging the internal scale of the Médoc:

> The gravelly soil of the Médoc may appear uniform in its original poverty, which borders on indigence. And yet these poor lands produce wines of very different qualities, so much so that a hierarchy of merit

was established more than two centuries ago. One cannot legitimately claim that the prestige of the owner by itself explains the reputation of the product;[34] this condition is necessary; it could not be sufficient. To speak only of gravel is to forget two essential factors of the natural environment: the age of the alluvial layers, on the one hand, and their more or less elaborate surface relief, on the other. Taking these things into account is to recall the influence of *sites de terroir.* We have shown that the surface relief of the best of these sites exhibits the most clearly rounded remnants of erosion in the gravel of the Quaternary [Period], and that for this dual reason [the] number [of such sites] is limited.[35]

On this view, the gravel upstream from Langon should have little value by virtue of the fact that it is uneroded and still covered with fine silt.[36] What are we to say, then, about Yquem or Pétrus, where little or no gravel is to be found?

The internal hierarchy of the vineyards of the Médoc is brilliantly defended. It is, of course, quite true that the first great vineyards of the Médoc (Lafite Rothschild, Latour, Margaux, Mouton-Rothschild), were planted on the highest ridges (those that "see the water"), which were covered by the thickest distributions of ancient gravel, and benefited from a subsoil sufficiently broken up for the old vines to take root there. Until the seventeenth century, these were the poorest lands in the entire region, devoted to the cultivation of rye or sheep grazing. And yes, it is true that this gravel is found only in the Médoc and that it confers its personality upon the great wines that are born there. But none of this justifies Enjalbert's assertion, enthusiastically seconded by Pijassou,[37] that "the comparative analysis of all the vineyards of great quality leaves not the slightest doubt: fine wines are made only on a small number of *terroirs* and the characteristics of these [wines] are so strictly defined that there is scarcely any hope, at the present time, of extending them to new sites."[38] Maître Enjalbert, a noted connoisseur, would have shuddered at the thought of tasting the new *"grands vins"* that are cropping up almost everywhere, not only in Aquitaine, but elsewhere in France and throughout the world. And even in those districts of the Bordeaux region that were the first to be developed and known, such as the Graves, it is still possible to create *terroirs* of outstanding promise that no one had thought possible. This is what happened, for example, in a wood of oak and pine belonging to Château Olivier at Léognan that was cleared in 2002, with 220 ditches, each two meters deep, being dug throughout the property by Laurent Lebrun, the new director there.[39]

IMPROVEMENT IN PEDOLOGICAL
AND CLIMATIC CONDITIONS

It must be admitted that, within a given wine-producing region, the natural facts do seem to explain the established hierarchy of *terroirs*. But what qualifies, or at least complicates, this acknowledgment is the fact that "good" *terroirs* have throughout their history been substantially improved in ways that are mostly artificial in nature. By chance, the majority of great vineyards in both Bordeaux and Burgundy have been discovered within estates that have grown up within an elaborate legal, economic, and technological context. The voluminous archives of these estates have to a large extent been preserved for several centuries. Rolande Gadille and René Pijassou have obviously not failed to consult these archives, nor to notice the evidence there of these improvements; but they assign relatively little weight to such evidence in comparison with the original state of nature. This greatly weakens their argument.

Apart from anti-hail cannons and, of course, as we shall see, the evacuation of rainwater that otherwise would stagnate in the soil, human attempts to compensate for the effects of climate in the Bordeaux region have been few.[40] The situation in Burgundy, with its much cooler climate, is different. I have already mentioned the role of walls in surrounding and protecting vineyards there since the Middle Ages. While the gradient of the slopes of the Côte d'Or and the direction of their exposure cannot be neglected,[41] some excellent wines come from vineyards lying on ground that is almost flat and well drained, such as Chorey-lès-Beaune, situated on deposits of limestone debris and sand below the Savigny pass; others come from vineyards that face west, or even north, as in parts of the Hautes-Côtes where high-quality viticulture has been practiced since at least the eighteenth century. Finally, like the Champagne region, Chablis is vulnerable to spring frosts. For several decades now, growers have installed heating devices and water-spraying systems on certain exposed slopes.[42]

In both regions the soils have undergone profound transformations. In Bordeaux, the enemy is clay: even the deepest gravel contains sills that retain small flows of groundwater. Drainage systems were therefore constructed from the seventeenth century onward, and vestiges of old drains are regularly found beneath the rows of vines *(regès)* in the best vineyards when they are replanted or drained.[43] The earliest ones were made out of hollowed-out pine trunks. They were later replaced with earthenware pipes, which in recent years have given way to plastic. The vineyard of Latour has been equipped with drains since the eighteenth century.

In Burgundy, outcrops of rock and, later, the low walls made from stone dug out of the slopes were removed by the owners of the best properties, such as Corton and Chambertin.[44] The parcels located on the upper slopes of the Côte, where the natural soil is too poor to support fine viticulture, were salvaged by bringing in cartloads of earth from elsewhere. But contrary to the traditional view, the very same expedient has been resorted to for the purpose of improving soils even where they are naturally suited to viticulture. One should not be surprised by this. Ever since the time of Philip the Bold in Burgundy and the seventeenth century in Bordeaux, even though it has been necessary only very rarely, if at all, to manure the best vines, it has long been recommended that earth be imported in order to enrich certain parcels.[45] In Burgundy, the earliest evidence of this practice, called *terrage,*[46] goes back to 1407; favored especially on the ducal properties of Beaune, Pommard, Volnay, and Chenôve, it survived until recently. We know, for example, that in 1749 André Croonembourg, then the owner of La Romanée, had spread in his vineyard 150 cartloads of good earth taken from the decalcified *terra rossa* found on the plateaus that jut out over the Côte, and that the Prince of Conti did the same when he acquired Romanée in 1760.[47] One can hardly agree with Aubert de Villaine, then, when he asserts that nothing has changed with respect to the thickness and the composition of the soil[48]—still less since at La Romanée, as at all of the great vineyards, this operation must have been repeated many times since the Middle Ages and since, owing to the slight gradient of its slope (between five and six degrees), erosion there is limited.

Reliance on external sources of soil was especially pronounced in Chablis at the time of the lax AOC classification of 1938.[49] Although prohibited today, the practice is still tolerated in certain villages, such as Aloxe-Corton, where the gradient is relatively steep and the associated degree of erosion high. Thanks to a system for recovering and decanting storm water in a quarry located at the bottom of the hill of Corton, growers are able to come and cart away soil that has been washed down with it. This earth is of mixed composition, however, since it comes from the entire hill. The INAO, ever the punctilious guardian of the temple, and sometimes inclined to a certain excessive purism in such matters, checks to make sure that the soils remain as they were, and scrupulous owners (among them Aubert de Villaine) approve of this regime. The problem is a familiar one for museum curators and preservationists in many fields. Almost all historical monuments and works of art have been repeatedly subjected to restoration and transformation, without which they would have been irremediably degraded; indeed, many would have disappeared. Have they therefore lost their authenticity? No, of course not. One must accept the idea that the soils of the *grands crus* are an indissociable mixture of an original state of nature and subsequent human modifications, including added material from external sources, and that there is no reason to take offense at this fact, provided that the wine is good.[50] If one wishes no longer to countenance such procedures, there can be no objection, but one must not conceal the history of the matter. Here we are faced with one of the rather fundamentalist aspects of the religion of *terroir* that is spreading today, and whose implications for quality need to be carefully considered.

The importation of foreign soils has been no less frequent in Bordeaux. In the Médoc the practice is well attested.[51] A thousand cartloads of earth were spread each year at Latour in the early nineteenth century, and roughly the same amount at Lafite (René Pijassou calls this "modest tinkering"). On the plateau of Saint-Émilion, the soil is very thin. Around 1750, in order to plant vines there, ditches were dug in the limestone and filled with good earth brought from outside.[52]

Some *grands crus* have nonetheless emerged from improbable environments with types of soil and exposure that would, according to the usual line of reasoning, predispose them to lesser quality. Such conditions are typical of some of the most famous estates: Château Pétrus in Pomerol, Château Cheval-Blanc in Saint-Émilion, Château d'Yquem in Barsac, and, in Burgundy, the Clos de Vougeot. Pétrus covers 11.4 hectares of land that is practically flat and barren of gravel over 90 percent of its surface. At a depth of 20 centimeters, the soil consists of sand (roughly 64 percent), silt (24 percent), and clay (13 percent).[53] The deeper one digs, the more abundant the clay—a paradox, considering that quality viticulture first developed in Bordeaux on gravelly soil, as in the Graves, Médoc, and even Pomerol, where Château Trotanoy has enjoyed a good reputation since 1760. And yet the ascension of Pétrus began in the nineteenth century, thereafter never to cease. Its wine has become by far the most fabled and the most expensive in all of Bordeaux.[54] The reason for this aberration has to do with hydrology. Instead of stagnating in impermeable soil, rainwater flows down the sides of the dome-shaped mound that cloaks the island of Pétrus, the clayey upper layer lying on top of a subsoil of gravel and sandstone. Nonetheless, because the clay swells when it rains and crushes the rootlets that have penetrated it, so thoroughly that the vines absorb little of the water, a network of drains was installed in the middle of the nineteenth century.

The vineyards of the Libournais had traditionally departed from the practice of the Médoc of giving preference to cabernet sauvignon, which even in the nineteenth century accounted for no more than one-sixth of the planted varieties; since World War II it has been phased out altogether. When the severe frosts of 1956 made it necessary to replant, a few owners had the brilliant idea of putting their money on merlot, renowned for its suppleness. At Pétrus the proportion was 95 percent merlot and only 5 percent cabernet franc, which imparts an incomparable bouquet to the wine, a mixture of truffle and violet. It goes without saying that the techniques instituted by Jean-Pierre Moueix and his son Christian are among the strictest in the world. Henri Enjalbert recounts the story of the extraordinary harvest of 1981. September was rainy, and harvesting under wet conditions is never recommended. Then came a sunny spell. Jean-Pierre Moueix managed the amazing feat of assembling 180 grape pickers at Pétrus and harvesting the entire vineyard in two days.[55] The results were commensurate with the scale of this extravagance, as Bernard Ginestet, a man of the Médoc, observed: "[The wines] stand out by their sober and alluring beauty, the infinite richness of their aromas, their splendid color, their unequalled softness, which, in the best years, places them ahead of all the red Bordeaux. For Pétrus is a wine that is respected, but it is also one that commands respect, with power, love, and delicacy being wonderfully united in it."[56] Good wines sharpen the talent of poets, it is true, but there are few wines from Bordeaux of which it has been written that they contain love—a phrase classically associated with Burgundy.

The choice of merlot to the virtual exclusion of other grape varieties, together with the expert methods of vinification employed at Pétrus, has attracted a following. A small estate, Château Le Pin, which does not cover more than two hectares,[57] produces eight thousand bottles annually of a "garage wine" that admirers describe as voluptuous and that is quickly bought up throughout the world at prices close to those fetched by Pétrus. The very idea of garage wine, as we shall see, exasperates some connoisseurs and critics. Their annoyance is misplaced, for no one is obliged to buy overpriced wines. Whether buyers are motivated by the feverish search for excellence of the true connoisseur or by mere snobbery, what matters is the pleasure taken by those who are willing to bear such expense; the rest is only talk and jealousy. No psychoanalyst will ever really succeed in explaining the sentiments that animate collectors, especially those for whom the emotional aspect is paramount and who buy such wines for the purpose of drinking them, not in order to keep them indefinitely or, worse still, to resell them at a profit.

Another apparent aberration is the success of the vineyard of Cheval-Blanc in Saint-Émilion. A great part of the wine of this *premier grand cru classé (A)* comes from soil having a very high proportion of clay—until the early nineteenth century it was poorly drained tenanted land in Figeac, *premier cru classé (B)*—planted not only with merlot, as is the custom in the region, but also with a preponderance of cabernet franc. The technical director of the château, Kees van Leeuwen, a recognized authority on the soils of the Bordeaux region, humorously remarks, "Surprising that such heavy soil can yield fine wines. . . . These plantings go against the rule of thumb of every popular textbook on winemaking: merlot must be grown on clay, cabernet on gravel."[58]

The terrain of Yquem is almost as paradoxical as that of Pétrus and Cheval-Blanc. Here again it appears that clay, far from being unfavorable, gives richness and fullness to the wine if properly treated. Planted on the highest hilltop of the region, around its fortified château, the vineyard of Yquem rests on a dome of clay and marl covered with a bit of sand and gravel. Charles Pomerol has well summarized the situation: "The impermeability of the clay caused sheets of groundwater to form above it that, through asphyxiation, would have entirely prevented the roots from developing if the property had not been entirely drained."[59] The length of earthenware drainage pipes buried in the soil is reckoned at about a hundred kilometers, or about a kilometer per hectare. When a vine weakens and its leaves turn white, one must dig immediately next to it to unblock or replace the nearest drain.[60]

In Burgundy, we have seen that the Clos de Vougeot has benefited from the cumulative effects of meticulous care over nine centuries. Situated at the bottom of the hill, it has not enjoyed the same opportunities of exposure and soil as Nusigny, located just above, but many of its eighty current owners, heirs to a tradition of exacting standards and prestige, have tried to make their wine in the image of its reputation, insisting on maintenance of the walls, proper drainage, good plants that are the product of varied selection and cloning, severe pruning, the controlled use of fertilizer (or none at all), frequent trimming, green harvesting of unripe grapes *(vendange en vert)* if necessary in July (otherwise at full maturity), careful vinification, and so on. The result more often than not measures up to expectation: Clos de Vougeot is truly a good wine, sometimes a very great wine. At domaine tastings, it would be shocking if the most prestigious *cuvée* by reputation were less dazzling than a *premier cru* or, a fortiori, a village appellation wine.[61] That said, Clos de Vougeot is incomparably more affordable than Pétrus[62] or indeed any of the *premiers grands crus* of the Bordeaux region.[63]

TALENT REINFORCES HIERARCHY

From the earliest times, attentive care has improved the quality of the wines of reputable vineyards. Rolande Gadille, despite the primacy that she accords the natural environment, is not insensitive to a reality that she describes very honestly, albeit in a footnote so as not to weaken the force of her principal thesis:

> The manner in which vinification is carried out plays an essential role in the quality of the product; from the same must wines of very unequal quality may be obtained. These differences of quality associated with the vinification process used to be more pronounced (hence the superior results achieved by certain owners, the Cistercians of Clos Vougeot, for example, who thus strongly contributed to the renown of the vineyard that they worked). Still today the wines made from a single *cru,* but vinified by various hands, meet with quite different degrees of success, since the inequalities in natural conditions are of much less importance than the skillfulness of the winemaking.[64]

One could not have said it better.

And this is not only true of Burgundy, where appellations are divided up into innumerable parcels cultivated and vinified by different owners. The same contrasts are encountered in Bordeaux. If Château Haut-Marbuzet, a simple *cru bourgeois* from Saint-Estèphe, reaches great heights today, it does so because the Duboscq family has been able to bring out the best qualities of its land. The same may be said of Château Lagrange, which had fallen into so pitiable a condition on being bought up in 1983 by the Japanese firm Suntory that it was openly said in Saint-Julien that fine wine could never be produced there. Today it is recognized throughout the world as a great Médoc, indeed one of the most elegant. Château Sociando-Mallet, a simple *cru bourgeois* from the Médoc, came in first at a major blind tasting in 1999, with a European jury, ahead of Margaux, Haut-Brion, and Cheval-Blanc.[65] Thanks to the determination of the somewhat iconoclastic oenologist Denis Dubourdieu, the modest labels of Château Reynon, in the Premières Côtes de Bordeaux appellation, and Clos Floridène, in the Graves, are worn by bottles superior to many of the classed *crus* of the region, for a quarter of the price. This is the same Denis Dubourdieu who, with his father, succeeded in raising Château Doisy-Daëne in Barsac, a vineyard classed in the second rank, to the level of the first without matching its prices. Château Climens, also in Barsac, has likewise attained—and, for certain vintages, in the judgment of some tasters, exceeded—the stature of Yquem for a price three to five times lower.

A final example, taken again from Bordeaux, ought to prompt the eternally glorious names of the region to reassess their position. The wines of the Côtes de Castillon, which have borne the misfortune of growing up in the shadow of Saint-Émilion, have long been considered far inferior to their illustrious cousins. Their controlled appellation dates only from 1989. Since then they have made great strides in seeking to create a typicity based on their soils and on the marriage of merlot and cabernet franc, so much so that many connoisseurs of fine wines admit their quality. Denis Pallaro, owner of Château La Croix-de-Louis, declared in 1992, "We are less well known, it is true. But this inferiority obliges us to outdo ourselves."[66] And so they have. This episode sums up the entire revolution that is now underway throughout the world—probably the only true novelty that has occurred since Roger Dion described the historical processes that affect the making of wine almost fifty years ago. It is still the customer who commands, because if he does not buy, efforts to improve quality are doomed to failure; but in this case the initiative comes back to the producer, who takes the risk of changing the tradition of a region and of trying to tempt the curious connoisseur. Pallaro, for one, recognized the challenge at the outset: "We urgently need to set ourselves apart. We have to strengthen our image: the quality is there, we simply have to make it known." Today there are Côtes de Castillon that find takers at the same prices as good Saint-Émilions and Pomerols. They are no longer blended in vintages of Mouton Cadet, which until quite recently was considered an honor for them.[67]

What has happened with a certain number of marvelous wines from appellations judged to be in the second rank is also taking place among the prestigious vineyards of Burgundy and Bordeaux. The contrasts that can be observed in the relation between quality and price delight the knowledgeable wine lover; they can also shock. They are explained both by the strong demand that is concentrated upon the best-known wines in the world and by the investments that are made when properties change hands, which turns out to be fairly frequently, especially in the Bordeaux region. Land values continue to depend much more on the INAO classifications and the classification of 1855 than on those of contemporary guides and critics.[68] A word to the wise (particularly the wise buyer unaffected by snobbery) is sufficient! Talent and hard work can raise up the lowly; inattention and complacency can spoil the finest hopes and topple the powerful from their thrones. Discrimination is a virtue that each connoisseur must learn to cultivate.

No clear conclusion emerges from this brief consideration of the importance of the physical environment, so intertwined are the natural conditions (subsoil, soil, climate, hydrology) that form the basis for the initial development of viticultural potential, improvements carried out over time, and methods of cultivation and vinification. John Locke, while visiting Bordeaux in 1677, noted in connection with Haut-Brion:

> The vine de Pontac, so much esteemed in England, grows on a rising open to the west, in a white sand mixed with a little gravel, which one would think would bear nothing at all; but there is such a particularity in the soil that at M. Pontac's, near Bourdeaux, the merchants assured me that the wine growing in the very next vineyards, where there was only a ditch between, and the soil, to appearance, perfectly the same, was by no means so good.[69]

Locke no more took issue with local opinion than did Thomas Jefferson, captivated by the charms of Chambertin and Montrachet on his journey through Burgundy in 1787, with the opposite point of view: "It is pretended that the adjoining vineyards produce [wines of] the same qualities, but that, belonging to obscure individuals, they have not obtained a name, and therefore sell as other wines."[70] Michel Feuillat, the great expert on the *terroirs* of Burgundy, modestly cautions against trying to settle this difference of opinion: "Let us delight in preserving, in this domain, a certain mystery."[71] Alas, academics seldom possess this sense of the ineffable, indispensable though it is when one finds oneself confronted, as Feuillat has been his entire life, with complexity and art, with theory and practice, with money and pleasure, with nature and culture.

A linguistic metaphor, drawn from the Spanish verbs *ser* and *estar* (both translated by the French *être*), may nonetheless point to a tentative conclusion. *Ser* is used for that which does not change (the Eiffel Tower is high) and *estar* for that which is transient (I am in a good mood). The owners of renowned vineyards, wishing to conserve the exceptional value of their landed capital and of the wines that make it profitable, opt for *ser;* the talented vine growers who produce fine wines in less renowned appellations prefer *estar.* At the risk of giving offense, let us say that there is more creativity, more of the future in *estar,* more self-satisfaction in *ser.* Considering the rate at which international competition in the world of wine is evolving, it is not clear that a half century from now one will still be able to use *ser.*

We have seen that even in antiquity it was possible to identify a certain number of *terroirs* that had been more or less favored by nature from the start. The hierarchy that was later established, in the belief that it was both objective and definitive, turned out to suffer from numerous exceptions. What cannot be disputed, however, as both ancients and moderns would agree, is that a fine wine, wherever in the world it comes from, is necessarily concentrated, complex, and original, which is to say it is a local, geographical wine—a *vin de terroir.* It differs from its neighbor and varies from one year to the next. As the great Loire oenologist Jacques Puisais is fond of saying, "A sound wine must have the face of the place where it was born and the year, and the guts of the fellow who made it."[72] Advances in agronomy and oenology have been rapid in recent decades, and much more is known today than in years past about how to arrive at such a result. To be sure, and fortunately so, there will always remain an element of trial and error, but many principles that once were mysterious are now well understood and applied by the best growers throughout the world. Far from standardizing their wines, this situation works more and more to differentiate them, as with everything that concerns globalization.[73] If René Girard is right in saying that scientists "search for invariance rather than difference," surely viticulturalists stand apart from other scientists.[74] Bordeaux and Burgundy have both been pioneers in this revolution, which has brought out particular methods adapted to local environments as much as it has universal laws. Their oenologists and schools have trained cohorts of able vine growers whose achievements, hesitations, and fashions will shape all those who come after them.[75]

Viticulture begins with the soil in which the vine is rooted. Enormous progress has been made in understanding the relationship between these elements. Apart from questions of granulometry and the role played by the subsoil in drainage, we know today that the only good soils are ones that are alive and teeming with microorganisms that multiply the number of mineral elements that can be mobilized in the vine's growth.[76] This discovery owes much to the work of Claude Bourguignon and Nicolas Joly.[77] Bourguignon notes that the majority of soils in Burgundy are dead, owing to excessive use of pesticides, as far down as at least forty centimeters. The current scarcity of snails is proof of this.[78] A certain number of domaines have embraced the methods either of organic agriculture or a still stricter version, biodynamics, formulated in the early twentieth century by the German philosopher and naturalist Rudolf Steiner, who nonetheless condemned the consumption of wine.[79] Altogether the domaines practicing organic agriculture represent only a small fraction of the total land area, some 2,000 hectares in Aquitaine and 370 hectares in Burgundy in 2002.[80] But they include some of the most prestigious names: Château Margaux and Château La Tour Figeac in Bordeaux; Vosne-Romanée (owned by Lalou Bize-Leroy and Aubert de Villaine) and Gevrey-Chambertin (owned by Jean-Louis Trapet) in the Côte d'Or. It is still too soon to know whether organic wines are consistently superior in quality to conventional wines, all the more since the estates I have just mentioned employ some of the best vine growers in France, but the initiative is deserving of respect and attention.

The working of the soil is a subject of serious study today. "Over-the-row" tractors (invented in 1934 by Joseph Boillot, a viticulturalist at Meursault, and mass-produced after the war by Léon Loiseau, son of a blacksmith at Meursault) have made many operations easier.[81] Some current models are huge in both size and weight. Though these machines treat the vines with increasing precision and care, they have the disadvantage of packing the soil a little more with every pass through the rows, making it harder for water to percolate down into the soil and nourish microbial life, which is already threatened by the inappropriate application of pesticides and so forth. A few domaines known for the excellence of their products, both in Burgundy and among those that make *vins de garage* in Bordeaux, have therefore gone back to using horse-drawn plows, following the example of Nicolas Joly at La Coulée-de-Serrant in the Loire. This may raise a smile, but it cannot be dismissed as a piece of modern folklore.

Viticulturalists in Bordeaux and Burgundy, as elsewhere in France, are also investigating the relative merits of clonal and mass selection of vines. The latter method consists of grafting shoots selected from vines found throughout the vineyard (rather than from a single mother vine) onto existing rootstock. Later I shall come back to the question of grape varieties. For the moment it suffices to note that for a quarter century now most viticulturalists in the world, those in France included, have preferred to plant clones, which is to say identical vines that have been selected and reproduced *in vitro* without any apparent genetic modification. The problem with this sophisticated procedure is that it propagates individual vines that are both resistant to certain diseases and productive; together with the abuse of fertilizers and antiparasitic treatments, it is the primary reason for excessive yields and therefore the dilution of wines, even in the most famous appellations.

As long as the majority of consumers were content to drink passable wines and concerned mainly with collecting their labels, clonal selection was a godsend. This is no longer true, however. Particularly in France, where growers are under pressure to produce very good wine as a result of the real international competition that has emerged with respect to both quality and price, attempts are now being made to minimize the disadvantages of clonal selection by planting several types of clones on renovated parcels or, better still, as at the Domaine de la Romanée-Conti, for example, by reverting to mass selection.[82] In this way greater genetic variety can be achieved, enabling vines to extract more of the mineral wealth that a *terroir* contains and so to improve the chances of producing rich and nuanced wines. These challenges present proponents of biodiversity with a fertile ground on which to test their arguments.

The best wines are obtained from the oldest vines, as growers have always known. Yields diminish with age, of course, but quality constantly increases. A vine from Volnay Santenots du Milieu, planted in the 1920s, still produces splendid wines today. Lalou Bize-Leroy, the fortunate owner of two parcels in this *climat,* describes the extraordinarily concentrated 1997 vintage thus: "The vine is rather scrawny, being seventy years old. Its grapes are small, magnificent. Its roots must be impressive to manage to 'dredge up' such juice."[83]

The use of fertilizers is now much reduced. Apart from their effect on yields, fertilizers dissuade the vine from plunging its roots deep into the ground in search of nourishment, with the result that wines are both diluted and thin. Should an unusually wet year come along, grapes fail to ripen and excessive chaptalization becomes unavoidable. Moreover, the large quantities of potash that growers in Burgundy have dumped on their soils over the years eliminate acidity, making it necessary to add tartaric acid to the wines.[84] The better domaines use compost (made from coppice wood and animal manure) and substances rich in certain minerals to amend the soil after an analysis of its deficiencies has been made. The question of whether or not to plant grass between vine rows has similarly been a topic of debate. Some domaines still use chemical weed killers despite their harm to soils. Others choose to leave the land alone, which has the advantage of creating a competitive environment in which the roots of the vine are forced to strike deeper into the ground, but the disadvantage of encouraging a veritable jungle of weeds to develop aboveground. Rye grass is therefore sometimes planted, and then mowed as one would a lawn. This is done in the Hautes-Côtes of Beaune and Nuits, for example, where tall vines two meters apart are authorized and very common. In prestigious domaines weeding continues to be done manually with a hoe, which is harnessed to and dragged behind a horse. The weeds are buried, the soil is aerated, and the vines are beautiful to look at—not a negligible consideration in regions whose viticulture is a major component of their attraction to tourists.[85]

Then there is the matter of pruning. The substantial rise in yields over the last few decades has been aggravated, among low vines, by the

Guyot system of pruning, which involves selecting a long fruiting shoot (or "cane") that contains between four and eight buds, and a short shoot (or "spur") containing three buds for the following year. Invented in the nineteenth century, when the means of fighting plant disease were limited, the Guyot system has today been abandoned in the best domaines in favor of the more severe Cordon de Royat method of training vine trunks along a wire. This method is practiced at Vosne-Romanée by François Lamarche, the Philippe de Rothschild of Burgundy, who in 1992, after eight years of work, succeeded—even more rapidly than Rothschild himself—in having his *premier cru* vineyard La Grande Rue promoted to the status of *grand cru*.[86] One interesting geographical feature of pruning deserves to be mentioned. Like most of the operations carried out on vines before harvest, it is done almost exclusively by men, with one exception: the Côtes de Nuits, where pruning traditionally has been, and often remains today, a job for women.[87] There it is felt that women are more careful than men and so may be counted upon to wield the knife and clippers with the strictness and precision that such work requires. When André Noblet served as vineyard manager and cellar master of the Domaine de la Romanée-Conti, it was to his wife, Madeleine, that he entrusted the task of pruning in this, the queen of Burgundy appellations.

The technique of trimming remained useful as a way of promoting the ripening of grapes, above all in Burgundy, in years when there was less sunshine than usual. Green harvesting, the removal of surplus bunches of grapes before veraison, is a direct consequence of excessive yields. When the flower has not yet fallen from the vine, and the fruit has just begun to form in the proper way, one often finds today that the vines have an excess of grapes. Growers who are concerned about quality and take care not to exceed authorized yields—indeed, who deliberately aim below these levels—are therefore obliged to begin cutting grapes in the month of July, selecting those that have the least chance of ripening as they should. This practice is very rare with vines that are forty years old or more, and with ones that have been propagated through mass selection. Everyone knows that the grapes from old vines, though few in number, are superior to others. The great winemaker at Vosne-Romanée, Henri Jayer, always advised against tearing out old vines, limiting intervention to the replacement of ones that had withered and died; good wine, he believed, can be made only from vines between thirty-five and fifty years of age. The grape bunches they produce have small, stunted berries with a thick skin, rich in tannins and color.[88]

Harvesting represents the moment of truth for growers, who have now learned to choose the right date by analyzing the juice of the grape with a refractometer. Only the sweet wine–producing area of the Garonne Valley delays harvesting until the end of September and early October, when the noble rot (caused by the microscopic fungus *Botrytis cinerea*) has concentrated the pulp and sugar. To increase quality, the best vineyards operate on a staggered schedule. At Château d'Yquem, for example, the grape pickers, armed with small scissors, make some fifteen passes through the vines, each time selecting only the most desiccated berries. Elsewhere harvesting is done in a single go. The difficulty of finding good pickers and the risks of rain and of gray mold have led many domaines in France, as in the great industrial vineyards of the United States and Australia, to invest in mechanical harvesting methods. The scale of the estates and individual properties in Bordeaux and the rarity of steep planted slopes explain why mechanized techniques have been adopted more quickly there than in Burgundy, and especially the Côte d'Or. Opinions differ, of course, but it cannot be disputed that entrusting the harvest of a future *grand cru* to a machine, no matter how sophisticated, is a very risky business. Nothing will ever replace a team of skilled *vendangeurs* who can choose the finest grapes while discarding the rotten parts of certain bunches. Once the grapes have arrived at the winery, another team working at a triage table must meticulously complete this process of selection. Château Valandraud in Saint-Émilion, for example, employs twenty-five pickers to harvest its two hectares under vines; destemming is then done by hand.[89]

Low yields, even if they are not by themselves a sufficient condition, are in any case an absolutely necessary condition of making a good wine, and even more so of making a great wine. In Burgundy, before the phylloxera epidemic, yields never exceeded twenty hectoliters per hectare; they should never exceed forty-five hectoliters for red wines and fifty hectoliters for whites. Every effort should be made to come in well below this level, even if the sale price or, for that matter, the profit margin, suffers as a result, which would not be the end of the world. A recent study has demonstrated the obvious link that exists between gustatory quality and yield from one vintage to the next.[90] Some domaines, such as that of Lalou Bize-Leroy at Vosne-Romanée, for example, deliberately seek to approximate pre-phylloxera yields. The results of the tasting that Alain Ducasse organized there a few years ago shows that by insisting upon such demanding standards, it becomes possible to bring out the differences between wines from different *climats* to their fullest extent.[91]

REGIONAL RESEMBLANCES
AND VARIATIONS IN WINEMAKING

Much of the success of wines today is due to the immense progress in oenology that has been made since the Second World War. In Bordeaux one must pay tribute to Jean Ribéreau-Gayon, who from 1949 to 1976 directed the station for agronomic and oenological research there (later the Institut d'Oenologie de Bordeaux), a training ground for young oenologists of immense talent not only from France, but also from countries around the world.[92] In 1946, Ribéreau-Gayon's first student, the brilliant Émile Peynaud, defended a doctoral thesis at the University of Bordeaux ("Contribution to the Biochemical Study of the Maturation and Composition of Wines") that described the mechanisms and function of malolactic fermentation, a discovery that was to revolutionize the making of wines and their taste. Together with a team of researchers that grew larger every year, Ribéreau-Gayon and Peynaud achieved decisive advances in vinification through the mastery of biochemical processes. Their work did not go unnoticed: the whole *noblesse du bouchon* attended their lectures and applied their principles.[93] In the course of his long career, only recently ended, Peynaud—"the father of modern oenology," as he is now known—advised the owners of 169 properties, principally in Bordeaux and a few other regions in France, as well as a great many cooperatives, merchants, and seventeen foreign wineries. No one has been more usefully influential in the domain of technology. His recognized successes include La Mission Haut-Brion, Smith-Haut-Lafite, Climens, Rieussec, Lafite-Rothschild, Lagrange, Margaux, Figeac, and Pavie. Among his imaginative and sensitive successors, veering off from the beaten path, are Denis Dubourdieu, Michel Rolland (an advisor to several dozen prestigious estates),[94] and Kees van Leeuwen.

In Burgundy the great authority was Max Léglise, also recently deceased, who directed the oenological station in Beaune in the same spirit. Like both Peynaud and Jacques Puisais, still active in the Loire Valley, Léglise was a gifted wine taster who adapted his techniques and advice in response to detailed sensory analysis. These three masters also published works of great beauty aimed at cultivating an approach to tasting that combines intelligence with pleasure.[95] If one adds to their number the late Jules Chauvet, who it must be hoped will one day be followed by all the producers of Beaujolais, one has the *ne plus ultra* of a profession that has too often tolerated complacency, if not actually encouraged it.[96] Léglise's successors in Burgundy include Michel Feuillat, Noël Leneuf, and Claude Bourguignon. There, as in Bordeaux, the torch has been passed on. It remains to diffuse its light as broadly as possible.

Although it is accepted today that great wines are born of the most "natural" processes possible, this has not prevented them from being tempered like the clavier of Johann Sebastian Bach. If yields have been held within their proper limits, however, there is no need for doubtful procedures such as enriching the must through cryoextraction[97] and reverse osmosis, nor for overchaptalization. Many viticulturalists, unfortunately, resort to cultured yeast, which has the advantage of permitting regular, rapid, and sure fermentation. The best ones reject it, however, or, having once used it, abandon it in favor of organic methods, which do a much better job of preserving the richness and variety of natural yeasts on the bloom of the grape. Artificially selected yeasts have the additional disadvantage of conferring exaggerated, coarse aromas that kill the nuances of a wine and reinforce already prominent characteristics, much like glutamate in bad Chinese cooking or a woman who wears too much makeup and perfume. An intrusive banana-scented yeast, for example, has for a long time now spoiled the pleasure of drinking Beaujolais. Michel Bettane has castigated these practices with his customary and salutary verve:

> Today, the sauvignons sauvignon more and more, and the pinots pinot furiously, to the point that they resemble those of the new worlds, and the chardonnays chardonnay diabolically and muscat at every possible opportunity with the aid of appalling microvinifications, detached from any notion of *terroir,* that make and unmake the reputation of our modern clones. Abundant yields, a source of great pride to the wine profession, serve to accentuate the "varietal effect" by diluting the *terroir* and by leading winemakers to compensate for a lack of maturity, intensifying aromas. . . . How long will it be before fine wine comes in the form of an aftershave spray dispenser or, better yet, a roll-on stick?[98]

This is why the French have no interest in imitating the methods of certain viticulturalists in North America and the southern hemisphere, whose unrivaled mastery has allowed them to bring doctored wines to market at affordable prices. There is still more work to be done to convince the profession as a whole, but common sense once more has the wind in its sails.

Careful control of fermentation temperature (ideally 18°–20°C [64°–68°F] for white wines, and 25°–30°C [77°–86°F] for reds) is a necessity during hot autumns, more common in Bordeaux than in Burgundy, for any rapid rise threatens to hinder the extraction of color and tannins, and also to impart undesirable flavors. In the past, the outer surfaces of wooden fermentation vats were sprayed with cold water to lower the temperature. As recently as thirty years ago, Raoul Blondin, the cellar master at Mouton-Rothschild, slept in his cellar throughout the period of *cuvaison* in order to be able to intervene at any moment in case the must bubbled over. "I am the wine's nanny," he declared. "I pamper it. . . . This is the job of the cellar master. I wouldn't do more for myself than I do for the baron."[99] Today, most domaines are equipped with stainless-steel vats and electronic systems of internal temperature regulation that trigger the circulation of cool water down the sides of the vat when the must becomes too hot. In Burgundy, some domaines whose buildings are naturally cool remain attached to traditional methods of alcoholic fermentation using wood vats. This is the case at Domaine de la Romanée-Conti, as well as in white wine appellations such as Meursault, Chassagne-Montrachet, and Puligny-Montrachet, where fermentation takes place directly in barrels and is accompanied by regular *bâtonnage*—the daily stirring of the lees, which gives more richness and fat to the wine. In Bordeaux, at Yquem for example, enough is harvested each day to fill a maximum of a dozen barrels, but sometimes only one.

For reds, the question of the color of the wine and of the extraction of the matter contained in the skins poses delicate problems, all the more since in Burgundy the addition of teinturier (or coloring) grapes and illicit blendings are now things of the past. The practice of *pigeage* used to be traditional in this region: men climbing naked into the vat and stamping down the cap of solid matter (skin, pulp, and seeds) in order to mix it with the liquid.[100] This procedure, also known as "punching" (which produces extraordinary sensations for the *pigeur* while exposing him to the danger of carbon dioxide poisoning from the fermentation), was carried out twice a day;[101] it is now increasingly mechanized, having been replaced by the technique, habitually employed in Bordeaux, of *remontage,* which involves pumping the wine up from the bottom of the vat and spraying the cap with it. In the best of all worlds it would be possible to maintain the tradition of trampling grapes underfoot, if only to preserve the experience of physical and sentimental contact between the winemaker and his wine.

Almost everyone now destems before fermentation. The Domaine de la Romanée-Conti sets itself apart, in this respect as in others, by vinifying with grapes and stems. To be sure, this imparts additional tannins and acidity to the wine, but the juice is so rich that it supports them very well and the wines gain in structure and longevity. A few years after they are bottled, the silky character of the *grands crus* of Vosne-Romanée prevails, without any loss of power.

Élevage—the series of operations that take place in the cellar following fermentation, up until the moment of bottling—is now carried out everywhere in the world upon wine in oak barrels, an acknowledgment of the important role played by the tannins in the wood and by the micro-oxygenation that occurs during the course of aging. The Bordeaux cask (225 liters) is very close in size to the one used in Burgundy (228 liters).[102] In all the great châteaus of Bordeaux and the leading domaines of Burgundy, the wine spends between eighteen months and two years, or even thirty months, in cask. The proportion of new barrels varies from one estate to another. It may be as high as 100 percent in the top vineyards, which then sell them after a year or two of use to owners of less prestigious properties. Confronted with a purchase price of €500 or so per barrel in the case of French oak, however, owners and their managers understandably think twice before buying.[103] It must nonetheless be realized that the advantages of a new barrel count for little or nothing if it is filled with mediocre wines. A few leading merchants in Bordeaux have taken to putting minor generic wines in new barrels of less expensive American oak with the words "aged in oak cask" on the label. These wines sell well, both in France and abroad, thanks to the pleasant flavor of vanilla that comes from the oak tannins. One thinks in this connection of Malesan, the mass-market brand created by William Pitters and subsequently sold to Castel, a commercial success (8 million bottles in 1999),[104] and especially Castel's Baron de Lestac (10 million bottles in 2001, a figure that it is hoped will rise to 25 million).[105] The use of oak shavings, common in the rest of the world, would, if authorized in France, make it easier to produce such wines, to the detriment of their bouquet and the distinctive taste of the land from which they came.

With wines of superior quality, however, the greatest caution needs to be observed. Too much new oak is liable to mask the delicacy of such wines, which are unable to support high levels of tannin. It is customary to accuse the famous American critic Robert Parker of promoting this tendency.[106] There is probably some truth in the charge, but his influence has been greatly exaggerated. Parker does not hesitate to defend his own preferences, as every critic does, but he is fully capable of appreciating, alongside very woody wines, the excellence of bottles in which the hint of oak is more discreet. "A certain myth has it," he once remarked, "that I like only powerful, woody wines that are high in alcohol. This is totally false. The twenty books that I have done on wine are proof of it."[107] Parker's wine guides are very extensively researched reference works. He readily acknowledges that his opinions have changed a great deal after a quarter century's experience: "Twenty years ago I found Haut-Brion too subtle and light. Now I'm crazy about this wine."[108] Evidently a man of taste!

There is a final nuance in the use of casks in the two regions. In the Côte d'Or and the Yonne, the bung always faces upward, ensuring a permanent ullage, or headspace, due to evaporation. In Bordeaux, as in the Mâconnais and Beaujolais, a stopper is placed on the side once the major rackings have been carried out; moistened by the wine, it prevents any air from entering. The process of clarification varies from one estate to another rather than between regions. To each his own ideal method: egg white, bentonite—or even nothing at all, the cold of winter being relied upon to precipitate impurities.[109] Unfiltered wines always have a greater richness of aroma and taste, but in this case perfect cleanliness is required, for they are apt to exhibit certain instabilities, particularly during transport.

Techniques in Bordeaux and Burgundy therefore do vary, but only marginally. Good winemakers seek now and then to exalt the virtues peculiar to their *terroir* and a particular vintage.[110] Curiously, they are not always conscious of belonging to a viticultural community beyond their own region, preferring to imagine that their work has no equivalent elsewhere. Jean-Bernard Delmas, director of Haut-Brion, sincerely believes this: "In the *grands vins* of Bordeaux, balance and harmony come naturally when one knows how to express the grape, to translate the messages of the summer. In this case, one obtains results that are surprising and unique in the world. I do not see it elsewhere."[111] An odd thing to think, that one is unique in the world, but pardonable perhaps when one manages the affairs of Haut-Brion.

DOUBTFUL DEALINGS, SMALL AND LARGE

A whole literature has recently appeared that is quick to denounce the disturbing technological developments that I have mentioned.[112] Not taking advantage of new technologies means taking certain risks, however. As the Alsatian grower André Ostertag remarks, "Wine in the old days was more capricious, more unequal, but it had an unmistakable personality."[113] Today the risks of technology-related manufacturing accidents in the winery are much lower than in the past. Yet many winemakers are happy to run other risks by going heavily into debt for equipment that is more ostentatious than it is useful.[114] Worse mistakes were made in the old days, however. One cannot account for the present-day production of quality wines in Bordeaux and Burgundy without mentioning the dealings that for decades, even centuries, called into question the seriousness, if not also the honesty, of their growers and merchants. It is true that until the 1930s government regulation erected certain barriers, but authorities remained silent about many practices that today are illegal.

For a long time quite different wines were sold under the same name to different clients. Even the philosopher Hegel, a connoisseur of Haut-

Brion, complained of this early in the nineteenth century. "I beg of you again," he wrote to his wine merchant, "to send me a *muid* of Pontac, but to ship it as soon as possible and in such a way that it travels during the night, for at this time of year it would go bad during the day. I beg you also to send me [wine of] good quality; for I notice that, for the same price, there arrive here from your firm wines of better quality than the ones I receive; and I believe myself worthy of receiving ones as good."[115] One can never know whether this difference in quality was due to the existence of different *cuvées,* made at the château but not blended for the purpose of marketing a uniform wine, or whether Hegel's merchant was in the habit of concluding private deals in the secrecy of his cellar. And what is one to make of this passage from a letter placing an order with Château d'Yquem, on behalf of President Washington and himself, that Thomas Jefferson addressed to the Comte de Lur-Saluces in 1790: "Kindly assure me of shipment, and assure me that it really does come from you"?[116] Jefferson had reason to be wary, having been advised that "The grower never adulterates his wine . . . but once a wine comes into the hands of the merchants, it never comes out without having been mixed."[117] Is there anyone who could claim with confidence today that, in all the châteaus of Bordeaux, even the most prestigious ones, all bottles of *grand vin* contain exactly the same product, the result of the assemblage decided upon by the proprietor and the cellar master? Chemical analyses could be performed, of course, but they are tricky and in any case do not seem to have been attempted. Besides, whatever nuances and differences might be detected could turn out to be perfectly legal.

A more serious matter is that wines were long sold under the labels of estates in Bordeaux and Burgundy that came only partially, or not at all, from these regions. Of course, this was for a good reason: one wanted to improve the ability of wines to tolerate the difficult conditions of long-distance transport, preserving their color and taste. This is the point that Flaubert sought to make with a well-aimed barb in his

Dictionnaire des idées reçues: "Wines. Subject of conversation among men. The best is Bordeaux, since doctors prescribe it. The worse it is, the more natural it is."[118]

Françoise Grivot, daughter of a Beaune merchant, is keen to justify the cellar work and assemblage carried out by the trade there, challenging the invidious comparison urged by self-styled connoisseurs who made a point of stocking up on "true wine from the small grower" in order to avoid the "merchant's cooking."[119] Until 1925 or so, almost the only wine growers made was for their own everyday consumption, and the little they knew about winemaking was no guarantee of its quality. All the wine from Burgundy that was put on the market came from the merchants, whose competence and integrity made them the only persons, according to Grivot, able to vinify *cuvées* of the same origin, no matter that the minuscule size of individual parcels obliged growers to mix grapes from neighboring plots.[120] In Grivot's view, "preventive, corrective additives" are necessary and do not call into question the article of faith that "the great Burgundies are characterized by the unity of their provenance." Inevitably, of course, there are some swindlers and cheats, but "the proportion of these undesirables is not higher than elsewhere."[121] Rolande Gadille maintains the same discreet silence, mentioning only the blendings that until the nineteenth century were made among vintages or (as in 1440–41, for example, in the cellar of the dukes of Burgundy) between *gros vin* and *vin fin,* both from local producers.[122] This can hardly be considered a grave offense, and in any case the statute of limitations has run out by now!

There is not a word from either one about the enormous quantities of wine, indeed whole harvests, from the Côtes de Rhône, Languedoc, and Algeria that for many years were dumped into Burgundian vats.[123] Nothing could have been easier, since local merchants also resold vintage wines bought legally in the Midi or in Algeria, without any indication of provenance. The firm of Patriarche in Beaune, for example, has long marketed brands of table wine from various regions, among them

Champlure and Cramoisay (about fifteen million bottles per year), Cuvée des Bons Papes, and the sparkling wine Kriter (about seventy million bottles), none of which contain a single drop of Burgundy, something that the labels in any case do not claim. By contrast, the priest Jules Gâcon, a colorful minor merchant from Nuits-St.-Georges still active in the late 1980s, confessed to missing the days when he could make real Burgundy, fortified by wine from the Midi.[124] It is not by chance that merchants are now prohibited by law from making AOC Burgundy in the same buildings as their other *cuvées*. Moreover, these buildings cannot be connected with one another, either aboveground or below, through their cellars. Consider, for example, the warehouses of Moillard in the rue Caumont-Bréon in Nuits-St.-Georges, where even the parking lots are separated by a wire fence.

Pierre George, in his thesis on the lower Rhône, noted the renaissance of the vineyard of Châteauneuf-du-Pape, which took place at the very moment that he was doing his research in the early 1930s. "Before the war," George writes, "the greater part of the harvest was bought up by Burgundy, where it was used to fortify the local wines and to correct their excess acidity in certain years."[125] There is a well-known story about a merchant from the Côte d'Or who imagined that Madame Le Saint, mother-in-law of Baron Le Roy, the savior of Châteauneuf-du-Pape and father of the Appellation d'Origine Contrôlée system, would be pleased to hear him say, "You here at Châteauneuf-du-Pape have become our branch office." "You are mistaken, sir," she replied, "we are the head office."[126] The honored gentleman whom Robert Sabatier ridiculed for his shaky knowledge of oenological geography was therefore not so ignorant after all when he suggested, "Why don't we drink a good Burgundy, a Châteauneuf-du-Pape, for example?"[127] The great Curnonsky himself concluded a brief 1948 article in praise of Burgundy with the words "But the time has come for the growers of Burgundy to put an end to this unbridled falsification, which risks compromising the glory of their wines."[128]

The Bordeaux geographers René Pijassou and Philippe Roudié have been more honest in discussing the surreptitious adulterations of the past.[129] The wines of Bordeaux were "Hermitaged" every bit as much as those of Burgundy, to the point that some local merchants settled in Tain-l'Hermitage; one merchant from this town, Jean Calvet, was to make a fortune in Bordeaux in the nineteenth century.[130] Bordeaux wines were liberally blended with wines from Spain, Sicily, and Algeria, all unloaded in great quantities on the Quai des Chartrons. In 1669, the English author and physician Walter Charleton noted that "Alicant" was called to the rescue in order to strengthen the color of claret.[131] Poitevin, the estate manager at Château Latour, wrote in connection with the 1800 vintage, "The *grands vins,* moreover, are dependent upon the success of helping wines [used] to work them in the English manner, as wines of Hermitage, Beni Carlo, etc., and to them we owe the sale of this year's wines, which in truth are thin."[132] His successor, Lamothe, was to say much the same thing in 1811. Pijassou finds the remarks of these two professionals, who acted in what was thought at the time to be a perfectly proper way of fortifying somewhat light vintages, excessive, if not uncalled for—a consequence perhaps of his reverential enthusiasm for the great vineyards.[133] Yet he is aware of the many proofs of fraudulent winemaking conserved in the archives of the Syndicat des Grands Crus Classés du Médoc. In 1901, for example, the merchant Nathaniel Johnson complained that the Gironde brought to market between six and seven million hectoliters of wine, whereas it only produced between two and three million.[134] At that time the difference was made up mainly by Algeria, much of whose wine was bottled and passed off as Bordeaux in addition to being blended with wines from the Gironde. As one critic in the 1930s put it, "The wine production of the Bordeaux region is so great . . . that it suffices to provide at least a quarter of what is consumed."[135]

In the late nineteenth century, the phylloxera crisis and the ensuing collapse of production aggravated this state of affairs. Some producers even went so far as to manufacture a wholly artificial wine containing not a single drop of grape juice. Gaston Roupnel lamented the practice:

And then there is something else that devastates us, that kills us: the fabrication of wine. Here you see the land and the sun unemployed, and the grower as well. The chemists of misfortune have done us great harm. Off they go to make wine, these crooks. First they set up their laboratories: empty vats, drugstore jars, little vials of poison, and large sacks of soft brown sugar. . . . Then they pump water up from the wells, and after a little make-believe fermentation there it is, the spigot at the bottom of the vat shamelessly pissing wine.[136]

The practice continued in the early twentieth century, owing to the laziness and greed of certain merchants.

The blending of wines from different sources cannot be considered on a par with the making of fake wine, however. Outright fabrication, once not uncommon in France, is revolting to the palate and dangerous to both health and viticulture. Mixing local wines with ones of foreign origin, on the other hand, while obviously dishonest since the contents of the bottle do not conform to the label, succeeded for a time in compensating for a shortage of domestic production. Philippe Roudié, though he is an advisor to the INAO, unhesitatingly justifies the practice: "Fraud was incontestable with regard to origin, but no one (not even the producers) complained about it until [the establishment of the AOC system in the 1930s], and besides, there does not seem, legally speaking, to have been any offense."[137] By contrast, certain newcomers to the world of wine did cause harm, at least from an ethical point of view, by giving their own products prestigious French names. Thus, for example, "Bordo" was sold in Japan in the 1930s.[138] It was not until the end of the twentieth century that champagne, Burgundy, and Chablis finally ceased to be imported from across the Atlantic or from the southern hemisphere.[139] Even the anathemas hurled by Raoul Ponchon were long powerless to dissuade foreign imitators:

You are too funny by far,
You huge Australians!
Screw your heads on tight down there
Where the insane idea reigns

That there is any other Burgundy wine—
Take it from a drunkard—
Than the one that we burgeon
On the slopes of Burgundy. . . .

You from Melbourne will plant
On your barbaric slopes,
The finest of our Gallic vine stocks,
Our rarest pinots,

In vain! For what these strapping lads,
These true gentlemen,
Are lacking is this prime land,
Land, thank God, that is ours.[140]

With the return to large-scale production in France at the turn of the twentieth century, and the birth of the AOC system between the wars, the repressive arsenal of regulation grew more complex. Thereafter penalties became more severe, periodically disturbing the staid dignity of the French wine world. One recalls the scandal that stained all of Bordeaux in 1975 involving Cruse, one of the most honorable Chartrons dynasties, convicted of illicitly blending and mislabeling local wines with ones from the Midi.[141] The Médoc merchant Jacques Hemmer was brought to trial on the same charges in 2002.[142] Scandal had similarly touched Beaujolais in 1973–74, and then the Côte d'Or in 1979, when the firm of Grivelet shipped sixty-four thousand bottles of fraudulent *grands crus* to the United States.[143]

That such practices are ever more harshly punished is naturally welcome. And yet it is widely known that *"vins médecins"* continue to be used to doctor disappointing vintages. It is not impossible in Burgundy, for example, so long as one pays in cash, to obtain wine made from the Spanish Alicante grape, a variety that is neutral in taste but highly coloring. This can help in cool years when the skins of the pinot grape yield only a deep pink color, which is no longer what customers expect from a red wine.[144] Pierre-Marie Doutrelant, known for his dry sense of humor, remarked not so very long ago that wines from small châteaus in Bordeaux "gain in quality from being softened with 5 to 10 percent Algerian or Italian wines or wine from Corbières [in Languedoc]."[145]

With regard to the adulteration of wine through the addition of various substances, much ink has been spilled in recent years. Two of the most prestigious estates, one in Burgundy, the other in Bordeaux, were found guilty of this practice in 1998. The Hospices de Beaune was charged with overchaptalization (more than two degrees of alcohol obtained by adding sugar) and illegal acidification of its celebrated wines. The no less famous Château Giscours in Margaux, then caught up in a messy affair arising from quarrels within the Tari family, made front-page news when its new owners were accused of fining their wines with milk, adding water, corrective acids, staves, and oak shavings to avoid the cost of aging them in barrels, and mixing vintages and appellations (old-vine Haut-Médoc was mixed with young-vine Margaux in order to improve the estate's second wine, La Sirène de Giscours).[146] Not all of these accusations turned out to be true, but the reputation of Giscours suffered greatly and tarnished that of the whole profession. Today this venerable estate is gradually regaining the quality for which it was long known. Claude Fischler, who analyzed the Giscours affair in detail, particularly with regard to the treatment given it in the French and foreign press, emphasizes the sense of uneasiness that such episodes of fraudulent activity arouse in the popular mind, which at the present moment has the disagreeable impression of no longer being able to trust anything or anyone.[147]

All the more, then, must credit be given to a certain number of domaines in Burgundy and châteaus in Bordeaux, and perhaps also to a few scrupulous merchants, who led the crusade for quality in the 1930s as sponsors of the AOC system; who very quickly collaborated with the first great oenologists of the postwar period, dazzling genuine connoisseurs; and who proved that it was not merely honest, but profitable as well, to make true local wines. That such commitment should have been found in every winemaking region in France, and that it should have been widely imitated, is a cause for rejoicing.

MORE BORDEAUX THAN BURGUNDY

With all due respect to partisans of each region, it must be said that the international reputations of Bordeaux and Burgundy are roughly equivalent. But there is another reality: far more Bordeaux is drunk throughout the world than Burgundy, quite simply because it produces much more, over a greater area. The 17,000 properties (including 5,000 châteaus) in the Bordeaux region comprise 115,000 hectares of land under vines (6.8 hectares on average) that produce, good year or bad, some seven million hectoliters of wine,[148] or on average the excessive yield of 60 hectoliters per hectare.[149] The 8,000 properties of Burgundy total 23,000 hectares, or an average of 2.9 hectares, which produce 1.5 million hectoliters (Beaujolais not included), or an average, still more excessive, of 65 hectoliters per hectare. The ratio of the two volumes of production is therefore about five to one. Officially, the division into appellations is inversely proportional: 46 in Bordeaux, 105 in Burgundy. Again, however, the reality is quite different. Counting the listed first-growth vineyards in the Côte d'Or, one comes up with several hundred denominations. As for the Bordeaux region, one might as well count the number of stars in the sky, since each château produces several *cuvées,* each of which is equivalent to an appellation of origin that is controlled solely by the proprietor, who seeks to impress upon it a personality that he values more than anything else.

It has always been the case that supply in Burgundy is much smaller than that in Bordeaux, which explains why it is so hard to come by good Burgundies, unless one can buy directly from the source or one is very wealthy. I do not even mention the great domaines (among them Comtes Lafon, Romanée-Conti, Ramonet, Leflaive, and Simon Bize) that have almost nothing to sell, or sell wines only within a prohibitively expensive range.[150] This is not true of the wines of Bordeaux, which as a rule are in ample supply at all prices and carried by all major distributors, including the greatest wines, which are never as hard to find as the top Burgundies, though sometimes special pleading is required.

Madame Edmond Loubat, the former owner of Pétrus, receiving a group of restaurateurs from New York who had come to complain that they were unable to buy enough of her wine, is said to have replied with equal measures of charm and candor, "Yes, I understand! But you put me in an awkward position. It doesn't make me very happy, you know, to deny my wine to anyone. You have all been very nice. You will have some. But you must send me a great deal of money. . . . For you, that's easy!"[151]

In general, however, it is impossible in Bordeaux to buy directly from the château. Nor is it necessary, since the brokers, merchants, and distributors play their assigned roles perfectly. The disproportion between the two regions has to do in part with the environment, which is more difficult in Burgundy owing to its more northerly latitude. It has also to do with history. For centuries Bordeaux was the cellar of England and the whole of northern Europe. Burgundy was only the supplier to the former duchy of the same name, the popes of Avignon, and high society in Paris. No doubt if demand had increased, every effort would have been made to develop new land suitable for the production of great wines. As we know today, such land can be found throughout Burgundy.

Although the subdivision of properties within appellations differs greatly between the two regions, real estate prices are roughly comparable.[152] In 2001, a hectare of AOC land under vines sold for €50,000 in Bordeaux and €73,000 in Burgundy. These are average figures; the Médoc and the department of the Côte d'Or are much more expensive. In the Côte d'Or, the official average transaction price, under-the-table deals excluded, reached €130,000 in 1997[153] and, in Clos de Vougeot, €1,500,000.[154] In 1993, François Pinault purchased Château Latour for €114,000,000. In 1999, when it was bought by Bernard Arnault's LVMH group, the value of Château d'Yquem was estimated to be €150,000,000. This is the same Bernard Arnault who the previous year, together with the Belgian banker Albert Frère, had bought himself Château Cheval-Blanc for the trifling sum of €130,000,000.[155] Land in Champagne is on average much more expensive than in either Bordeaux or Burgundy, at €360,000 per hectare,[156] whereas the Côtes du Rhône is somewhat less expensive, at €30,000. By comparison, land in the southwest and Languedoc-Roussillon is a steal at €13,000 per hectare. This is a reality that must be taken into account if one is to make sense of the dynamics of the global market. How are French winemakers to compete when excellent properties in New Zealand and Australia can be had for ten times less than the cheapest French vineyards? The same is true for Romania and Bulgaria, where labor is ten times less expensive as well.

Because they are in shorter supply than Bordeaux wines, Burgundies are less well known by connoisseurs in France and the rest of the world. Considering, too, that there is a greater chance of being unlucky when one buys a Burgundy, and that one is apt to become light-headed more quickly when drinking it, it is unsurprising that most people who build up a personal collection of wines for entertaining at home should choose Bordeaux; and less surprising still in the case of purchasing agents responsible for catering banquets and receptions at royal palaces, presidential residences, ministries, and embassies throughout the world.

CHAPTER 4
INCOMPARABLE WINES

Over time, despite the different environments from which they emerged, Bordeaux and Burgundy came, as we have seen, to follow parallel paths. Both routes led to the production of quality wines, even if some regrettable detours have made it necessary to qualify this picture somewhat. But if one now stops to consider the wines themselves, one cannot help but notice that for the most part they do not resemble one another. Attempts to explain this fact by appealing to differences in climate and soil are simplistic, all the more so as some Bordeaux wines do in fact happen to resemble certain Burgundies. As Gérard Bélivier, president of the producers' association of Pomerol, wrote in 1949 with regard to the wines of his appellation, in an astonishingly Burgundo-philic flight of fancy, "The gastronome ... is brought up short, surprised by a bouquet of merlot and cabernet in a body of exceptional power, the finesse of a great Médoc, but also the vigor of a Saint-Émilion! And what generosity! Does it not put one in mind of the most exhilarating Chambertin?"[1]

Jacques Puisais, a man of the Loire, and therefore neutral in the quarrel between Bordeaux and Burgundy, once teasingly organized a tasting that he called Pommard-Pomerol, in the course of which he did his utmost to confuse his guests.[2] But he would not have dared to play such a game with a Médoc and a Chambolle-Musigny, or with a Puligny-Montrachet and a fine white Graves.

NEITHER CHANCE NOR NECESSITY

The pattern of planting in Bordeaux and Burgundy today is generally considered to be something very old and logical, and in any case impossible to challenge. Present-day grape varieties are thought to be so well adapted to the pedological and climatic environments of their respective regions as to constitute a fact of nature: this is the way things are, and a good thing, too. It seems not to have occurred to anyone to ask what would happen if Bordeaux were to be planted with pinot and chardonnay. This would pose no technical problem; the grapes would grow quite well, and the wines made from them would be powerful and full-bodied. The limestone plateau of Saint-Émilion, for example, would probably be hospitable to Burgundian varieties. And why not plant Burgundy with merlot, a well-traveled grape that is found in regions with a similar climate, such as Austria and Hungary, and in colder climates such as Canada and Long Island, New York? With proper selection it might even be possible to adapt cabernet sauvignon—a late-fruiting variety that is therefore relatively resistant to spring frosts, little affected by gray rot, and harvested fairly early—to such conditions; it does well in Anjou, for example. Cabernet franc, which thrives in the Loire Valley no less than in Provence, would certainly have no difficulty.

The scientific literature concerning grape varieties in relation to soils and climate is often unsatisfactory, not least for its reluctance to acknowledge the capacity of grapes to adapt to different environments. And yet even an agronomist as able as Jacques Fanet is sometimes taken in by the "reputations" of certain varieties. He will forgive me for citing several amusing examples, taken from his fine book on *terroirs,* that border on paradox. "In Burgundy," he says, "the chardonnay grape is very fond of soils that are rather heavy, clayey, and deep. . . . In the

Mâconnais . . . it produces powerful wines on shallow, chalky soils and more ethereal ones on land that is clayey and sandy."[3] With regard to pinot noir, he writes, "This grape does not put down roots just anywhere; it establishes itself only on the chalky formations of the Jurassic." A little further on, however, he mentions its success in the United States: "It is above all in the state of Oregon that this grape has found favorable ground: in the Willamette Valley, south of Portland, on basaltic soils and in a cooler climate, it produces wines that are full-bodied, fruity, and structured."[4] Life, whether of plants or animals, is indeed capable of remarkable adaptations.

The history and geography of grape varieties remain to be written for the most part. Not all places of origin have been identified, and some paths of diffusion are only approximately known in their modern history; but emphasis needs to be placed above all on the decisions that at a particular moment favored one variety rather than another, and in some cases rendered its planting obligatory. Not all of these decisions, which are justified today by a concern with quality, are known. The fact that they corresponded to preferences of taste has perhaps not been sufficiently stressed. This is an area of research that has been relatively neglected until now because it falls under the head of culture, and therefore of the imagination and pleasure.

Until the end of the nineteenth century, despite the dominance of certain grapes, a great many different vines were planted throughout the wine-producing regions of the world. Mixed planting was practiced even within individual parcels. Many ancient grape varieties have now totally disappeared. White grapes were eliminated from the Médoc by the end of the eighteenth century.[5] Vines originating in the town of Tain and the present-day appellation of Hermitage disappeared from Château Lafite after 1820,[6] the camerouge grape from Château Margaux toward the end of the nineteenth century, and elsewhere in the Bordeaux region the wonderfully named chalosse, grapput, folle, mansin, boutignon, and enrageat, over whose demise we shall never know whether to weep or rejoice. Malbec (known as cot in the Loire valley), a very productive grape that was commonly found in the early twentieth century in vineyards of lesser rank, is now no more than a memory; petit verdot presently accounts for only 1 percent of the vines at Latour and Lafite-Rothschild, and 2 to 3 percent at Léoville Les Cases, Margaux, and Mouton-Rothschild.[7]

The same pattern may be observed in Burgundy, where melon, gouais, césar, beurot (pinot gris), and enfariné have virtually disappeared. Gamay and aligoté are found to a smaller and smaller extent in the Côte d'Or and the Yonne; they also survive, though as a minor variety, in Saône-et-Loire. One still encounters pinot planted together with gamay in certain parcels of the Côtes d'Or, on properties of the eastern plain (at Boncourt, for example) and of the Côtes de Couchois and the Hautes-Côtes (at Segrois, for example). Combining pinot and gamay is the traditional way of making the pleasing, thirst-quenching wine known as Passetoutgrains.[8] Chardonnay has not been planted together with pinot at Clos de Vougeot since the late nineteenth century, and it survives in this juxtaposition only in a single parcel of Domaine de la Vougerie. Jean-François Bazin explains its former presence very nicely: "Rare on the Côtes de Nuits, the white vines probably owe their existence here to the habit of producing reds and whites at Vougeot. The monks of Cîteaux almost surely wished to be able to enjoy both and compelled nature to bend to their wishes. [Nature] eventually became accustomed to the idea and even took some pleasure from it."[9] Seldom is a fundamental topic of geography treated so concisely and poetically.

The reason why cabernet sauvignon came to be the preeminent grape of the Médoc, Graves, and other areas of the Bordeaux region remains somewhat obscure. Lamothe, the manager of Latour, bought eight thousand plants in 1808, calling it the "best grape variety."[10] In the eighteenth century, the most prestigious estates had all recognized the advantage of planting cabernet sauvignon on the gravel hilltops, where it gave very distinctive results, with a bouquet rather closer to cedar than to green pepper. But what did it matter, to the extent that merlot and cabernet franc also did very well here? A slender guide to the world's grape varieties that appeared a few years ago in German offers this confident assurance: "From the thirteenth and fourteenth centuries, the courts of England and Aquitaine preferred wines that came from combining cabernet sauvignon, cabernet franc, merlot, petit verdot, and malbec."[11] This notion of preference is worth noting, for it holds the key to a process that continued until recently.

Cabernet sauvignon was predominant until the mid-1980s. Today it is merlot that has the upper hand.[12] To be sure, the former thrives on the well-drained gravelly soils of the Médoc and ripens satisfactorily in the climate of the Bordeaux region, but the main thing is that the wine that is made from it appealed to customers in northern Europe. The *cuvées* made from cabernet sauvignon are characterized by a lovely deep ruby color and a very vigorous and pronounced structure, thanks to an abundance of hardening tannins when they are young. They are hardly agreeable to drink at this point, still less if they have undergone a long period of fermentation and then been left to age in new barrels, further strengthening the tannin content. It is for this reason that they are generally blended with a certain amount of merlot (between 20 percent and 40 percent) for suppleness and roundness, and cabernet franc (between 2 percent and 15 percent), malbec, and petit verdot for a tart, slightly acidic freshness. Nonetheless, great Médocs with a high proportion of cabernet sauvignon should not be drunk until they have aged in bottle for years, or even decades. Before this time they are dark, lacking in bouquet, bitter, and generally unpleasant. Brokers, merchants, and critics, used to tasting young wines in the cellar, engage in the highly perilous practice of anticipation—rather as though a company were to recruit its staff among children coming out of elementary school. What customers in northern Europe like about cabernet sauvignon is precisely its elegant austerity, its severity, the necessity of waiting a long time for it to mature, and therefore of drinking relatively little of it—a consequence of the rise in price during the interval. All of this raises questions about the place of wine in these societies and how people think about it. It should be added that starting in the seventeenth century the wines of Bordeaux met with competition on the English market in the form of good Portuguese wines that were very dark in color as well. These are the main reasons for the success of cabernet sauvignon.

Saint-Émilion and Pomerol opted instead for merlot, blended with other varieties in proportions inverse to those of the Médoc. There were pedological reasons for this, in particular the greater proportion of clay in the soil, which is well suited to merlot; but the distinctive commercial orientation of the Libournais district, which historically had been less concerned with the English market owing to its domination by producers from the Médoc, was decisive. Merlot's suppleness made wines from the Libournais attractive to a clientele eager to surrender itself to their pleasures sooner. The fact that the wines made from this grape were ready to drink more quickly presented an enormous economic advantage as well—not a negligible consideration, given the amount of capital that otherwise would have been tied up in inventory.[13] Cabernet sauvignon had been much more common in the Libournais before the great freezes of the spring of 1956. When replanting was undertaken, the INAO encouraged growers to increase the proportion of cabernet sauvignon, but in the end it was merlot that prevailed in the great vineyards, owing to the efforts of Jean Capdemourlin, a prominent magistrate and president of the producers' association of Saint-Émilion.[14] In Saint-Émilion today, as at Pomerol and Fronsac, merlot is very much the leading variety, indeed almost the exclusive variety in certain *grand cru* vineyards such as Clos Fourtet, La Mondotte, Le Tertre Roteboeuf, Troplong Mondot, and, of course, Pétrus. But the distinctive feature of the region is the number of different grapes planted within a particular appellation. Thus Figeac, like the Médoc, is equally planted with cabernet sauvignon, cabernet franc, and merlot, whereas Ausone and Cheval-Blanc are divided almost evenly between merlot and cabernet franc, cabernet sauvignon being excluded. These patterns, the product of long and deliberate reflection by a former or present owner, are what give the wine of each château its personality, no less than nature and the depth of the soil. Surely this state of affairs is due more to human choice than to any dictate of nature.

The selection of noble grape varieties is both older and better known in Burgundy. I have mentioned the role of Philip the Bold, signatory of the famous ruling of 1395 that banned the unlawful gamay and imposed, by logical deduction, the grape known until then as noirien (or, in the Île-de-France, morillon) and that took the name of pinot in Burgundy.[15] The mixing of pinot with other grapes that were considered much less distinguished was already a serious offense by this time; in 1394 a young grape picker from Auxerre, fifteen years of age, had been beaten so violently by his master for disobeying orders on this point that he died.[16] The text of the charter of the following year is very clear: "Foreign and other merchants, believing themselves to supply good wines, have found in the cellars of our aforementioned subjects and others these bad wines mixed together with the other good wines from the good plant."[17] In this context there can be no doubt about the identity of the "good plant," even if the word *pinot* is not used.

These wines from the pinot grape enjoyed an immense reputation at the time, from Flanders as far south as Avignon, and notably in Paris and Dijon. In 1459, Duke Philip the Good was "reputed [to be] Seigneur of the best wines of Christendom"[18]—propaganda, probably, but the same was not said about the wines of Bordeaux, no matter that they had long been exported in great quantity to England. The reason for this, quite simply, was that during the Middle Ages techniques of viticulture and vinification were more advanced in Burgundy than in Bordeaux. The wines of Burgundy did not travel across the English Channel at this time, and those of Bordeaux, whose quality was not commented upon, went neither to Paris nor to Avignon, still less to Dijon. It is now impossible to compare the two, for even if at some point in the past such a comparison were feasible, there is no trace of it in the texts that have come down to us. The adjustment in their reputations did not occur until the seventeenth century. In the meantime, the superior delicacy of the pinot grape justified Roger Dion in asserting with regard to the late Middle

Ages and the Renaissance, which is to say the eve of the Reformation, that "the result of these determined and skillful efforts was that, in the minds of people at the end of the Middle Ages, the position of Beaune at the summit of the hierarchy of wines was as unassailable as that of the pope at the summit of the hierarchy of human beings. This sentiment was echoed in formulas such as . . . *vinum belnense super omnia recense,* which were popular in the time of François I."[19] The likening of the authority of the wine of Burgundy to that of the pope is not to be taken lightly; it counted for a great deal.

The charms of chardonnay and pinot blanc were slower to take hold in Burgundy than those of pinot noir. It was only in the eighteenth century that the delicate chardonnay grape came to dominate the properties of Puligny, for example, and not until the mid-twentieth century in the case of the *premier cru* slopes in Chassagne. Like pinot, it possesses remarkable aromatic qualities when cultivated in northern regions such as Burgundy. In a certain sense, pinot noir and chardonnay, by virtue of their sensuality, and because they have the added advantage of good acidity, can be thought of as occupying a place roughly equivalent to that of merlot in Bordeaux. The austere cabernet sauvignon has never had any counterparts in Burgundy, at least not any successful ones. Beurot (pinot gris), though it produces some of the finest Alsatian wines,[20] does not easily open up; and the very tannic césar, which used to prosper only at Irancy and Clamecy, is planted today to a still smaller extent.[21] These grapes evidently were not what the customers of Burgundy were looking for.

All of this goes to show that the historical geography of French grape varieties deserves greater attention. Burgundy and Bordeaux have no variety in common apart from sauvignon, which is abundant in the Gironde and found in isolated patches in Saint-Bris-le-Vineux (Yonne) and Pouilly-sur-Loire (Nièvre). By contrast, both regions share some of the varieties planted in the Loire Valley. Pinot and gamay are found in Burgundy and Touraine. Melon (or muscadet) originated in Burgundy. Cabernet franc, cabernet sauvignon, malbec (cot), and sauvignon are found in the Loire and Bordeaux. By contrast, chardonnay is planted exclusively in Burgundy, Champagne, and now the Rhône and along the Mediterranean. Aligoté is exclusively a Burgundian variety. Chenin and romorantin are restricted to the Loire. Sémillon exists only in Bordeaux and the southwest.

LOTS LARGE AND SMALL

Apart from differences in the volume of overall production today, Bordeaux and Burgundy are distinguished by the quantity of wines produced by individual estates. Since the Revolution, this contrast has steadily become more marked: production is ever larger in Bordeaux (with the exception of garage wines), ever more limited in Burgundy.

Beginning in the late seventeenth century, winemaking in the Bordeaux region came to be organized in great estates centered upon châteaus, with their huge adjacent warehouses for vinification and aging. Initially it was the wealthy parliamentary magistrates (Pontac, Ségur, Aulède, Rauzan, and so on) who sought to amass substantial landholdings. The existence of a vast supply of land that was uncultivated or restricted to grazing allowed them to acquire and consolidate lots totaling 30 to 50 hectares or even more; and since in the late seventeenth century and for most of the eighteenth century land suitable for viticulture was relatively cheap, they had money left over to invest in agronomic development (deforestation, deep plowing, drains, roads, planting) and the construction of a rationally laid-out series of buildings for winemaking. This complex typically included an elegant and comfortable manor house that enabled proprietors to survey their domain, spend agreeable periods of time in the country, and entertain guests, among them current or potential clients. Michel Réjalot has well described the main impulse of this passion for building: "The true genius of the bourgeois class [during this period in Bordeaux], and above all of the parliamentary magistrates, was perhaps not so much that they discovered and promoted the qualitative potential of gravelly hilltops as that they landscaped their vineyards in such a way that eventually the wine itself acquired the image of aristocratic ownership."[22]

The château came to constitute the soul of the Bordeaux countryside and the source of its charm. Merchants from England and other northern European countries who settled in the Chartrons district fairly quickly established themselves and made fortunes. Following the example of the first *seigneurs des vignes,* the Gascon aristocrats and bourgeois parliamentarians, they invested in land and constructed or bought châteaus. They were succeeded in the nineteenth century by bankers (Rothschild, Pereire, Fould), then in the twentieth century by industrialists and other businessmen who had made their fortune in all sorts of activities.[23] Foreigners, resident there in large numbers since the eighteenth century, managed over time to become accepted members of local society. Today they come from all over the world.

The historic core of medieval castles (Yquem, Fargues, and Agassac), renovated in the eighteenth century, was enlarged by a magnificent garland of beautiful neoclassical houses built in the same century (La Louvière, Laroque, Figeac, Beychevelle, Malle) and under the Empire (Margaux). Later came theatrical facades (Cos d'Estournel) and neo-something châteaus (Pichon Longueville, Palmer, Cantenac Brown, Giscours).[24] Today, the concern for appearances has been carried underground with the hiring of famous architects to build cellars, the more impressive the better. Éric de Rothschild, for example, who called upon Ricardo Bofill in 1982 to construct Lafite's extraordinary new circular *chai de deuxième année,* justified his choice in this way: "All refinement is cultural. The pleasure of [making] fine wines, like the pleasure of building. And here, with this cellar and Ricardo, I have a great deal of pleasure." These few words distill the essence of the Bordeaux region and the importance of the link between wine and château, without which Bordeaux would not be what it is, and without which it would not arouse the images that it does in the minds of those who buy and drink its wines.[25] Witness a recent piece by the journalist Pierre Veilletet, who dips his pen into pure fantasy in declaring that "Yquem is Nervalian, Pomerol is redolent of Corrèze, Malle has Italian accents, Cos d'Estournel is oriental."[26]

Among the classed growths, most of the châteaus of Bordeaux cover an area that is rarely smaller than 10 hectares. Estates are larger in the Médoc (Lafite, 100 hectares; Latour, 65; Margaux, 90; Mouton, 82; Lagrange, 109) than in Graves (about 50 hectares) and in Saint-Émilion, Pomerol, and the Sauternes district (7 hectares at Ausone and 11.4 at Pétrus, between 20 and 30 for almost all the others). The result is that the majority of châteaus are capable each year of marketing between 100,000 and 200,000 bottles bearing their most prestigious label. The best *cuvées* are blended to make the *grand vin,* which is to say the wine that enjoys the honors of the official classification. Selection among the *premiers grands crus* is rigorous, and in a lean year may go as far as to withhold two-thirds of the harvest from the top bottlings *(tête de cuvée),* as at Château Margaux, for example. The rest is used to make a second wine (Pavillon Rouge de Margaux, Carraudes de Lafite, Les Forts de Latour, La Demoiselle de Sociando-Mallet, Les Hauts de Smith, and Le Petit Cheval de Cheval-Blanc, for example). Only Yquem refuses from time to time to sell a vintage under its own label, when it is not judged worthy of the name (nine times during the twentieth century, including two years in succession, 1951 and 1952), or sacrifices to the trade 80 to 90 percent of an already slight harvest (given that yields do not exceed ten hectoliters per hectare).

In less prestigious appellations, which differ by reason of their soil and by the fact that they did not attract buyers looking to consolidate properties in the early eighteenth century, individual holdings rarely exceed a few hectares. Paradoxically, then, it is easier to find a bottle of Lafite-Rothschild, available *en primeur* for €200, than an agreeable Château Beaulieu, a good generic Bordeaux from an estate of 23 hectares (about 57 acres) in Salignac that goes for €10. By contrast, what is now called garage wine is almost unobtainable in Bordeaux.[27] Pétrus was arguably the first such wine, having consistently maintained its reputation for excellence while continuing to fetch the highest prices (€600–

1,200). The fashion for garage wines was launched some twenty years ago by Jacques Thienpont at Château Le Pin in Pomerol, with a planted area of only two hectares and prices comparable to those of Pétrus. Other owners followed: Château de Valandraud (originally 2.5 hectares, now a dozen), Château La Mondotte (4.5 hectares)—both in Saint-Émilion, and both selling their wines for as much as €500 a bottle at one point—and, more recently, to the great displeasure of owners in the Médoc, Château Marojallia and Domaine Porcheron in Margaux.

How were such results achieved, particularly in Saint-Émilion, on parcels of land that were rather poorly regarded by the INAO classification commission?[28] In the main they are due to the expert care lavished on every vine, very restricted yields (16 hectoliters per hectare at La Mondotte), very late berry-by-berry harvesting, a lengthy period of fermentation marked by high extraction, and prolonged maturation in new barrels that have been rather heavily toasted (that is, heated at a high temperature to strengthen the presence of the wood's tannins in the wine). All of this produces extremely concentrated wines that are nonetheless, in the judgment of their admirers, well balanced. A few favorable notices by prominent critics (Robert Parker, for example) and the desire of certain wine lovers to try something unusual did the rest. A doubtful relation between quality and price is one thing; the law of supply and demand is another. Whether one likes it or not, it is supply and demand that prevail in the end.

Unsurprisingly, scathing attacks from established interests predicted the rapid collapse of what were called "ostentatious" or "showy" wines. The critics were right not to applaud wildly; they were wrong not to taste them with an open mind, however. Perhaps the new style is nothing more than a flash in the pan, but it may also be a direction worth exploring for French viticulture: the pursuit of absolute excellence and devotion to *terroir*. The same choice has been made by some producers of fine leather goods, such as Hermès, who have resisted competition from manufacturers that use ordinary raw materials and cheap foreign labor. In the case of wine, this choice makes sense only if concentration and complexity do not do away with elegance and finesse, and with them the graceful beauty that alone makes wine a moving experience.

Things are entirely different in Burgundy. The largest properties are those of the Hospices de Beaune (a bit more than sixty hectares)[29] and those of a few prominent merchants who, unable any longer to buy fine wines in cask from the producer because of the growing profitability of estate bottling, have managed to add to their real estate portfolios. At Chablis, Michel Laroche owns 100 hectares and William Fèvre 47 hectares; Louis Jadot, a merchant in Beaune, has 144; Faiveley, of Nuits-Saint-Georges, 120 (much of it in the Côte Chalonnaise); Joseph Drouhin, 60; Louis Latour, 50; Jean-Claude Boisset, 37. The other domaines content themselves with small holdings, between 5 and 20 hectares, which are nonetheless perfectly viable in view of the prices Burgundies presently command.[30]

Regardless of its size, a property is typically divided into innumerable parcels, some of them amounting only to a few acres (several hundred square meters). The buying up of adjacent properties is much frowned upon in Burgundy. What little consolidation does occur is the result of transactions among local owners or merchants, almost never of sales to large firms, as in Bordeaux. These are offset by the division of properties among heirs to an estate. Large parcels belonging to the same owner in the same appellation may be counted on the fingers of one hand; at bottom, they are analogous to the garage wines of the Bordeaux region. There is Château de Pommard, for example, exceptional for its 20 hectares under exclusive ownership; Clos des Lambrays, recently purchased by the Freund family from Koblenz, Germany (8.8 hectares); Clos de Tart, wholly owned by Mommessin (7.53 hectares); Romanée-Conti (1.85 hectares), controlled by the domaine of the same name, like La Tâche (4.6 hectares) and Château de Meursault (8 hectares)—and that is more or less it for the Côte d'Or. One finds a few single-owner domaines in the Côte Chalonnaise, such as Clos Salomon in Givry, which occupies 7 hectares.

The other appellations are divided into a great many, often minuscule, parcels. Clos de Vougeot belongs to about eighty different owners, Chambertin to thirteen, Clos-de-Bèze to fifteen, Montrachet (covering eight hectares) to a dozen, and so on. The majority of growers in the Côte d'Or own land in several appellations, sometimes as many as a dozen, even if the total does not exceed ten hectares. This stands in striking contrast to the scale of the lands worked in the Bordeaux region. Fiona Beeston, rounding off the numbers a bit, is not wrong to summarize the situation thus: "In Bordeaux there are 200 large châteaus, and that's it, whereas in Burgundy there are 200 large appellations multiplied by 200 owners [each], or about 40,000 different wines."[31]

This system of ownership implies a vast multitude of fermentation vats whose contents develop at different rates, since harvests are staggered over two or even three weeks. There is obviously no possibility, then, as in Bordeaux, of choosing the best part of the harvest upon which to confer the appellation's prestigious name. The slightest negligence has irreversible consequences, for there are no reserve lots of grapes within individual domaines. As in fresco painting, second thoughts are not permitted. The differences from one vintage to another are therefore more appreciable, except in the best domaines, where the custom is to downgrade a part of the harvest in disappointing years. This explains why for a long time it was necessary to resort to "Hermitaging" in order to rescue substandard *cuvées*—in the extreme case, even to substitute non-Burgundian wines for them altogether. Some parcels of a given appellation are so small that they yield only a few hundred bottles of wine a year. Domaine de la Romanée-Conti owns 0.85 hectares in Montrachet, which each year produces a dozen casks of wine, fewer than three thousand bottles of the greatest white wine in the world. Here again supply and demand determine price. In order to satisfy a few more clients, the domaine had the idea of selling its wines only in mixed cases containing just one or two each of the rarest *grands crus* that it produces: Romanée-Conti, La Tâche, Montrachet. Many prestigious domaines, though not Romanée-Conti, are fully subscribed and refuse new customers.[32] Standing customers who fail to buy their assigned quota find their privileges cancelled.

The problem posed by this splitting up of property is not a trivial one from the buyer's point of view. An appellation of controlled origin and a vintage do not by themselves constitute a sufficient guarantee of quality. Nor are all producers equally talented and painstaking. This is why for a long time, rightly or wrongly, connoisseurs of Burgundy placed their trust in merchants. Many people, restaurateurs and importers in particular, continue to do this today. Some merchant houses are unanimously recognized for their integrity and rigor in the selection of the lots of wine they buy and bottle.[33] It is no secret that other merchants are happy to sell inferior wines, but the unwary consumer cannot tell the difference, since the information required by law to appear on their labels is exactly the same.[34] These houses, which market a large share of Burgundy production, go unmentioned in the press. This is a terrible shame, for their wines, overpriced for what they are, harm the reputation of Burgundy as a whole. Some of them have invested in prestigious small domaines that produce excellent expensive wines, but that does not save the rest from mediocrity. The practice of inflating the price of undistinguished wines is also encountered in Bordeaux and other regions.[35] The fact remains that it is difficult to buy a good Burgundy at an affordable price from the large retail outlets. The *foires aux vins* that draw wine lovers into the hypermarkets every fall in France are generally much better stocked with Bordeaux than Burgundies.[36]

A large share of the wines available from volume retailers is sold under the simple name "Burgundy" and comes mainly from the Mâconnais, a region that could get better results than it does from its fine land. Its growers care little about quality, however. What they want, as do many growers in the south of France, are subsidies and price supports. At the general assembly of the Bureau Interprofessionel des Vins de Bourgogne (BIVB) in 2002, Gilbert Vincent, president of the producers' association of the Saône-et-Loire, angrily declared, "Some appellations are experiencing difficulties, particularly in our department. The BIVB must take steps. . . . Growers will not go away without making themselves heard. We are ready to take to the streets. This could get messy. We will do everything necessary to protect our young people." To which Pierre-Henry Gagey, president of Louis Jadot and of the merchants' association of Burgundy, sensibly replied, "It is the demand for quality that has changed. We must be aware of this and proceed in this direction. We must help you."[37] Until now it has been a dialogue of the deaf. Timid winemakers who likewise persist in burying their heads in the sand, demanding guaranteed prices as part of negotiations over the reform of the INAO, can be found elsewhere in France as well.

And yet there are unmistakable signs of vigorous competition with respect to quality and price. Philippe de Rothschild saw this more than twenty years ago, stating bluntly, "On the American market, which is the largest, ordinary French wines lag behind Italian, German, and Chilean wines. The reason for this is that, for the same quality, French wines are more expensive. Advertising campaigns won't change anything: at the very most they will make it possible to go on selling for a while, but over the long term they will fail."[38] Foreigners—who are now more discerning than they used to be, while French consumers have hardly progressed—are no longer fooled. Consider this recent editorial in a Canadian wine journal:

Living off their reputation for some time, Burgundian producers underachieved from the late sixties to the earlier eighties, often supplying us with light-coloured, lean-bodied, and short-lived wines. For many producers quantity overruled quality. The choice of high-yielding pinot noir clones combined with the exaggerated use of chemical fertilizers helped deplete the Burgundy *terroir*. Producers claimed that "finesse" was the style in which these wines were created. Unfortunately, more often than not, "finesse" became synonymous with thin, weak wines. . . . Luckily, this trend is now reversed. Since the early nineties we have noticed an obvious change. Conscientious producers have gone back to old methods and techniques (aided by new technology) to produce more deeply coloured wines with more concentration and potential to age. . . . Not all the producers have chosen this direction, but the most reputed and highly rated winemakers are part of this group.[39]

In order for France to continue exporting, the way forward is entirely mapped out: success depends on emphasizing quality and paying careful attention to consumers and critics.

Lovers of quality Burgundies that resemble the land they come from, their vintage, and their owner have only one sure option, namely, to employ an expert agent and, whenever possible, to go to individual properties and taste their wines on the spot.[40] In Burgundy a relationship of personal trust is essential; in Bordeaux no such need arises, since wines from a classed vineyard there can be bought anywhere in the world at virtually no risk. This is obviously an advantage for the consumer. That said, some large foreign buyers have found a way to get around the obstacle by stocking up on Burgundies directly from the producers themselves. This is the case in Canada, for example, where a public company, the Société des Alcools du Québec, holds the monopoly on the sale of alcoholic beverages in that province. In its catalogue and its extraordinary network of stores, which stock hard-to-find wines from small producers in Burgundy, one finds evidence of a far greater meticulousness in selection than in the large retail outlets in France.

One should also mention the occasionally remarkable achievements of certain cooperatives in the Bordeaux region (Rauzan, for example) and, in Burgundy, at Chablis, along the Côte Chalonnaise, and in the Mâconnais. It is difficult to find dazzling wines, given the location of these cooperatives away from the great vineyards as well as their habit of blending harvests and the volumes of wine they produce; but, as in Alsace and Languedoc-Roussillon, they have encouraged small growers to improve their methods of cultivation and to supply grapes of better quality. Some of these growers, having declared their independence, now aspire to take their place among the best.

Looking to the future, the only solution is to make appellations of controlled origin much harder to obtain and to require producers to make wines that are notable for their concentration, personality, and elegance. Consumers, for their part, must educate their palates and sharpen their critical faculties.

BOURGEOIS VINEYARD, PEASANT VINEYARD

It should perhaps not come as a surprise, in view of the historical differences between the two regions, that estate owners in Bordeaux and Burgundy seldom resemble one another. Exaggerating only slightly, it is fair to say that in Bordeaux they have university degrees, speak English (and sometimes another foreign language), read the daily financial news, travel frequently to Paris and abroad, dress in the style of English gentlemen farmers, and play tennis or even polo; in short, their manners are sophisticated. Most of their counterparts in Burgundy, by contrast, have no higher education, dress in a rustic or sporty way, in any case without any concern for fashion or affectation, and proudly display their peasant manners. The former spend their time mainly in the office and rely on employees to do the work of the vineyard and cellar; the latter, even when they have the assistance of hired staff, take pleasure in getting out of the office and rolling up their sleeves. Although both are devoted to making good wine, they approach the task in quite opposite ways.

The accent of the southwest of France is very attenuated among owners in Bordeaux and the majority of their executives,[41] all the more so as many of them are not native to the region, often coming from northern Europe or elsewhere in the world. By contrast, the accent is still strong among the old estate managers, cellar masters, and employees. In Burgundy, many of the owner-growers continue to roll their *r*s and to accentuate *a* and *e* sounds, even if the youngest among them, influenced by the Parisian accent familiar from television, are more careful about their pronunciation. This observation applies, of course, only to families of old Burgundian peasant stock, not to the few families of aristocratic lineage whose manners are much more those of city dwellers, or to the new generation of winemakers whose families settled in the region only a generation or two ago. Local accents are now heard less and less among merchants; indeed, when one encounters them in the aisles at Vinexpo, the world's largest wine fair (held every other year in Bordeaux), it is often difficult to tell at first sight where they are from. To judge from their way of dressing and conducting business, most merchants today are interchangeable. But not quite all of them. It is hard to imagine the descendant of a Chartrons dynasty negotiating the purchase of three casks of a *grand cru* with a grower from Gevrey-Chambertin, who has no need of a merchant in order to sell his wine. This would be a fine scene for the stage or cinema. Nor would it be any easier for an experienced merchant from Nuits, proud of his family's century and a half of success, to buy two thousand cases of a Saint-Julien *cru classé* from a broker who has already established his network of sellers and buyers, according to a web of unwritten rules of the greatest complexity.[42] The economic aspects of the wine trade are intimately intertwined with its cultural side, and if daring is permitted, improvisation is not. The one may work wonders, but the other is apt to lead to catastrophe.

At this juncture the question arises whether a relationship between the style of a given wine and that of its makers can be asserted without oversimplifying. Can one say that Burgundy is more a product of the countryside than Bordeaux, on the ground that winemakers in the two regions do not share the same social and cultural background? Probably not, and fortunately so. Neither history nor literature furnishes proof that such a contrast has ever been perceived or declared. The wines of Bordeaux and Burgundy have both been valued by royal and princely courts, as well as by members of the bourgeoisie throughout Western Europe. If the king of England and his court liked "French claret," the king of France and the emperor of the French delighted in good Burgundy. One might say that Burgundy is rural because of its tiny lots and comparatively small-scale transactions, and Bordeaux urban since its enormous volumes of uniform wines from individual vineyards and contracts totaling tens, indeed hundreds, of thousands of euros exert greater influence on market prices. Yet the wines of Burgundy are apt to be no less sophisticated and refined *au palais,* in both senses of the term (palate and palace), than those of Bordeaux.

Just the same, the wines of Burgundy are rural by virtue of the whole culture that goes with them. They are the wines of hard-working and cheerful peasants. Gaston Roupnel, in his preface to *Le Clos de Vougeot,* by his friend Camille Rodier, says:

> Everywhere here you will find a little something that bespeaks good humor: a smile, a certain gaiety, a wink of the eye, a certain mischievousness, a bit of good-natured bantering. A reflection of the wisdom of our forebears, of their ironic and doleful outlook on life, animates and colors the work, impresses it with the turn of mind found among us, the mark of the countryside . . . , reminds us of where we live . . . , makes us breathe the smells of the Côte and the flowering vine . . . , fills our soul with the sunny spirit of a strapping Burgundian lass, pleasing as the musky harvest![43]

Here, limned with Roupnel's distinctive brand of lyricism, is the picture of the people of Burgundy that the people themselves, and especially the region's men of wine, wish to present to the world. One finds the same tone in *Colas Breugnon* by Romain Rolland, in passages that Colette devoted to Burgundy and its wine, in *La billebaude* and *Le pape des escargots* by Henri Noël, and in the work of so many other earthy authors born and raised in Burgundy.[44] It recalls, too, the verve of Gaston Gérard, mayor of Dijon before the war, and his wife, Andrée (la Dédée), an omnipresent figure in Dijon and the Côte who survived her husband by many years; of the canon Félix Kir, who succeeded Gérard as mayor; of Bernard Barbier, an eloquent and colorful mayor of Nuits-Saint-Georges and senator, who was also an indefatigable advocate of the wines of the Côte d'Or; of the founders of the Confrérie des Chevaliers du Tastevin, foremost among them Camille Rodier and Georges Faiveley. All these Burgundians rolled their *rs*—those famous

Burgundian *r*s that, as Colette said in *Prisons et paradis,* "have remained
in my throat for half a century."[45]

Marion Demossier has written perceptively about the distinctive culture of the winemakers of Burgundy, which represents the core of a
regional identity that they claim to be uniquely their own.[46] This privilege is generally conceded to them by the population of France as a
whole. When they travel and tell people where they are from, the people of Burgundy feel a sense of pride at being able to raise a smile and
turn the conversation at once to wine and food. The elegant Lalou Bize-
Leroy, less a merchant now than a viticulturalist, creator of some of the
greatest wines of the Côte d'Or, well illustrates this marriage of immense professionalism with the spontaneity inherited from Burgundian
tradition. No one in Bordeaux would dare to confess the childhood
memory that she unhesitatingly confided to Alain Ducasse: "Every time
a party was given at the house, there were very great wines. . . . When
we had guests, I used to get up from my nap and go to the dining room
while my parents and their guests were in the living room. I used to
empty the glasses, and I liked that—a lot."[47] Another scene that would
seem out of place in Bordeaux comes to mind. On 11 June 1999, the
merchant house Moillard celebrated its one hundred fiftieth anniversary
at Clos de Vougeot. The hundreds of guests included executives, clients,
and friends of the house, as well as a few important local figures.
Toward the end of a cordial dinner at which the wine flowed freely, the
three bubbly daughters of Denis Thomas, the president, came up to
the microphone and began singing a ballad that their father had composed in honor of the patriarch of the dynasty, to the tune of Serge
Gainsbourg's "Poinçonneur des Lilas":

> I'm the merchant Yves Thomas,
> Specialist in wine, not plonk.
> There's no sun underground,
> Strange sort of cruise.
> I'm never bored—my head's full of
> The names of wines I repeat to myself.[48]

Thunderous applause. By unanimous request, the full text was sent to all the guests. Four years later, Philippine de Rothschild celebrated at Mouton the one hundred fiftieth anniversary of the purchase of Château Brane-Mouton by her ancestor Nathaniel. Two thousand guests were present. All the French Rothschilds were there, along with Bernadette Chirac and the upper crust of political life, society, and the arts. At dessert, the baroness pulled back a curtain and there appeared Placido Domingo, who launched into an aria from *La Traviata* with words by Jean-Pierre de Beaumarchais. The two scenes, each moving in its way, could not have been more different.[49]

Bordeaux is urban and distinguished by the personal style of its winemakers and their fashionable admixture of Anglomania with the French spirit of the eighteenth century.[50] Wearing red suspenders, as Claude Ricard of Domaine de Chevalier used to do, is not done in Bordeaux.[51] Whether or not their owners are year-round residents, the châteaus of the Bordeaux region entail a certain standard of living and upkeep. One can make fun of all this, as Mauriac, Doutrelant, and Ginestet have done in their different ways, but it has ever been thus, and the great foreign buyers would surely not wish it otherwise.[52] Mauriac and the others have given the proprietors of these châteaus a reputation for being stingy, calculating, and artificial, but the proportion of estate owners fitting this description in Burgundy is just as large as in Bordeaux. Credit must be given to the affectionate portrait that Jean-Paul Kauffmann has drawn of the Bordelais, which, it must be admitted, contains the barest hint of smugness, tempered, happily, by a touch of irony: "The world of wine in Bordeaux is the most hospitable, the most open that I know. The whole problem comes from the fact that the owners are convinced deep down that they make the best wine in the world. The worst of it is that it is true. This awareness of their excellence paralyzes them to a large extent. . . . The admiration that the whole world lavishes upon them makes them rather shy. They don't want to be admired, they want to be liked."[53] Let us like them, then, if this is the condition of their continuing to make great wines for our delight.

Within this world there cross the paths of men (and a few women, who are now increasingly numerous) from quite different backgrounds. Although they do not all come from the same mold, they fairly rapidly acquire a family resemblance and adopt a behavior that enables them to blend in with their executive staff. At least seven kinds may be distinguished. There still exist a few families of the old Gascon aristocracy, landowning and Catholic, but there are fewer and fewer of these; the Lur-Saluces, who have lost Yquem but yet hold on to Fargues, are among the last. Still, they have become Bordelais only through marriage. Next came the old Chartrons dynasties, most of them originally from northern Europe and Protestant (Barton, Cruse, Schyler, Lawton); they have lost much of the immense power that they once enjoyed and no longer really set the tone for the wine community in Bordeaux. Then came the Parisian and English bankers who began to invest in prestigious châteaus in the nineteenth century. Without the Rothschilds, whose three branches have carried on a tradition of their own with panache until the present day, the Médoc would not be what it is.[54]

Then came trading families from other regions of France, who, by dint of hard work and imagination, created empires (the Moueix from Limousin, the Cazes from Ariège). Later, in the 1960s, a few families of *pieds-noir,* the Tari family among them, managed to give new life to abandoned châteaus. Bordeaux has always welcomed foreigners, a tradition that in the twentieth century was sustained by the arrival of proprietors from previously unrepresented countries: the Mentzélopoulos family from Greece, along with others from the Americas, Australia, Japan, and elsewhere. Finally, and among the most dynamic of today's owners, there are the great French patrons who took over prestigious estates that were in financial difficulty or at the center of stormy inheritance disputes: Bernard Arnault, Claude Bébéar, François Pinault, and so on. In this way they were able to provide their corporate portfolios with an extra measure of prestige, as well as an additional source of income, having seen that these estates, properly managed, could be something more than an expensive hobby.

Unlike Burgundy, which owes very little to the tranquil cultural life of Dijon, the whole wine culture of the Bordeaux region is strongly influenced by the city of Bordeaux.[55] The very names of the two regions betray this difference. One speaks of the wines of Bordeaux, but never of the wines of Dijon; the expression "wines of Beaune" has not been used for centuries, except for those that are produced within the narrow confines of the commune of Beaune. One speaks instead of the wines of Burgundy, that is, of an entire region, which underscores its more rural character.[56] The city of Bordeaux, by contrast, is strongly marked by the presence of the wine industry, not only because of the Quai des Chartrons, even if it has now been deserted by the merchants and one no longer sees barrels being loaded at the Port de la Lune, but also on account of the abundance of architectural details alluding to vine and wine.[57] Very happily, a wine festival is now held every year in the spring on the wharves, in the shadow of one of the most handsome settings of stone architecture in all of France. The great merchant houses have now relocated to grand new quarters on the outskirts of the city, and the shores of the lake are the site of a huge exhibition hall that hosts Vinexpo every other year in June.

In Burgundy the trade's presence is more spread out, divided among Beaune, Nuits, and Meursault. In Dijon one encounters few visual allusions to wine, apart from the statue of the *bareuzai* (vintager) treading grapes with his feet atop the fountain on the Place Rude. Unlike in Bordeaux, it is rather difficult to buy good wine there. For that one must go to Beaune, which, along with Saint-Émilion and Vézelay, now once again planted with vines thanks to the efforts of the chef Marc Meneau, figures on the UNESCO list of World Heritage Sites.

To have a sense of the soul of the wines made in these regions, one must walk the vineyards and trace the necklace of the châteaus of the Gironde countryside and the picturesque villages of the Côte d'Or. Châteaus are few in Burgundy; there are no grand avenues lined with hundred-year-old trees, no great stone cellars, no rosebushes at the head of the vine rows (or only very rarely), no majestic, lazy estuary. One does find, on the other hand, beautiful vine growers' houses, Roman and Gothic religious edifices with stone or glazed tile roofs in the style of Central Europe, charming views of the Hautes-Côtes and the plain below, of the Jura and Mont Blanc, the beautiful days of winter. Above all, in Burgundy as in the Gironde, there are the vines themselves, which, better than other plants, mirror the passing of the four seasons and testify to the harshness of the struggle to master nature, and so to extract from it the noble beverage that is at the heart of Western civilization.[58]

WHERE ARE THEY CONSUMED?

The distribution of drinkers of Bordeaux and Burgundy remained stable for a long time, evidence of a particular European geography and of boundary lines that seem to exist only with regard to the wines of these regions. Bordeaux, thanks to its ancient association with maritime navigation, was drunk in England and in the riverine lands of the Atlantic (Brittany, Ireland) and the North Sea (Nord Pas de Calais, Belgian Flanders, the Netherlands, northern Germany).[59] Burgundy was drunk in the continental regions of the former duchy, in Paris, in central and southern Germany, and, during the Middle Ages, by the popes in Avignon.[60] Although it is no longer true today, Jean-Paul Kauffmann is correct to say that while Burgundy was a French wine, Bordeaux was not: "Invented by the English, adored by the Dutch, it was long a 'foreigner's wine.'"[61]

Bordeaux was, and still is, so obviously the wine of the English court that the Duke of Clarence, brother of Edward IV, executed in 1478 for having hatched a plot, is credited with uttering the following words before his death—words meant to offend the king and his entourage: "I desire to be drowned in a barrel of wine from Beaune so that my death will be easy and good."[62] Even today—and I do not say this insultingly—the English are poorly acquainted with Burgundies. At Emmanuel College, Cambridge, for example, whose cellar is so richly stocked, when a Côtes du Rhône (such as Châteauneuf-du-Pape) is served at official dinners instead of Bordeaux, it is called simply Burgundy![63]

Since the early nineteenth century (some say since Louis XV, who began to appreciate Bordeaux on the advice of the Duc de Richelieu), the wines of the Gironde have penetrated farther into France and beyond, into Central European countries. But the swing in Parisian consumption toward Bordeaux, at least in the case of red wine, is a recent phenomenon. In 1791, the wine list of the restaurant Véry, at the Palais-Royal, leaned more toward Burgundy than Bordeaux: of the seventeen unfortified wines on offer, eleven were Burgundies, four Bordeaux, and two champagnes.[64] This proportion is consistent with the holdings of the cellar of Louis de Bourbon, Duc de Penthièvre, inventoried at his death in 1793: 207 bottles of Haut-Brion, 524 red and white Graves, and 238 Sauternes, as against 260 Clos de Vougeots, 480 white Beaunes, 592 Meursaults, and 450 Montrachets.[65] In addition to these were bottles of Côte-Rôtie, white Hermitage, Málaga, and so on. The list of the Restaurant des Trois Frères Provençaux ou de Beauvilliers, under the Restoration, conformed still more closely to this proportion, as did the menus of official banquets during the nineteenth century.[66] The reason, according to Jean-Paul Aron, is that "there is a certain affectation, a certain sophistication, about Bordeaux; Burgundy seems more virile, and so more acceptable. Until 1850, it was the preferred accompaniment for the great dinners."[67] Bordeaux slowly began to gain ground in the capital in the second half of the nineteenth century and the first decades of the twentieth century. As late as the interwar period, however, Parisian banquets were no less likely, and perhaps even a bit more inclined, to serve Burgundy than Bordeaux. At a banquet held in the autumn of 1932, for example, Chablis, Montrachet, and Clos-de-Bèze were served along with Lafite-Rothschild and Yquem.[68] Another banquet, held in the summer of the same year, featured Fleurie, Meursault, and Corton, as well as Côte-Rôtie, Château Chalon, and champagne—but no Bordeaux.

It was only after the Second World War that Paris switched allegiance and Burgundy, particularly red Burgundy, became scarcer at official banquets. The proportions came to be inverted, even to the point that Burgundies were occasionally excluded. At the dinner given by François Mitterrand for the queen of England on 9 June 1992 at Élysée Palace, the wines included Yquem 1981 (a vintage dear to the president's heart), Latour 1978, and Krug champagne. For the party celebrating the millionth duck served at the Tour d'Argent restaurant in Paris, on 29 April 2003, Claude Terrail organized a lavish dinner at which the following wines were served in succession: Montrachet 1985, Ausone 1995, Cheval-Blanc 1985, Haut-Brion 1979, Lafite-Rothschild 1978, Mouton-Rothschild 1975, Pétrus 1989, and Yquem 1986. A 1990 Laurent-Perrier champagne concluded this impressive procession of seven Bordeaux and one Burgundy. Even granting that the intoxicating reputation of Burgundy red wines may be justified, one wonders how many guests managed to keep their wits about them after so many magnificent Bordeaux, of which not even the least well-informed connoisseur could have left a drop in his glass, much less—something unimaginable in this sanctuary of gastronomy—spit it out.

The triumph of Bordeaux in Paris is dramatically expressed by the holdings of the cellars of the Republic. The cellar of the president of the Senate is supposed to reflect the output of France as a whole. This it does, but Bordeaux wines nonetheless make up 70 to 80 percent of the some seven thousand bottles conserved there.[69] There are Meursaults and white Chassagnes, but not a single bottle of red Burgundy among the 6,500 laid down in the depths of the Quai d'Orsay.[70] The same is true at the Hôtel de Ville de Paris, whose cellar contains some twenty-four thousand bottles; white Burgundies are plentiful, but only three red Burgundies find a place alongside ninety-eight red Bordeaux.[71] By contrast, the great restaurants of the capital have more balanced reserves; cellars such as the one at the Bristol prove that trained sommeliers have more eclectic tastes than government purchasing agents.[72] The gradual reduction in the variety of the wines accompanying official banquets—a champagne served as an aperitif, a white Burgundy or a Sancerre, and a red Bordeaux—points to a certain cautiousness on the part of the political class and their stewards. Winemakers in many other regions of France should complain.

Outside France, the United Kingdom remains very attached to Bordeaux, but even so it is the leading European customer for Burgundy. Heading the list of non-European importers of both Bordeaux and Burgundy is the United States, followed by Japan, where the fashion of fine wine is booming, particularly among women—so much so that in 1998 the Bureau Interprofessionel des Vins de Bourgogne organized an amusing advertising campaign around the theme "The Wines of Burgundy Are Japanese." A photo of a glass of red wine taken from above against a white background, meant to suggest the Japanese flag, was accompanied by this text:

> You were afraid? That's a good sign! Let us explain. Burgundy is THE wine. France is the country of wine. Yet most wine from Burgundy is drunk elsewhere in the world. Sixty percent of the harvest is bought and consumed abroad. The English and the Americans drink enormous amounts of it. The Japanese more and more. Yes, the Japanese. They've more than doubled their buying in the last year! Let's face it, when it comes to the wines of Burgundy, you've sometimes said some stupid things: "Burgundies are heavy and very expensive red wines." You've got it all wrong.

One curiosity associated with this pattern of consumption, which no one seems to be able to explain, has to do with the names of colors. In France, *bordeaux* is commonly used as an adjective to denote purplish brown-red.[73] In Great Britain and the United States, however, the adjective *burgundy* is used, and *bourgogne* is used in Quebec.[74] A small mystery . . .

Rather than undertake joint ventures and promote cross-investment, companies from Bordeaux and Burgundy have a long tradition of investing in other regions in France and abroad, but never together. Jean-

Louis Vignes, the son of coopers in Béguey, in the Gironde, settled in Los Angeles and planted Bordeaux grape varieties in the 1830s.[75] Paul Masson, born near Beaune, settled in California in 1878, founded a wine empire, and flooded the United States with a "champagne" called Eye of the Partridge.[76]

Immigrants from Bordeaux created the vineyards of central Chile and Mendoza, in Argentina, in the second half of the nineteenth century. These two countries then ceased to import wines from Bordeaux. Winemaking in the Rioja region of Spain was modernized by natives of Bordeaux during the same period as well.[77]

In the course of recent decades, many houses in Bordeaux and Burgundy have looked to diversify and invest in regions where land suitable for vine growing is less expensive than in France. Philippe de Rothschild was a pioneer in this regard, entering into partnership in 1979 with Robert Mondavi to create the Opus One vineyard in California's Napa Valley. There each year 360,000 bottles of fine wine are produced, the first *grand vin à la bordelaise* in California. Rothschild's daughter, Philippine, founded the Almaviva vineyard at Puente Alto in Chile, in 1992, in association with the Chilean winery Concha y Toro.

Within France itself, Éric de Rothschild, François Lurton, Philippe Dourthe, Philippe Courrian, and many others from the Bordeaux region have a strong presence in Languedoc-Roussillon, as do the Burgundians Michel Laroche, Laurent Max, and Denis Thomas. Louis Latour has successfully planted chardonnay in the Ardèche region, profiting from the international fashion of this grape and the taste of the Anglo-Saxon market for the type of wine that can be made from it in hot climates. The famous domaine Mas de Daumas Gassac, established by the Millau glove manufacturer Aimé Guibert at Aniane, in the Hérault, succeeded in grafting the spirit of Bordeaux onto the land of Languedoc. The soil, consisting of small limestone pebbles and very well drained, was enthusiastically appraised some years ago by Henri Enjalbert,[78] then planted partly with Bordeaux grape varieties, which explains why Mas de Daumas Gassac is still classed as a table wine despite the use of vinification methods originally recommended by Émile Peynaud. It is in any case far and away the most expensive table wine in France.

A great many French investors, from Bordeaux and Burgundy in particular, have made their presence felt throughout the world, typically where the price of land and labor does not weigh too heavily on manufacturing costs: Argentina, Chile, South Africa, Romania, Bulgaria, Hungary, China, and so on. One oddity deserves to be noted: the Bordeaux oenologist Michel Rolland acts as a consultant to Grover Vineyards, a domaine that produces a Bordeaux-style wine, and a full-bodied wine at that, near Bangalore in the south of India.[79]

Finally, there is the exportation of French winemaking expertise. Since 1957, the Institut d'Oenologie in Bordeaux has dominated the national and international training of oenologists, along with, to a lesser degree, the school of agronomy at Montpellier. Today the Institut Jules-Guyot at the University of Dijon is beginning to exert its influence at the international level as well. But it must be recognized that many oenologists now learn their trade at excellent universities in Italy, Spain, the United States, South Africa, New Zealand, and even Japan (at Yamanishi University in Kofu); indeed, a certain number of renowned French wine houses now employ talented foreign oenologists who have not necessarily been trained in France. In Bordeaux, for example, the oenologist at Château Carsin, Amanda Jones, is Australian, the daughter of a winemaker and herself educated in Australia. After working in Portugal, she entered the service of this château in the Premières Côtes de Bordeaux, owned by a Finn, Juha Berglund, in 1993. Jones makes the wine (which, as it happens, is not too woody) to suit the tastes of a clientele that is overwhelmingly found in the Nordic countries and England. Just the same, she ages some of her *cuvées* of white wine in two-year-old French oak casks purchased in—Burgundy![80]

This is an aspect of globalization to which one must pay attention. There is nothing disturbing about it in and of itself; it simply shows that as the taste for wine spreads throughout the world, so does the taste for making it. French standards of training will need to remain permanently on the crest of the wave—a rather stimulating challenge, everything considered.

BOTTLES AND GLASSES, ROUNDED AND SLENDER

The wines of Bordeaux and Burgundy began to be bottled toward the end of the seventeenth century, as we have seen, just when improved techniques of vinification had made it easier to produce and stabilize wines, but also when the glass industry had learned to make bottles of thick, dark-colored glass. Champagne had taken the lead in the matter of glassmaking early on, with Bordeaux and Burgundy following, but bottle shapes in these regions long remained similar. The oldest bottles, manufactured in England and the Low Countries, were onion-shaped and could only be stored standing up. To combat the risk that the stopper would dry out, letting air in, most glassmakers abandoned the semispherical shape in favor of cylindrical bottles once cork came generally to be used. Burgundy gradually came to choose the same model as Champagne and Bordeaux, big-bellied with sloping shoulders and a moderately slender neck—the easiest shape to produce in a mold by blowing into a bubble of molten glass. The upper part is a bubble drawn in the form of an egg; the lower part, resembling an inverted truncated cone, emerges easily from the mold before it is pressed with a punty in order to form a stable base with an inverse indentation that allows the sediment to collect at the bottom and so, for the most part, to avoid contact with the wine. Finally, when the bottle was held by the bottom, the neck could be heated and given a collar of spun glass that reinforced it for sealing.

The decisive event in the geography of bottles (see map 4) was the invention by Bordeaux glassmakers of a tall cylindrical bottle with narrow, square shoulders, originally called *frontignane* and today *bordelaise*.[81] This shape, which dates from the time of the Empire in the early nineteenth century, reflected the strong differentiation of French re-

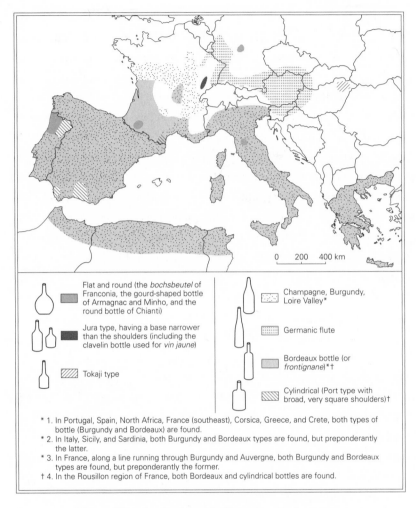

Map 4. Wine bottle shapes in Europe at the beginning
of the twenty-first century.

gional cultures with regard to dress, diet, and so on, a much more recent
phenomenon than is generally believed.[82] The new bottle presented certain advantages as a result of recent changes in French viticulture. Up
until that time, exporters had used barrels exclusively. English and
northern European buyers, having understood the value of aging in bot-

tles, became increasingly interested in purchasing old wines already packaged for shipment in this form in the cellars of the Chartrons. Though casks were easy to handle, they required regular topping off, without which the wine was very likely to turn sour despite being sulfured and shipped during cool months. One of the reasons for the appearance of the cylindrical bottle in Bordeaux was the ease with which it could be stored in piles and put into wooden crates that held twelve bottles each. But this seems not to have been decisive, for the body of Burgundy bottles likewise assumed a cylindrical shape during the course of the nineteenth century, simplifying storage and crating there as well.

The real reason is probably to be sought elsewhere. We know that improved methods of vinification during the eighteenth century grew out of a desire to clarify wines more carefully. Bordeaux was more attached to this practice, for its Nordic clientele demanded it. Nonetheless, despite settling, sieve filtration, racking, and clarification, wines still contained a good deal of suspended solid matter that was deposited in the bottle in the course of aging. Despite the precautions taken just before tasting (the bottle was brought up from the cellar forty-eight hours in advance and laid down in a basket), there was a great risk of pouring cloudy wine into the glass. This was the origin of decanting, which is to say the careful transfer of wine from the bottle into a glass or crystal carafe (called a decanter by the English). The practice originated in England, where it was the object of a meticulous ritual, as in the case of the tasting that followed it, and led to the invention of curious contraptions, plated with silver and equipped with a screw and a crank, that made it possible to tilt the bottle horizontally. The ideal setting for transvasing wine was a room illuminated by burning candles in silver holders placed on a table of varnished mahogany, where the wine was carefully poured in turn from the decanter into a glass made of crystal. Against this brilliant background, the color of the wine was brought out by the flame of the candles.

It was altogether natural that Bordeaux high society, whether or not it was connected with the wine trade, should have adopted these

English—and Dutch—customs. The mayor of Bordeaux in the 1840s, M. Duffour-Dubergier, was an astute connoisseur. According to the Maréchal de Castellane, the "prince of Aquitaine [as Duffour-Dubergier was known] reasoned better than anyone else about the wine of Bordeaux and the manner of swallowing it."[83] On his death in 1860, the inventory of his cellar revealed holdings that went beyond the regional.[84] Of 4,372 bottles, 3,758 were Bordeaux vintages from the period 1825–54. Next came small quantities of sherry, champagne, Madeira, port, Málaga, wines from the Rhine Valley, and twenty-one unfortunate bottles of Burgundy. The poet Biarnez described the way in which Duffour-Dubergier personally prepared the bottles that he wished to offer to his guests, taking infinite pains and precautions. The scene unfolds at his country seat, the Château de Gironville, in Macau:

> Before the bottle that he holds ever horizontal,
> He presents at once a small flagon of crystal;
> With attentive eye, fixed on the sparkling liquid,
> His hand lets it flow so long as it runs clear.
> If ever a particle of tartar or lees appear,
> He stops—what's left isn't worth worrying over.
> Thus must it always be, transparent and ruby red,
> That the vinous drink comes out of an old bottle.[85]

The English manufactured black bottles with shoulders clearly more pronounced than those of Bordeaux, borrowing from the bottles used for port, a wine liable to contain even more deposits than claret. The slender bottle with square shoulders nonetheless managed during the nineteenth and twentieth centuries to acquire an image of elegance that harmonized well not only with the distinctive etiquette of drinking Bordeaux, but with the manners of the elites of Bordeaux and of northern Europe as well.

In Burgundy and Paris, by contrast, wine has continued until the present day to be served in bottles that are placed on the table, together with the dust and patches of mildew that deepen the impression of age. One almost never sees a bottle of Burgundy decanted, in part because the generally softer tannins of the red wines made from the pinot grape require less oxygenation than ones made from cabernet sauvignon, particularly when they are young. The gastronome and gastronomical philosopher Grimod de la Reynière, who cannot be suspected of uncouthness or abandon, was firmly opposed to the practice of decanting:

> Pouring [wines] into crystal flagons, in order to produce them with a greater flourish on the table, causes them to lose their bouquet, and a part of their spirit and quality. This kind of extravagance, unknown to our fathers, could have been adopted only by men who were wholly unacquainted with the great art of living well. The true beauty of wine resides in its great age rather than in the sparkle of the vessel that contains it. How much better, too, to drink it out of ash-fern glasses, which is to say very thin ones. Glasses made of crystal, in putting too much space between the drink and the lips of the drinker, are the great enemies of degustation.[86] True gourmets ought to proscribe their use, which was introduced only through an ostentation more sumptuous than sensible.[87]

Grimod de la Reynière himself, in keeping with the Parisian habits of the day, almost surely drank more Burgundies than Bordeaux.

That vine-growing areas outside Bordeaux and Burgundy should have hesitated between the two shapes is unsurprising. By tradition, allowing for small variations in form and decoration, the northeastern part of France, the Loire Valley, and the Rhône Valley as far as Châteauneuf-du-Pape—regions dominated by the Parisian market— were loyal to the Burgundy bottle *(la bourguignonne)*. Despite the injustices to which it had long been subject at the hands of the wine trade in Bordeaux, the southwest—including, with only a few exceptions, the region of Armagnac and, to a somewhat lesser extent, of Cognac and Pineau des Charentes, which was always open to new ideas—remained attached to *la bordelaise.* Those regions converted more recently to the idea of bottling—Languedoc-Roussillon, Provence-Alpes-Côte d'Azur, and Corsica—were divided in their loyalties. The same was true abroad. Both styles were found in roughly equal proportions in

Spain, Portugal, and Italy, again with regional variations, but *la borde-laise* gradually gained the upper hand.

Currently some ten billion bottles of the Bordeaux type are manufactured worldwide each year, as opposed to three to four billion of the Burgundy type.[88] There may be a financial reason for this: a machine for putting a single label on a bottle, often the practice in Bordeaux, costs less than €15,000, whereas a machine that can also attach a second label around the neck of the bottle sells for €40,000.[89] What is more, in the company of other wines on display in a shop, a Bordeaux-style bottle immediately catches the eye of the customer. At Beaumes-de-Venise, for example, near Avignon, producers generally present their wines in Burgundy-style bottles, except for Domaine de Durban, which for decades has chosen fine transparent *bordelaises* of the sort used for Sauternes. Similar exceptions may be noted in other regions. The cellars of Pouilly-sur-Loire contain a *cuvée* sold in fifty-centiliter Bordeaux-style bottles. Still more provocatively, perhaps, Château de Cléray in the Muscadet region sells its wines in *bordelaises,* as do the makers of certain white wines from the German valley of the Moselle, which until recently were bottled exclusively in the Germanic flute.[90] Wine buyers are attracted to this style for its elegance, according to Michel Creignou, who speaks of its "mythical" quality: "It has charmed the world with its aristocratic appearance. . . . In many respects, the *'bordelaise'* resembles and is identified with the wine it contains. Its austerity is fitting and its breeding is evident."[91] This perception explains why many winemakers and merchants throughout the world increasingly look to the Bordeaux-style bottle in order to give themselves an air of distinction.

For a long time the labels on bottles of Bordeaux and Burgundy were very different as well. Not in the beginning, which is to say in the eighteenth and nineteenth centuries, for then only the name of the wine appeared on the label, soberly printed on a rectangle of white paper, sometimes with a simple decorative border. Later, owing to advances in lithography and silkscreen printing, the styles came to be sharply distinguished. Differences in the shapes of the labels—almost all labels in

Burgundy were horizontal and surmounted by a smaller, usually oval neck label bearing the year of the vintage, whereas many labels in Bordeaux were vertical—accentuated differences in the shape of the bottles themselves.[92] Until the Second World War, almost all wine was bottled by merchants at their warehouses. In Burgundy a simpler style was generally favored than in Bordeaux, where *négociants* sought quite early to adorn their labels with a picture of a château. All that changed with the advent of estate bottling. The idea, revolutionary at the time, was first put into practice in 1924 by Baron Philippe at Château Mouton-Rothschild, a property lacking a castle or manor house that could lend a bit of flair to a label. Confident in his artistic tastes, the baron commissioned a cubist design from the poster artist Jean Carlu that same year. After the war, from 1945 onward, he entrusted the task of illustrating the label for the year's vintage to a contemporary artist; the first, conceived by Philippe Julian, elaborated the theme of "V" for victory.[93]

Bottling by the producer became as widespread in Bordeaux as in Burgundy, and it was in the decades between 1950 and 1990 that the contrast between the two regions was most pronounced: lofty graphic design in the one case, the archetype of which was the label of Château Latour; popular art in the other, the style long favored by growers, consisting of yellowed and curling parchment lettered with Gothic fonts.[94] The most elaborate example of this style is associated with the wine tastings sponsored by the Confrérie des Chevaliers du Tastevin, which commissioned designs from the Alsatian artist and illustrator Hansi. There are, of course, exceptions, such as the plain style of Domaine de la Romanée-Conti. Conversely, some of the greatest wines of Bordeaux conceal themselves behind overcrowded labels, sometimes adorned with a black-and-white or sepia photograph of the château. The design of an estate's label often says something about its taste and how it sees itself, but it is seldom enough to enable one to form an idea of wine's style in relation to its appellation.

The language on these labels is regulated by antifraud statutes, which require that a certain amount of information be displayed in a specified range of point sizes. Only Château d'Yquem enjoys a special dispensation, which since 1975 has allowed it to indicate, on a rectangle of cream paper with cut corners and plain thin gilded lines, only the name of the domaine, the name of the owner, and the vintage, the whole of the text surmounted by an earl's coronet. But the sale of Château d'Yquem by the Lur-Saluces family to the French luxury goods giant LVMH in 1996 has left its future in some doubt.

For at least a large part of the twentieth century the contrast between bottles was echoed in the shape of drinking glasses. The very idea of placing before each guest the glasses needed for the successive courses of his meal goes back to the eighteenth century and the highly sophisticated Duc de Richelieu.[95] Before then, at the guest's request, servers retired to a sideboard and there poured wine, more or less diluted with water, into a glass that was apt to be very refined, indeed sumptuous in the Venetian style of manufacture known since the Middle Ages, but that did not appear on the table before the beginning of the meal.[96] Starting with the regency and then the reign of Louis XV, which saw the intimate supper party become fashionable, servers were fewer and more discreet. Bottles were placed in ice buckets nearer the table, as may be seen in the painting by Jean-François de Troy depicting a supper given by the Prince of Conti at the Temple.[97]

In the course of the nineteenth century it became customary to include several glasses, one for each style of wine, in the place setting. The habit of cutting wine with water was only very slowly lost, probably in association with the new enthusiasm for sparkling champagne, and it was not until the twentieth century that it came to seem shocking. Diluting wine in a cup or glass, it will be recalled, goes back to antiquity, when drinking pure wine was considered a sign of barbarousness.[98] Diodorus Siculus mocked this Gallic practice: "Loving wine, they fill themselves up with what the merchants bring without mixing it with water and, their passion impelling them to use the drink in all its brutal force, they become inebriated and lapse into sleep or into delirious states."[99] One should therefore not be surprised to learn that Montaigne diluted his Bordeaux with water. He remarked that the wines from Basle were so light that the people of that region "never help themselves to water with their wine, and they are right in a way, for their wines are so small that our gentlemen find them still weaker than the heavily watered-down ones of Gascony."[100] Louis XIV thought it quite natural to drink his Vosne wine with water and ice, and Napoleon drank his Chambertin in the same way.[101] Today only priests still add a little water to the wine used during mass.

Glass and crystal makers in the late nineteenth and twentieth centuries began to offer sets of glasses for purchase, particularly as wedding presents for young middle-class couples. It was obviously in their interest to recommend a different type of glass for each wine.[102] It is amusing to note the gradual acceptance of the idea of using an open tulip-shaped glass for Bordeaux and a balloon-shaped glass for Burgundy, shapes that recalled somewhat the respective bottles from these regions. The *Larousse des vins* recommends the use of two different glasses, justifying the principle in the least convincing manner possible: "[A] Bordeaux glass, whose ample form allows red wines to blossom. . . . A Burgundy glass, easy to twirl, allowing the aromas to escape more readily."[103] Shocking though the suggestion may seem, the only justifications for such a preference are aesthetic and cultural. The proof of this is that professional tastings today at all vineyards in France are done with a glass having the shape of a small closed tulip.[104]

GOURMETS, GOURMANDS

There is an old saying that, despite its obvious exaggeration, summarizes the contrast between the two regions rather well: "In Burgundy, everything is for drinking and nothing for sale, whereas in Bordeaux everything is for sale and nothing for drinking!"[105]

Drinking habits tell us a great deal about the cultural background of both producers and consumers. Alain Juppé, a native of the Aquitaine countryside who was mayor of Bordeaux before becoming prime minister of France, and who therefore has ample experience of official hospitality, confessed to being surprised by the way his guests drank—or did not. "One of the things that struck me on coming back to Bordeaux," he remarked, "is that here wine is more talked about than drunk."[106] Valuing this sign of a good Bordeaux upbringing, he remains faithful to the philosophy of his distant predecessor Michel de Montaigne, who wrote in his *Essays,* "I cannot understand, for all that, how people come to prolong the pleasure of drinking beyond their thirst, and forge themselves in their imagination an artificial and unnatural appetite."[107] Montaigne points here to a cultural trait that has persisted in his native region until the present day.

In Bordeaux, wine is drunk at table; in Burgundy, it is drunk when one is thirsty, or even when one is not.[108] Louis Veuillot used to say, "[A] jeweler sets his precious stones, a man of Bordeaux sets his wine; the setting is the meal."[109] The Burgundian custom of drinking wine between meals, at friendly gatherings, is common to the vineyards of the Loire, the Saône, and the Rhône as well.[110] At bottom one finds the same contrast between the traditional habits of drinking in Bordeaux and Burgundy as in antiquity between the Greeks and Romans, on the one hand, and barbarians on the other. The bearded Gauls and, later, the Germanic invaders were renowned, as I have said, for their love of pure wine, undiluted by water in the Mediterranean manner, and for their intemperance. It is probable that the people of Burgundy conserved not only the cultural inclination to excess of their ancient ancestors, but also, and especially, the peasant character of ancient vineyards. In all the literature of Bordeaux there is no hero comparable to Gaston Roupnel's Nono, at once so good, so moving, and so intemperate—unsurprisingly, perhaps, for the people of Bordeaux learned from their merchant elite to practice restraint. An exception, albeit a very sophisticated one, was the old Club des Oenarques, a merry sort of brotherhood—almost a secret society, full of erudition and eloquence—that used to gather regularly to taste the greatest wines of Bordeaux, its members dressed in highly eccentric Scottish kilt suits.[111] But this club no longer exists.

Another considerable difference is that Burgundy, unlike Bordeaux, has inspired innumerable drinking and dancing songs, more or less bawdy, that ring out at the end of banquets, though this fashion is now beginning to die out a bit. The most famous of these songs, "Joyeux enfants de la Bourgogne," rhymes "Bourgogne" with "trogne" (face or mug) and "ivrogne" (drunk), and dares to imagine bathing in a glass of wine and drinking oneself not merely into the grave, but carrying on drinking in the grave after death.[112] One recalls, too, the eighth stanza of the "Chant des vendages":

> What surprise, then,
> That a vine grower's son
> Should come into the world
> About ten months after autumn![113]

There is also this excerpt from a rather sycophantic song, probably written by the parish priest of Pommard in honor of the dauphin Louis, son of Louis XV, born during the grape harvest of 1729:

> This cheerful child of September,
> Twin brother of our grapes,
> Will see to it that beyond the Sambre
> Do our wines sell and pay us well.
> In La Micande, in La Rufaine,[114]
> Along the red strand that never ends:
> Long live the king, long live the queen,
> Long live my lord the dauphin! . . .
>
> Without speaking here of champagne,
> Let him who will, for his part,
> Take Beaune, Nuits, Chassagne;
> For mine, I keep to Pommard.
> Of this nectar a full bottle
> For your gurglings that never end:
> Long live the king, long live the queen,
> Long live my lord the dauphin![115]

There is nothing similar in Bordeaux, where wine seems not to have inspired such a folklore.[116]

If the habits of drinking are revealing, those of eating give away still more. One cannot help but notice that, in wine circles, one eats more at banquets in Burgundy than in Bordeaux. Alfred Contour, in *Le cuisinier bourguignon* (1896), suggested a few menus for each day of the week, varying from one month to the next. For a Monday lunch in February, for example, he recommended:

Hors d'oeuvre
Marinated Calf Brains
Goose Stew with Turnips
Sausages with Fried Potatoes
Sautéed Salsifies
Pastries

This is followed by an agreeable dinner arranged in the following manner:

Puréed Soup with Croutons
Beef with Tomato Sauce
Sweetbreads with Spinach
Lentils with Lard
Roast Chicken
Sweet Rissoles

For lunch the next day, probably to make up for a dinner that was too light, he recommended:

Hors d'oeuvre
Grilled Pig's Feet
Sautéed Kidneys
Roast Leg of Lamb
Green Beans in the Breton Manner[117]
Potato Salad
Herring Fillets[118]

Still today, at the gatherings of the chapters of the Confrérie des Chevaliers du Tastevin, three large appetizers and a main course are always served, something no longer seen elsewhere in France. Here, for example, is the menu of the *châpitre des tulipes* held on 15 April 2000:

First Course
Frogs' Legs with Watercress in Ramekins
Accompanied by a Brisk and Spirited
Bourgogne Aligoté des Hautes-Côtes de Nuits 1997

Second Course
Pike Cakes with Crayfish Coulis
Escorted by a Chassagne-Montrachet Premier Cru
Les Vergers 1997, Proud of Its Breeding

Third Course ("Entremets")
Eggs Poached in Red Burgundy Wine Sauce
Moistened with a Cool and Fragrant
Pernand-Vergelesses Premier Cru
Les Fichots 1994—Tasteviné

Main Course ("Dorure")
Farm-Raised Guinea Hen Thighs with Cèpes
Washed Down with a Nuits-Saint-Georges Premier Cru 1994
A Distinguished and Smooth Les Didiers—
Hospices de Nuits—Cuvée Jacques Duret

Cheese Course ("Issue de Table")
Fine Cheeses from Burgundy and Elsewhere
Enhanced by a Clos de Vougeot Grand Cru 1988 of Noble Lineage

Dessert ("Boutehors")
L'Escargot en Glace
Savarin with Raspberry Liqueur from the Hautes-Côtes
Petits Fours
Black Coffee, Vieux Marc, and Prunelle de Bourgogne
Highly Suitable for Stimulating the Subtle Vapors of the Brain

Four courses rich in cream and butter (not to mention cheeses and dessert)[119] for a dinner that lasts until two o'clock in the morning[120]—a far cry in quantity, it goes without saying, from the dinner, probably marvelous for the subtlety of its flavors, given in June 2003 by Philippine de Rothschild for her two thousand guests on the occasion of the one hundred fiftieth anniversary of the purchase of Château Brane-Mouton by her ancestor Nathaniel:

Aspic of Sea Bass—Pauillac Baron Nathaniel 1999
Duet of Veal with Chanterelles—Château Margaux 1996
and Château Mouton Rothschild 1982
Caramelized Peaches[121]

In each case one must not forget to mention the drinks served as aperitifs and on the occasion of toasts at the end of the meal, champagne in Bordeaux and crémant de Bourgogne in Burgundy.

The word *gastronomie,* adapted from the Greek, came into the French language in 1801 under the pen of the amiable Burgundian poet Joseph Berchoux, author of a poem of more than a thousand alexandrines in praise of good food.[122] Berchoux insisted on the necessity of having an agreeable château in Auvergne or Bresse in order to be able to eat well. It is true that over the centuries the people of Burgundy have created an image of themselves around values of conviviality and lavish feasts washed down with abundant quantities of good wine. Famously Rabelaisian characters such as Gaston Gérard and Canon Félix Kir were notable contributors to this tradition. Gérard, mayor of Dijon from 1919 to 1935, inaugurated the Foire Gastronomique, held every fall since, and, in his capacity as undersecretary of state for tourism in 1931–32, did a great deal to enhance the gastronomic reputation of Burgundy.[123] The national highway that passes through Burgundy is punctuated with great restaurants. Before the war, innovative chefs set themselves up in the old post road inns, attracting the cream of Paris society headed down by automobile to the Côte d'Azur: Jollandeau at the Écu de France in Sens, Chapuis, a student of Escoffier, at the Poste d'Avallon, Dumaine (known as "the Pope") at the Côte d'Or in Saulieu, and Lameloise at the Commerce de Chagny.[124] To this day Burgundy and the area around

Lyons remain a temple of gastronomy and abundance, where creativity has not ruined tradition. At Georges Blanc's restaurant in Vonnas, on the edge of Bresse and the Mâconnais, the spoon still stands up in the unforgettable cream sauce that accompanies the poulard.

Until recently there has been nothing comparable in Bordeaux. The top restaurants were hushed places in the city itself, dominated by the towering reputation of the Chapon Fin and Dubern, with the notable exception, of course, of Louis Oliver's famous restaurant in Langon.[125] Nonetheless, the true gastronomy of the southwest has always found a devoted audience among estate managers, cellar masters, and château foremen. The grape pickers, for their part, are as well fed in Bordeaux as they are in Burgundy, and the closing banquet (known as *l'aoucat* or *la gerbebaude*), enlivened by regional songs or ones from the French— or even the Spanish—Pyrenees, is no less well served with food and wine than its counterpart *(la paulée)* in Burgundy. Christian Coulon recalls the *aoucats* of his childhood in the Médoc, at which the menu always included a soup, charcuterie, a cold fish with mayonnaise, a roasted meat, a meat with sauce, cheese, and assorted desserts, all of it accompanied by a great deal of wine and brandy.[126] It was hardly any different in Burgundy in the 1960s. The fine art of creative cooking has recently been rediscovered in the Bordeaux region, albeit with some difficulty. Jean-Marie Amat managed to raise the Saint-James in Bouliac to new heights before going bankrupt, in part because he failed to attract enough of the region's major proprietors and merchants to his table. Today the culinary reawakening seems to come mainly from the vineyard itself, with the opening by Jean-Michel Cazes of the Château Cordeillan-Bages, a luxury hotel adjoining Lynch-Bages, where the kitchen is presided over by Thierry Marx, a talented chef who divides his time between this property and the Chapon Fin, now a part of the Cazes galaxy. Florence and Daniel Cathiard, owners of the Domaine de Smith-Haut-Lafite, have opened an extraordinary hotel and spa on their property, Les Sources de Caudalie, to which guests are now flocking for its many comforts, including "barrel baths" of grape extracts and fine food. From this point of view at least, the gap between Bordeaux and Burgundy is now being bridged.

On 16 November 1934, a time of plunging wine sales, a group of growers and merchants in Nuits led by Georges Faiveley and Camille Rodier created the Confrérie des Chevaliers du Tastevin.[127] This merry band has since become an institution. Its neo-medieval style (mocked everywhere else, but a source of delight to the some five hundred guests invited to the banquets of the various chapters) has served to effectively promote the wines and gastronomy of Burgundy among celebrities and dignitaries from around the world.[128] There is hardly a great film actor or opera singer, or an ambassador of the United States, the Netherlands, Great Britain, or Japan, or a member of a royal family who has not been honored as a special guest of the Confrérie, and who has not taken immense pride in beating the famous Burgundian drum with his hands while singing "la-la-la-la-la-la-la-la-lalère!"

The society's immediate success inspired imitators. On 13 September 1948 the producers of Saint-Émilion revived a local assembly dating from the ancien régime that had disappeared with the Revolution: the Jurade, created by John Lackland, king of England, in 1199.[129] Since then, in imitation of these two prestigious engines of commerce, friendly brotherhoods have been established almost everywhere in Bordeaux and Burgundy for the purpose of establishing a sense of solidarity among producers and as a good-natured way of promoting the wines and food of individual appellations. Some fifteen such fraternities are now found in each of the two regions. Others, more numerous in Burgundy, are more strictly gastronomic: the Confrérie des Poulardiers in Bresse, the Confrérie de l'Oignon in Auxonne, the Chevaliers de la Pôchouse, and so on.[130]

The traditional cuisines of Bordeaux and Burgundy resemble each other only in their shared love of garlic. There are environmental and cultural reasons for this. In Bordeaux one finds more grilled and roasted dishes made with oil, the fat of ducks and geese, and shallots; in Burgundy, more sauces calling for cream, butter, and onions.[131] But it cannot seriously be maintained that harmonious combinations are possible only among the dishes and wines peculiar to each region.[132] Quite to the contrary, pairings across the two regions can be magnificent: a Montrachet with foie gras; lamprey or eels cooked in Givry; a *pôchouse* or *escargots à la bourguignonne* with a fine white Graves; a cockerel (or beef) stewed in Margaux lees; roasted wood pigeons accompanied by a Volnay; *cèpes à la bordelaise* with a Morey-Saint-Denis, and so on. For once, one cannot approve of Raoul Ponchon's fervent Burgundophilia:

> Trusting in a woodcock
> Unenlivened by some Corton,
> Might as well gnaw the carcass
> Of a cardboard fowl.[133]

A fine Pomerol or a Saint-Julien would in fact make a splendid companion for this noble and enchantingly fragrant bird—a species of game that, alas, is no longer to be had in a restaurant.

SENSUAL WINE, CEREBRAL WINE

Enjoying a wine is a matter of appreciating its objective organoleptic qualities, which depend on its physiochemical properties. One may be sensitive to this or that one of the thousands of molecules of which it is composed, liking or disliking the effect it produces as the case may be. At the same time, of course, one enters into the domain of the subjective—of upbringing and images and the power of evocation. It is well known that the physiological effects of drinking wine are intimately associated with psychological dispositions. On the one hand, the feelings expressed while drinking are frequently unreliable, varying not only according to one's mood or momentary state of mind, but also to what one is looking for in a wine, and what one finds (or believes one finds) in it. On the other hand, wine drinkers may also be subject to uncontrollable physical reactions, triggered by the alcohol in the wine, for example, or by certain component molecules.[134]

It is commonly believed that whereas Burgundies are heavy, Bordeaux are light, and therefore to be recommended for people in ill health. This opinion is a holdover from the days (before 1955) when, in addition to being blended, Burgundies were heavily chaptalized and rarely sold at less than 12 percent alcohol, whereas Bordeaux were chaptalized to a much smaller extent, with even the *grands crus* seldom exceeding 10 percent alcohol.[135] In this respect, parity has now been reestablished, but a notable difference remains between the effects these wines actually produce and what people think they perceive. Additionally there is the fact that consumers of Bordeaux rarely have personal and physical contact with the growers, unlike consumers of Burgundy, who, when they visit the domaines, find themselves exposed to a massive dose of local culture. For a city dweller of a certain social and cultural background this is far more disorienting than encountering the culture of Bordeaux, which has been shaped to a greater extent by polite manners and courtesy.

Bordeaux, it is alleged, allows one to reflect and to keep a cool head; Burgundy does not. "Burgundy is a drug," one connoisseur recently confessed. "It really takes you up there."[136] Rabelaisians, may their coarseness be forgiven, put it differently: "Bordeaux makes you piss, Burgundy makes you fuck."[137] The description of the effects of a wine in relation to its place of origin goes back at least to the Middle Ages. Guillaume Breton, court poet to Philip Augustus, sang of "Vinous Beaune, whose wines enflame the temper."[138] A seventeenth-century physician from Beaune, Daniel Arbinet, described the wine of his native region thus: "It comes before all the others, because it charms first the eyes, then the nostrils and the palate; and then because it lessens the melancholic juice that is the author and abettor of sadness, and very quickly restores those who are exhausted by cares or by the work of the mind, whence the joy of the heart, euphoria."[139] Clearly the pinot grape of Burgundy produces wines that go to the head and elsewhere—a quality highly valued by its admirers, good physicians that they are.

Gaston Roupnel breached another boundary of decorum in explicitly comparing Burgundy (a Clos de Vougeot, in this case) to the body of a woman: "This sumptuous velvet color, is it not the sensual gown of a voluptuous nudity plump with adorable and profane flesh? . . . But, on the other hand, do you not sense in it an immaterial purity, and the sort of generosity that suggests the human mingled with the divine?"[140] The British writer Roald Dahl, in *My Uncle Oswald,* describes a memorable picnic on the low, white, dry stone wall of Romanée-Conti accompanied by a bottle of wine from the great vineyard: "Smell it! Inhale the bouquet! Taste it! Drink it! But never try to describe it! It is impossible to put such a flavour into words! To drink a Romanée-Conti is like having an orgasm in the mouth and the nose both at the same time."[141]

All the old growers joyfully wield this sort of metaphor; younger ones shrink from it somewhat today, for fear of being accused of a politically incorrect machismo. André Noblet is well remembered as a virtuoso of the genre. One thinks, too, of the observations of a merchant friend reported by the artist Henri Vincenot: "'Look at that!' he says to me. 'It quivers like a woman! It pouts with lust. . . . The second one's got some mischief about it—when you roll it around in your mouth, it pushes back, like a terrific lover! Slurp it! A real kidney-knocker, eh?'"[142] There is nothing new about Roupnel's association of these risqué images with the spiritual climate of Burgundy, where neo-Jansenism made few inroads and where the Chambolle-Musigny *premier cru* "Les Amoureuses" practically abuts the Clos de Vougeot of the Cistercian monks.[143] An old song from the 1890s in honor of Saint Vincent ventures these lyrics:

> Talk of a good grower
> You mean a good fellow,
> A merry fellow, a bon vivant
> Who drinks some
> And loves some,
> Passing from wine to sex—
> And a votary of Saint Vincent.[144]

One peculiarity should be noted. Metaphorically speaking, the wines of Bordeaux and Burgundy are hermaphrodites. Connoisseurs and poets characterize both as masculine and feminine, depending on the appellation and the vintage. For the nineteenth-century poet and gastronome Charles Monselet, "Burgundy is masculine and Bordeaux is feminine."[145] The gastronome Henri Clos-Jouve found "Burgundy still virile in its old age," and Père Maurice Lelong remarked that "if Bordeaux is of the class of *grandes dames,* Burgundy belongs to the breed of *seigneurs.*"[146] But Jean-François Bazin, comparing various *grand cru* vintages of Romanée-Conti, considered that the 1987 was "a Romanée of good family, raised at the [Couvent des] Oiseaux, her knees stubbornly held close together," whereas the 1962 had lost "a bit of its gown, while exposing lovely shoulders [and] preserving fragrances in which the musk and fur have not yet overshadowed the black fruit," and that the body of the 1970 "endlessly stretches out in an astonishingly amorous languor."[147]

The sensuality of a good Burgundy leaves no one indifferent. Aristide Bruant sang of Chablis in decent but unambiguous terms:

Chablis, I would that in your arms
A cross of honor did appear,
For by your divine tears
Your lads have become heroes;
And then in peacetime that
The juice of your vine stocks
Did infuse supreme courage
In your red- and round-nosed growers,
And the desire to repopulate France![148]

The mystique of Burgundy is felt even in the Far East. The memories and torrid fantasies that fill Takeshi Kaikō's famous novel *Romanée-Conti 1935,* for example, are not unlike those experienced by people in Burgundy and other Westerners like Roald Dahl. What propels the plot of this tale is not in fact a Romanée-Conti 1935, an unremarkable vintage (for by this point, alas, its charms have faded), but a Tâche 1966, at the height of its splendor and dazzling effects. The exoticism—and eroticism—of Burgundy and its wines exert a peculiarly powerful fascination. Even the great Inoue, not one known for letting himself go, says just before his death, "Go to Burgundy and you will know the true joy of living."[149]

These testimonies, chosen from among a thousand others, make it unmistakably clear that Burgundy stands out for its power to dilate the senses: it makes the temples throb, flushes the face, raises one's tone of voice; it arouses amorous feelings and induces a euphoric outlook upon the future. Those who have experienced its effects are likely to go back for more.

Nothing of the sort usually occurs while drinking Bordeaux, the wine of wise men and of all those who wish to preserve, if not actually to improve, their faculty of reasoning; of all those who seek pleasure while wishing to remain in control of themselves; of all those for whom letting oneself go amounts to a minor sign of moral decay.[150] The novelist René Benjamin, who boasted that he had never become drunk, wrote more than a half century ago, in keeping with the realities and prejudices of his time, "Of all nectars, Burgundy consumes me quickest and weighs me down . . . whereas a Bordeaux enlightens me."[151] By the mastery of his emotions and, indeed, by every aspect of his behavior, the statesman Alain Juppé betrays his attachment to Bordeaux, which when he was a child constituted 80 percent of his father's cellar. Juppé himself has confessed to a preference for the wines of Saint-Julien and Saint-Estèphe, which he admires for their equilibrium: "I am often reproached for having a sense of proportion and balance: I find these things in my love for wine. . . . Burgundies always seemed to me less profound than Bordeaux . . . until I discovered Romanée-Conti. Here, I said to myself, *here* is a degree of perfection, of richness, of complexity on the level of the greatest Bordeaux. In a different way."[152] This is proof that even the most deeply anchored convictions can lose their mooring, at least to some small degree.[153] The fact that Alain Juppé resembles the wines that he likes surely explains at least in part, too, why he was able to win election as mayor of Bordeaux—something that Canon Kir could never have done, had he ever been tempted by such an ambition in the first place.

"Remember," Lucien Farnoux-Reynaud wrote, "one gargles with Burgundy, whereas Bordeaux is something one almost chews, like a flower petal. . . . [154] [Bordeaux] is not a skull-crusher, a stupefier; without being excessively heady, it predisposes one to both a measured gallantry and a slight impertinence, the two faces of a perfect education. . . . It does not give off the sensual whiff of Burgundy, but it harbors a lucid passion that encourages you to do well while knowing what you are doing."[155] Like his counterparts in Burgundy, Farnoux-Reynaud devilishly likened wine to the body of a woman. The difference of tone may be judged by this passage: "One has only to spend an evening in the Cours de l'Intendance in order to be convinced that the women of Bordeaux possess the most beautiful bottoms in France and that, in carrying themselves proudly, yet without showing off, they manage to observe decorum at the same time."[156] Like a great Médoc, in a way— but this is a far cry from Rabelais!

One may be less inclined, however, to concur with one of Farnoux-Reynaud's earlier judgments: "We do not come as enemies of Burgundy, but as loyal friends of Bordeaux. We are drawn to it by a secret affection; it exalts our exceptional qualities and delights our weaknesses. It alone . . . satisfies our sense of reasonableness. Burgundy is a wine for kings and financiers; Bordeaux is the wine of cultivated men of independent means, diplomats, and philosophers . . . ; the wine of men who know how to think."[157] Let us overlook for the moment the false modesty of this apology. Even so, one can hardly agree with its characterization of the two camps. The kings and princes of Europe are equally divided among lovers of Burgundy and lovers of Bordeaux. Financiers have for a long time been rather numerous in the vineyards of the Gironde, which have nothing to complain about on this score; indeed, Burgundy could use a few bankers who would say to their estate managers, as some do in Bordeaux, "Spare no trouble to make the very best wine possible." And in view of what we have just said about the intoxicating power of Burgundy, more than Bordeaux it is a wine for the man of leisure who has no need to go back to work after lunch.

Philosophers, for their part, drink many things (water, beer, whiskey, wine, and so on), and what they drink no doubt influences their philosophy. If Montaigne and Montesquieu drank Bordeaux (which did not have the same taste in the sixteenth century as in the seventeenth), Diderot and Voltaire preferred Burgundy, as did the Parisian elite of their time. (It seems a safe bet that Condillac, the father of sensualism, relished it as well.) On the other hand, we may concede the point to Farnoux-Reynaud in the matter of wine and diplomacy: few ambassadors are willing to run the risk of serving red Burgundies at their table.[158] Diplomats have only themselves to blame if their influence is compromised by their own hand.

Farnoux-Reynaud points out a genuine difference between the two wine-producing cultures, however, when he writes, "When a man from Burgundy feels admiration for his wine, he says of it, 'It's got love'; and when a man from Bordeaux takes pride in his *cuvée,* he murmurs simply, 'It is distinguished.' By no means would I wish to speak ill of love . . . but it is not something that lasts. . . . But distinction, with all due respect, is a result. It is transmitted to you only as a consequence of [the labor of] earlier generations and daily discipline."[159] In the face of such confidence there is nothing to be said, for here one touches upon the very heart of the dispute between Bordeaux and Burgundy. These two positions are difficult to reconcile. One must not even try.

And yet there are a few austere winemakers in Burgundy, and a few voluptuaries among their counterparts in Bordeaux, who dare to oppose tradition. Henri Duboscq, the owner of Château Haut-Marbuzet in Saint-Estèphe, planted his vineyard with merlot and devised novel techniques for producing wines with soft, silky, sensual tannins, particularly by shortening the length of aging. The proof was in the tasting: critics found it unique, and customers acclaimed it as the most Saint-Émilion in style of all the Médocs. A Médoc that "merlots" is a little bit like a Morgon that "pinots." As one would expect, however, the profession stood on its dignity and disparaged a wine that it judged too pretty. "I was the whore of the Médoc," Duboscq says with a smile. "I made the wine with the slashed skirts. After five or six years, I realized that my wayward girl could become a *grande dame*. Still a whore, to be sure, but a sincere one, sincere in the way she expresses the *terroir* from which she came, and a whore who has remained faithful with the passing years. Isn't that the ultimate fantasy of every man?"[160] To be able to get away with saying such things in the Médoc, the cloak of respectability must weigh heavily and be difficult to lift up! Thanks to his well-deserved success, Duboscq is now better accepted than he once was, and, more to the point, his methods are discreetly copied.

In view of the effects produced by Burgundy, whether unforeseen or intended, one cannot pass over in silence the question of the drinker's age. Outside the wine-producing regions themselves, connoisseurs of Burgundy often turn toward Bordeaux as they get older, ruefully declaring that Burgundy no longer likes them. Curnonsky, when he was sixty years old, drank Bordeaux *crus bourgeois* ("Among the most charming wines that one can drink while eating! The older I get, the more I like them"). He insisted, moreover, on the restraint of the great Bordeaux, "which never jab you in the ribs with an elbow." Nor do they resemble those interminable public speakers who succeed in showing only that "it is impossible to say fewer things in more words"; a great Bordeaux, by contrast, "knows how to say everything without going on and on."[161] François Mauriac, a native of Bordeaux and a master of understatement, illustrated this virtue perfectly. With exquisite self-control and boundless talent, he contented himself with hinting at his unkind thoughts, while regretting them at once. Could this have been an effect of the wine from Malagar?[162]

And what of the relationship between the two wines and health? This question has fascinated physicians since antiquity, and continues to do so today.[163] The recent debate about the "French paradox" is but the latest evidence of this.[164] Bordeaux is usually thought of as a wine for people who are ill or, more exactly, a wine prescribed for the sick and for convalescents in order to assist their recovery, whereas Burgundy is counter-indicated. The medical reality is more complicated. Several decades ago the physician E. A. Maury developed a posology of wines corresponding to different illnesses.[165] Maury particularly recommended Bordeaux for allergies, anemia, throat infections, anxiety, lack of appetite, bronchial conditions, depression, diabetes, diarrhea, purpura, tuberculosis, typhoid, hives, and many other complaints. But Burgundy he found appropriate to prescribe for weight loss in the case of obesity, hypotension, cardiac insufficiency, demineralization, and hemorrhages, and, contrary to popular opinion, as a drink for the elderly. Bordeaux, and especially wines from the Médoc, are therefore considered more effective against a host of disorders, whereas Burgundies are considered more effective in treating general bodily illness. Alain Juppé recalls being made to drink wine after an attack of bronchitis when he was eight or nine years old: "As I began my convalescence, it was a small finger of Bordeaux. They went and poured me the last drops from the bottle, because they were a 'pick-me-up,' they put you back on your feet."[166]

The relationship between music and the wines of Bordeaux and Burgundy expresses another form of cultural difference. Drinking songs are more popular, as we have seen, in Burgundy than in Bordeaux. A local group, the Cadets de Bourgogne, has led the singing at the dinners of the Confrérie des Chevaliers du Tastevin since the 1930s. Its risqué repertoire, which includes traditional songs from the region and elsewhere in France in addition to original compositions, does not prevent conversation—far from it, so long as from time to time the guests sing a chorus in unison and beat the *ban bourguignon* before refilling their glasses and refreshing their voices. There is no equivalent in Bordeaux, as one may imagine. But classical music is no longer neglected in Burgundy. The Festival des Grands Crus de Bourgogne combines concerts with tastings; established at Meursault in 1986 under the title "From Bach to Bacchus," it has now spread to Gevrey-Chambertin, Chablis, Cluny, and Noyers, attracting more listeners every year. And Beaune has its baroque music festival, which, though it is not directly associated with wine, takes place in the courtyard of the Hospices.

Finally, one should not forget that great musicians have drawn inspiration from the wine of Burgundy. E. T. A. Hoffmann, for example, who held that "Chambertin is the true poetic wine," drank it in a way that no Burgundian today would disapprove, but that one has a very hard time imagining being countenanced in a *chai* in the Médoc. During his stay in Bamberg, Hoffmann frequently went down to the cellar of his friend Kuntz, who tells us, "It sometimes happened that the two of us sat facing one another on opposite ends of the same barrel, exultantly straddling it. . . . I can also assure you that we did not drink in the usual fashion, but enjoyed the pleasure of the moment in the most comfortable and spiritual way."[167]

Proprietors in Bordeaux have for a very long time held chamber music concerts at parties and receptions in their châteaus. But the writer Ylan Schwartz has gone farther, pairing musical instruments and wines in lengthy recital tastings, as they might be called, which indicate harmonious agreement between cabernet sauvignon and violin, cabernet franc and viola, and merlot and cello. From these experiments he composed a quite remarkable work whose harmonies may be difficult for many people to reproduce, unfortunately, on account of the rarity of the wines it calls for, a series of *grands vins* from 1970 and 1982.[168] But one may follow his example and drink a Sociando-Mallet while listening to a Haydn quartet, or marry Lynch-Bages and Schumann. Supreme refinement, in either case. The Canadian singer Leonard Cohen confessed that the wonderful performances of his 1993 tour were due to the fact that every evening with his musicians he drank Château Latour 1982—and gulped down his aspirin with it as well![169]

Generally speaking, the connection between wine and the fine arts has been pushed much further in Bordeaux than in Burgundy. Once again, this is a matter of culture. Philippe de Rothschild brought together in a sublime little museum at Mouton the world's most beautiful collection of objets d'art relating to wine. Edmond de Rothschild, for his part, assembled a splendid collection as well, part of which came from the Neapolitan branch of the Bourbons. It is not currently on display, sadly, except in the form of a lavishly illustrated book published the year he died, 1997.[170] One should also mention the collections of fine furniture, paintings, sculptures, tapestries, porcelain, and silverware housed in the five thousand châteaus of the Bordeaux region.[171] Taken as a whole, they cannot be compared with the treasures of Burgundy, which reside instead in churches and museums. Only a few domaine and private cellars in Burgundy match the elegance of *chais* in Bordeaux, such as the one at Château Margaux; many of them, such as the vat hall and cellar of the Clos de Vougeot and the cellar of Gilly-lès-Cîteaux, date to the medieval period. As for reception halls and tasting rooms in the two regions, they are exact opposites with respect to comfort and sophistication, to say nothing of aesthetic quality: some prefer to drink their wine (like Hoffmann, and as one still says today in Burgundy) *"au cul du tonneau,"* others on a varnished mahogany table or a fine tablecloth of starched white damask.

CATHOLIC WINE, PROTESTANT WINE

The question of wine in relation to religion is a sensitive one in France, though not, as one might suppose, because of the official separation of church and state that has regulated public life for more than a century. It is still common to see the religious roots of viticulture used as a promotional tool, especially in Burgundy, not only at the Clos de Vougeot, for example, but also at Beaune (home to the *premier cru* Vigne de l'Enfant-Jésus) and in advertising copy generally.[172] Nor is anyone shocked that the Rothschild family should own the Château l'Évangile in Pomerol. Just the same, the suggestion that past and present links with the Catholic Church are stronger in Burgundy, and links with the Protestantism stronger in Bordeaux, is not to everyone's taste, as I recently discovered to my surprise on agreeing to write a piece on the subject for *L'Amateur de Bordeaux.* The article, entitled "Is the Wine of Bordeaux Protestant?" was meant to be dryly humorous, and its publication met with no public outcry. An amusing and complimentary notice appeared in the Protestant journal *Réforme,* and the following week one of its readers described it as "particularly enjoyable."[173] My late friend François Guichard, a wine geographer from Bordeaux and himself a Protestant, found it entertaining as well. The message therefore seemed to have been acceptable to the Protestant community, and perhaps even to parishioners of the Temple du Hâ, the Protestant church in Bordeaux, whose congregation includes a few eminent members of old Chartrons families. In private correspondence, however, I received a sound thrashing from certain other geographers of this region.[174]

What accounts for the difference in their reactions? The essential point to keep in mind is that Protestants, like Jews, are a minority in Bordeaux. The majority, regardless of class, are Catholics by conviction and family origin, even if their relationship to the religion is somewhat strained. Like the majority of people in France, even if they are anticlerical or actually atheist, they quite like the familiarity of a Catholic atmosphere on the occasion of family weddings and funerals. To suggest that Protestant culture, with its insistence on ethical behavior and strict morality, might be dominant in the world of wine is perceived as a confiscation of their identity.

It needs to be stressed at the outset that Bordeaux remained a Catholic, indeed very Catholic, city under the ancien régime, unlike neighboring regions such as the Saintonge. Moreover, even if Jansenism was a temptation for a few members of the city's elite (Arnaud de Pontac, for example), its influence must not be overstated. Though it shared certain features with Protestant doctrine, its emphasis on the necessity of withdrawing from the world to some extent did little to encourage secular industry. By contrast, the merchants from the north who settled in the Chartrons were mostly Protestant and, in some cases (as Michel Espagne and Michel Réjalot himself have shown), they perfectly exemplified Weber's argument concerning the link between the Protestant ethic and economic success, construed as a sign of God's love.[175] Money was a reward, but it was not intended primarily as an instrument of pleasure.[176] Its purpose was to allow society to function harmoniously and to provide work for as many as possible. The atmosphere of the Chartrons, whose residents in the eighteenth century sought to act upon this ethic, was nonetheless not one of dreary moral rigidity. Lorenz Meyer, a German who visited Bordeaux in 1784–85, noted "the good taste, elegance, and naturalness of the manners" he found among the merchants there, whereas the old Catholic *familles de robe* in the center of the city were remarkable for "the arrogance of the nobility and an overbearing manner that came from attendance at Court."[177] This contrast no longer exists today, since the manners of the old Quai are now those of practically the entire elite of the Bordeaux wine world.

The devotion to sport among this elite is remarkable: squash and tennis at the Villa Primrose, polo at Giscours, sailing and swimming at Arcachon, and, for a few, the Marathon du Médoc in September. There is nothing comparable in Burgundy, unless one counts the annual *marche de Ladoix,* billed as a "Gourmet Walk," which takes place on the first Sunday of July. A crowd of strollers wearing straw hats, each one armed with a plated cup and a fork in a pouch slung around the neck, traverses the entire Corton slope, merrily pausing at the various *climats* to enjoy their wines and partake of a bit of fortifying nourishment. The tour ends with a blissful nap under the trees surrounding the church, Notre-Dame-du-Chemin, followed by a village dance. This discipline has not yet been added to the roster of Olympic competitions.

Only a few customs specifically associated with the Chartrons that testify to the northern origins of the immigrant merchant families survive, and even these have begun to fade away, if not actually disappear.[178] One observes a propensity for marrying within local society; a tendency to give one's children certain first names (Daniel, Édouard, Anthony, William, Charles, Diane, Nancy) and to send them on regular visits to England to perfect their English; a habit of campaigning on behalf of social causes, of belonging to a Masonic lodge, of attending more or less faithfully the worship services at the Temple du Hâ, and of keeping in the family an honorary consulship of a country in northern Europe. The Chartrons style that has conquered the entire bourgeoisie of the Bordeaux region is perhaps best seen in their dress: Ralph Lauren polo shirts, hunting or riding costume for visiting the vineyards, tuxedos and long gowns for receptions, with magnificent family jewels being worn on special occasions.[179] A certain standard of tasteful ostentation continues to be upheld. One may still hear the heiress to a celebrated Chartrons dynasty speak demurely of the beauty of her grandmother's starched damask tablecloths and napkins, or of the thrushes—deboned, stuffed, then poached and allowed to cool—that her cook is preparing. Life in her beautiful château unfolds in luxury and tranquility. The exquisite pleasure is understated, but it is only the more thrilling for that.

The late Raymond Dumay memorably described this innate sense of restraint, so perfectly expressed in the Médoc: "One day . . . a Château Margaux was served with the meal that did not lie. My hosts looked at me. One minute passed, then two, then three. I had still found nothing to say. Finally, a look of relief came over their faces: they had found someone with whom one did not need to speak. After a long pause, I murmured: 'Yes.' There were approving nods, in silence. Perhaps this is not the worst way to appreciate the wine of Bordeaux."[180]

It is also reasonable to suppose that the ease with which ownership of almost all châteaus in Bordeaux changes hands is, if not a Protestant peculiarity, at least a Germanic one, and reflects the juridical customs of the Anglo-Saxon world, where wealth is earned by merit and courage.[181] In the Latin world, possession—of the soil, in particular—is culturally vital, being transmitted chiefly by inheritance. It is one of Burgundy's contradictions that the region remains attached not only to certain "barbaric" customs but also to the old Roman law. Michel Réjalot very judiciously suggests that, when it comes to wine, the Anglo-Saxon world is more attached to companies and brands, whereas in the Latin world the love of products rooted in the soil led to the creation of the controlled appellation system, with its insistence on *vins de terroir.*[182] This idea, which remains to be developed, may turn out to be extremely useful in understanding the world geography of wine.

Another aspect of Protestant influence on the world of wine in Bordeaux is the characteristic form of its bottles, which I have already mentioned. Pierre-Marie Doutrelant used to gently poke fun at their rather strict and awkward style, which some find elegant: "Look at the shape of Bordeaux and Burgundy bottles. The first, Protestant and prim. The second, ecclesiastical and potbellied. There are two French schools of good wine."[183] A caricaturist would have no trouble drawing a Bordeaux bottle dressed in a minister's robe with a thin, dignified face penciled in above the neck, and a Burgundy bottle cloaked in an ample cassock and surmounted by a round face resembling that of Canon Kir. Is it unreasonable to imagine that the shoulders of a Bordeaux bottle, which assist decanting and therefore contemplation of the color of a claret, suggest the Puritan concern with transparency that is manifested, for example, by the frequent absence of window curtains in northern Europe and by the light that floods the churches of England and the dining halls of the medieval colleges of Oxford and Cambridge? In a moral universe in which absolution for one's sins cannot be received from a priest, it matters that one lives in the plain sight of others and of God—an idea expressed metaphorically by the taste of clear wine, presented in a crystal glass and drunk from it.

Little importance is attached to the notion of transparency in Burgundy, by contrast, where what counts most of all is the bouquet and taste of the wine, even if a silver tastevin was traditionally used to detect possible defects in the wine by examining its color. No one who drinks wine in the rear of a cellar there finds the thought of tasting a bit of the sediment in a bottle or a glass at all repugnant. Very recently, in fact, I witnessed a great Burgundian cellar master ask to be poured the last of a superb 1971 Échezeaux with its abundance of lees—in his view the richest and most flavorful part of the wine! There is an analogy here with the ancient Catholic practice of confession: the absolution of black sins in a dimly lit church, inside a confessional as dark as the stable of Bethlehem.

The choice of cabernet sauvignon in Bordeaux, and in the Médoc in particular, derived, as we have seen, from the need to please an English and northern European clientele. The wines that are made from this grape, far from encouraging lasciviousness (something that in any case has no place in a Puritan view of the world), inspire instead a noble asceticism: the quest for a perfect mastery of the impulses and for the pleasure that is obtained through a vibrant, but fully conscious, communion with complexity. It is in this sense that Péguy's notion that the Protestant constructs his faith, whereas the Catholic bathes in it, can be transposed to wine.[184] Cabernet sauvignon wines, if they are well made, are undrinkable when they are young. It is therefore necessary to allow them to age so that they can be appreciated and, ultimately, liked. As Musset used to say, "I think highly of Bordeaux, especially in its old age."[185] But then, because the aging process tied up capital, they became expensive. Exploiting this circumstance for personal enrichment was unimaginable, and in any case in the worst possible taste: fortunes were not made to be spent for private amusement, but in order to create additional wealth and employment, and to increase the general prosperity.

In England today, as in the United States and other countries of Protestant Anglo-Saxon tradition, one finds connoisseurs of Bordeaux who buy *grands vins* on the futures market, before they are bottled, then warehouse them and long afterward sell them at auction—just as they do with old bottles that they have bought in auction rooms, selling them years later in response to fluctuations in price. A great many specialized journals (such as *Decanter*) and price guides publish quotes on an annual basis.[186] The French investment bank Société Générale recently decided to enter this market, creating a financial product called SGAM Premier Cru, whose portfolio consists of wines rather than shares, mainly ones from Bordeaux, purchased *en primeur* and sold later at a substantial profit.[187] This is the opposite of the Gospel parable of the talents (Matthew 25:14–30), observed more faithfully in Burgundy than in Bordeaux: silver buried in a cellar grows and returns a profit to its owner, without any effort other than an intuitive feel for quality.

All of this may well be supposed to confirm the judgment of the nineteenth-century Italian gastronome Giovanni Rajberti, who in 1850 called Bordeaux the "prince of serious wines," whereas champagne seemed to him the "prince of amusing wines."[188] He said nothing about Burgundy, surely the prince of sensual wines, the wine of every kind of danger. Even so, one needs to be very cautious in insisting upon a straightforward relationship between consumers and the presumed character of the wines they prefer, to the extent that many European Catholics today have embraced a more austere conception of their religion, especially with regard to food and drink. They feel it is indecent to take pleasure in such things, which are denied to so many poor people, and that it is therefore their duty to share the misery of the world. By contrast, as in the Protestant world, license in the arts and sexual behavior has generally been approved by Catholics.

There can be little doubt that, if the wines of Bordeaux are attractive to customers in northern Europe, this is to some degree due to the historical contingencies of navigation and commerce. But one should not be satisfied with asserting a simple determinism based on geographical proximity alone. The fact that in the Netherlands, for example, Protestants drink Bordeaux while the Catholic minority favors Burgundy points to a sociological dimension that awaits further inquiry. It is nonetheless fair to say, in a general way, that northern Europe has fashioned Bordeaux in its image, while France and continental Europe have fashioned Burgundy in their image. But if the boundary separating the Catholic and Protestant worlds of European Christianity coincides in large part with the boundary between these two families of wine, there are, of course, important exceptions. One of the best known of these is literary: the upsetting effects of an 1846 Clos de Vougeot on the members of a small, rigorist Protestant sect on the Norwegian coast that Isak Dinesen portrayed in "Babette's Feast."[189]

The very limited role of the Catholic Church in the birth and development of the vineyards of Bordeaux is another striking point of difference.[190] In Burgundy, by contrast, the world of wine remained much more attached to its ancient links with the Church.[191] These went back to the bishoprics and chapters of Autun and Langres, and the great abbeys of Cluny and Cîteaux as well as of Bèze and Saint-Vivant, but most of all to the papacy in Avignon.[192] Despite the fact that Clement V, the first pope to take up residence there, had been archbishop of Bordeaux and had given his name to an estate (Pape-Clément) on his death in 1314, wines from Bordeaux were never drunk in Avignon or Rome. Petrarch was exasperated at the fond regard shown by the princes of the Church for their stays in Avignon, where the wines of Burgundy flowed: "Why should the cardinals hasten to come back to Rome," he asked in 1366, "deprived as they would be there of this precious drink that they consider a second food, like the Olympian nectar? In Italy there is no wine from Beaune."[193] And Gregory XI, the last French pope, who left Avignon for Rome in 1377 shortly after his election, confessed to missing "the generous wine of Burgundy ... more agreeable than the thick, plain drinks from Roman vines."[194] This fondness was to persist. In 1485, Innocent VIII thanked the Duke of Burgundy for a shipment of wine: "The wine of Beaune that you sent us was of good and agreeable flavor. ... We have used it more or less regularly during our last illness, by way of medicine."[195] The association with the Vatican has been sustained in modern times by three families of vine growers, Senard at Aloxe-Corton, Lafon at Mersault, and Armand at Pommard, each of pontifical nobility, holding the title of papal count.

In the years just prior to the Wars of Religion in France in the mid-sixteenth century, the great majority of Burgundian viticulturalists supported the Catholic Church.[196] Of 234 persons voting in the mayoral elections held in Dijon in 1560, twenty-one were vine growers, of whom three cast ballots for the Protestant candidate Antoine Brocard and eleven for the ultra-Catholic candidate Bénigne Martin. The following year, among 496 electors, 10 vine growers voted for Brocard and 188 for Martin, who was elected with 92.6 percent of the votes. What accounts for such a decisive victory? The historian Mack Holt suggests that the political weight of the growers had increased along with the reputation of their wines. They appreciated the interest shown by the Church in wine and commensalism as a means for uniting the community and binding it more easily to God. By the same token, the Protestant mistrust of the social use of wine aroused strenuous opposition among growers.[197] Tellingly, the principal decorative pattern on the west portal of the magnificent church of Saint Michel in Dijon, completed in the sixteenth century, was the pinot noir grape. The same pattern, as we noted earlier, is found at the Hôtel de Cluny in Paris. Nor was there anything exceptional about the resistance of vine growers in Burgundy to the Reformation; their counterparts in Rouen, Amiens, Troyes, Montpellier, Béziers, Toulouse, and Bordeaux reacted in the same way. Not a single grower's name appears in the registers of the *parlement* of Bordeaux among those accused of heresy between 1523 and 1559.[198] This is one reason why the Protestant merchants who came later from the north of Europe settled outside the walls of the city, in the Chartrons, where they were to take a stunning revenge.

Until the Revolution, the Church remained a great owner of vineyards in Burgundy. The remark, probably apocryphal, of Cardinal de Bernis is well known: "I say my Mass with a fine Meursault so that I will not wince in the sight of the Lord while partaking of the sacrament." Dom Goblet, the last cellar master at Cîteaux, who lived in Dijon after the closing of the abbey, still under the Empire offered his guests Clos de Vougeot that he had made himself. The abbey was subsequently reoccupied by the Cistercians, following renovations that began in 1898, and local growers continue today to supply good wine to the monks. Not long ago I asked one of them if he regretted that his monastery no longer owned the Clos de Vougeot. "No," he replied, "for thanks to the great kindness of our father abbot, I have been able to taste almost all the *grand crus* of the Côte."

The Hospices de Beaune is, of course, a secular institution, which is why it was able to retain control of its vineyard, but for many years it was run by nuns, who until the 1970s wore the robe and wimple of the fifteenth century. Their association with the wine of the Hospices was immortalized by the film director Gérard Oury in *La grande vadrouille* (1966). Generally speaking, the parish priests of the villages of the Côte d'Or did not despise good wine, nor did they avoid talking about it, even in their sermons. This was probably also true in Bordeaux, but there we have fewer written proofs of it. The writer Jean-Claude Pirotte, a Walloon and therefore a lover of Burgundy, recalls his visits with the priest of friends in Marsannay: "'Come along,' the *curé* used to say to me, 'we'll go say hello to my vineyard, at Chambolle, in the *climat des Amoureuses*. Then, when evening falls, we'll come back to the presbytery, listen to a mass by Bach, open a bottle, and with God's help meditate upon music and wine.'"[199]

Two clerics are particularly remembered for the major role they played in promoting the wines of Burgundy, good eating, and the art of living well: Félix Kir and Édouard Krau, both born in 1876 and united both by the first letter of their surnames and by their earthiness. Kir, who died in 1968 at the age of ninety-two, was an exceptional figure.[200] A country priest, fascinated by politics, he won his first term as mayor of Dijon in 1945, when he was sixty-nine years old (Gaston Gérard, having voted to give full powers to Marshal Pétain, was ineligible to run again). Kir served as deputy mayor of the Burgundian capital for twenty-three years, and for much of this time he was the doyen of the National Assembly in Paris, its last clerical incumbent. It was his habit on certain occasions to serve guests in the kitchens of the Palais des Ducs a concoction of local wine and black currant liqueur, typically two-thirds aligoté and one-third *crème de cassis de Dijon*. Very quickly this drink came to be known by the mayor's name, and it has since spread throughout the world, albeit in somewhat modified proportions (rather less black currant liqueur is preferred today). However one may feel about the taste of a kir, there is no gainsaying the fact that it has held the colors of Burgundy and its vineyards high in France and abroad. The canon's impromptu speeches in praise of wine delighted the whole nation, even those who disliked the clergy. "The charm of France," as he once said, "comes from the quality and innumerable variety of the whites and the reds . . . in its barrels and in its government."[201]

Édouard Krau, ordained in 1900, became the parish priest of Vosne-Romanée in 1919. In 1938, the newly formed Confrérie des Chevaliers du Tastevin decided to revive the feast of Saint Vincent, which was to take place in rotation among the villages of the region. The first celebration took place at Chambolle-Musigny. The members of the brotherhood asked Abbé Krau to preach, which he did with such lyricism that he was made chaplain of the Tastevin.[202] The following year he hosted the ceremonies in his church at Vosne. His sermon on that occasion is a superb piece of Christian and vinous eloquence that begins with this flight of fancy: "In your crusade on behalf of the wines of Burgundy, concerned to convince public opinion, hesitant as it may be, that you are spiritualists, not merely spiritual;[203] that your activity is not limited to promoting spirits; and that it pleases you to ennoble your young and knightly society with an element of high spirituality, you have resolved to restore, in our villages of the Côte, the feast—only the true, and therefore the religious, feast—of Saint Vincent, patron of the vine and of vinegrowers."[204]

Since then, one or several bishops have come every year for the occasion, marching in procession amid the banners and statues of Saint Vincent, in the cold of January, before celebrating mass, listening to a colorful sermon, and, finally, sitting down to a fortifying banquet accompanied by ample quantities of wine. The complexion of the princes of the Church then takes on the color of their cassocks, and their faces are lit up with joy. One thinks especially of Cardinal Gerlier, primate of the Gauls, at Beaune in 1955. Regional and political figures often make an appearance as well, making the event a good-natured combination of religion, politics, and wine of the sort that is still much beloved in Burgundy.

CONCLUSION
FAREWELL TO PAROCHIALISM

For a long time the French, whether they were from Bordeaux, Burgundy, or somewhere else, never for a moment believed that great wines could be produced in other regions of the world. Alas, many people in France continue to think that. One might perhaps still maintain that the great Bordeaux and Burgundies constitute the finest imaginable expressions of cabernet sauvignon, merlot, chardonnay, and pinot noir. But even this is becoming increasingly hard to do.

In 1987, Christian Millau convened in Paris an international jury of thirty-two judges who conducted a blind comparative tasting of twenty-nine white wines and thirty-six red wines. The results were instructive.[1] The Mondavi 1984 chardonnay from California came in second, just behind a Leflaive 1983 Chevalier Montrachet. Among the cabernet sauvignons, the 1984 Santa Rita from Chile and the Torres 1981 Gran Coronas Reserva from Catalonia in Spain finished ahead of the Cos d'Estournel from the great vintage of 1982. "There's nothing to be overly proud of," Millau rightly remarked about the results from the French point of view, noting that the venture had been undertaken against the express wishes of certain estate owners in the Médoc.[2] David Cobbold, in his study of the world's greatest vineyards, selected forty-four wines for comparison.[3] Overall, the French can congratulate themselves on accounting for twenty-four of these, among them eight Bordeaux and three Burgundies. To be sure, the choice is a subjective one; and the author, though he is English, lives in France and loves his adopted country, all the more as his ancestors were Huguenots. It is probable that in comparable evaluations by authors in the United States and other countries, French wines would not fare so well.

There is no doubt that more is known today about making wine than in the past. It would be a shame if French viticulturalists were not to profit from all the wonderful contributions of new technologies, which do not in the least prevent them from expressing their own personality in the wines that they make. It would be a still greater shame, however, if these modern methods were used to standardize their wines with a view to imitating certain styles currently popular in North America and the southern hemisphere. In that unfortunate event, the whole of French viticulture would soon disappear, the victim of relatively high land and labor costs. And what a loss this would be for everyone! Humanity would be deprived of one of the most effective and agreeable ways of fathoming the world's complexity, and therefore reality itself, since wine is above all an expression of life on earth.

Far from harming the reputation and trade of good wines, a willingness to abandon the belief in the intrinsic and automatic virtue of *grands terroirs* should strengthen ingenuity and favor talent. But on no account can winemakers afford to pay themselves compliments, or seek to extract them from slavish admirers in the media. Nobody is more suspect than a winemaker who boasts of his own wines too insistently. One must accept the give-and-take of competition, with its international juries and blind tastings; listen to constructive criticism and disinterested advice; and make a point of frequently tasting wines from near and far in order to compare. There are so many immensely talented yet modest people in Bordeaux and Burgundy. They can only gain from being known and recognized.

The time has finally come to bury the hatchet and to be done with the quarrels of another age. Bordeaux and Burgundy are different, just as brothers and sisters in a family are different. So be it! Both vineyards came into being as a benign consequence of Roman conquest and have survived through the centuries thanks to the patronage of the Catholic Church. The wines of both vineyards were favored by dukes and kings. Bordeaux borrowed more from the refined manners of the English elite. Burgundy preserved more of its country manners and the memory of its medieval past. There is some of the angel and some of the beast in both. Cannot the same be said of France itself? Of Europe?

All the greater the pity, then, if either of these distinctive facets of Western culture were to disappear and blend into the other or, worse, into some reductive conception of globalization. It needs to be said, without the least hesitation, that Bordeaux and Burgundy are equally necessary to the construction of Europe. If these two worlds spoke to each other more, exchanging ideas while retaining their separate personalities, their wines could only be the better for it.

For years now there has been much talk about the need for Europe to assert itself as one of several centers of power in the world. Its reputation as a living cultural palimpsest, altogether justified, is a source of special strength. Europe can assert itself more effectively, however, through seduction than by force. The diversity that its wines magnificently express, through a mosaic of *terroirs,* is an insuperable advantage in this regard, of which it has every right to be proud.

Is it unimaginable that this concern for a tolerant and shared diversity might one day spread throughout the world? Not at all—but on one condition: that the world's wines be very good, that they invite humanity to acknowledge the necessity of giving the best of itself in all things. It is a bit the same with languages. Nothing would be sadder than a planet that speaks only a basic English, not to say a rudimentary pidgin. Multilingualism sharpens the mind's agility and aids the understanding of one's fellow human beings. After centuries of fratricidal combat, the French, English, and Germans have turned their backs on war and become, with their neighbors, the pillars of a Europe that the majority of its inhabitants wish to see united in diversity and respect for identities. No one any longer seriously maintains that some people are more worthy than others. Just so, the people of Bordeaux and of Burgundy must at long last put aside their differences.

In a world of wines that fortunately becomes more various by the day, the profession of viticultural geography is a delight, and one that is not likely soon to fall into decline. Let us hope that, by its inherent humanism and the intimate familiarity with local realities that it requires, it will not only breathe new life into geography as a whole, but that it will continue to invigorate the fascinating world of wine, many of whose professional members have acquired a genuine geographical education in the course of their work. One can only hope, too, that the philosopher René Girard, despite his great wisdom, is wrong in supposing that to be scientific means searching for invariance rather than for difference. For a certain number of geographers today, it must be admitted, detecting and describing differences, and trying to explain them, seems a futile enterprise, promising nothing more than a tedious and profitless inventory of the world. In these pages I have sought in my own modest way to show that the opposite is true. Bordeaux and Burgundy, fraternal enemies, are two faces of a stimulating dialectic and debate that one must hope will not soon cease.

And so, long live Bordeaux and Burgundy! Alongside all the other wines of France, they are incomparable expressions of the country's—and the world's—cultural and natural wealth. For, as the Gospel says (John 14: 2), "In my Father's house are many mansions."

NOTES

CHAPTER 1. WEIGHING THE EVIDENCE

1. Brillat-Savarin, *The Physiology of Taste,* Varieties VIII, 362.

2. Et de Beaune et d'Aï les rives fortunées,
   Et la riche Aquitaine, et les hauts Pyrénées
   Sous leurs bruyants pressoirs font couler en ruisseaux
   Des vins délicieux mûris sur leur coteaux.

From *Hymne à la France,* quoted by Bernet, *Anthologie des poètes du vin,* 78.

3. See Ginestet, *Thomas Jefferson à Bordeaux,* 123–26.

4. This verse, to which Xavier de Planhol has drawn my attention, is probably a sign of the growing practice of putting labels (containing geographical information) on wines sold in bottles.

5. Amis, c'est en préférant
   La bouteille à la carafe
   Qu'on voit le plus ignorant
   Devenir bon géographe.

   Beaune, pays si vanté,
   Chablis, Mâcon, Bordeaux, Grave,
   Avec quelle volupté
   Je vous parcours dans ma cave!

From *Ronde de table,* quoted by Bernet, *Anthologie des poètes du vin,* 81.

6. Il est une heure où se rencontrent
Tous les grands vins dans un festin,
Heure fraternelle où se montrent
Le Lafite et le Chambertin

Plus de querelles, à cette heure,
Entre ces vaillants compagnons;
Plus de discorde intérieure
Entre Gascons et Bourguignons . . .

Ils ont dépouillé leurs astuces,
Tout en conservant leur cachet.
—Passez, monsieur de Lur-Saluces!
—Après vous, mon cher Montrachet.

Pommard, en souriant regarde
Glisser le doux Brane-Mouton.
Nul ne dit à Latour "Prends garde!"
Pas même le bouillant Corton?

From a long poem entitled "Les vins de France," quoted by Andrieu, *Le livre d'or du bourgogne,* 61–63.

7. Quoted by Bazin, "Le bordeaux, un sujet interdit à table," 73.

8. Quoted by Kauffmann, *Voyage à Bordeaux,* 95.

9. Ginestet, *Les Chartrons,* 28.

10. The Bordelais *confréries* were received on two occasions at the Clos Vougeot by the Confrérie des Chevaliers du Tastevin. Jean-François Bazin recalls the banquet of 1952 at which a few of the finest Bordeaux were served along with Burgundian dishes, in particular a Léoville-Les-Case 1945 with the cheeses. See Bazin, "Le vignoble des Hautes-Côtes de Nuits et de Beaune."

11. This is why, for example, the Bordelais Alexis Lichine says of the Burgundian *négociant,* "He can buy grape harvests from small parcels that are not commercially viable" (*Encyclopédie des vins,* 222)—as though Romanée-Conti (1.85 hectares, wholly owned by a single domain) or Montrachet (7.99 hectares, shared among a dozen owners) are not sufficiently famous that their happy owners could not sell them in bottles at an exorbitant price, under the table if they liked.

12. Kauffmann, *Le Bordeaux retrouvé,* 130–31.

13. In the course of the same interview (2 February 2004), he related with much amusement a line that one of his friends was particularly fond of: "When

I drink Burgundy, I piss Bordeaux"—not a nasty remark, but not a very affable one either.

14. Beer, "Des odeurs dans tous les sens."

15. Lelong, *Le pain, le vin et le fromage,* 123–24.

16. François Mauriac, *Revue de la Société des agriculteurs de France* (July 1937), 7; quoted by Réjalot, "Le modèle viti-vinicole bordelais dans sa filière (1980–2003)," 353.

17. Sollers, "Je suis né dans le vin," 203–4.

18. These remarks, from 1986, are quoted by Bazin, "Le bordeaux, un sujet interdit à table," 72–73.

19. Pijassou, *Un grand vignoble de qualité,* 2: 1094.

20. Though, it should be noted, *négociants* in Burgundy do not hesitate to blend wines from several different producers.

21. Oh! n'avoir jamais dans le dos
   Un laquais m'offrant du bordeaux;
   Surtout, je le dis sans vergogne
   Que je préfère le bourgogne.

Quoted by Coulon, *Toute la muse de Ponchon,* 112.

22. Bazin, "Le bordeaux, un sujet interdit à table." The author points out that for several centuries the wine of Burgundy was never compared with that of Bordeaux. Its great rival on the Parisian market (and particularly at court) was the wine of Champagne, then made from red grapes and light claret-colored. Louis XIV was urged by his doctor, Fagon, to drink Burgundy, and it was not until the Regency, and then the reign of Louis XV, that champagne became fashionable. In the meantime, however, champagne had become white and sparkling, while the competition with the red wines of Burgundy died out, and both were now consumed at the sophisticated tables of Paris.

23. Ibid.

24. Laplanche, "Oui, nous sommes des culs-terreux," 45.

25. It is true that since the introduction of the new French clarets at the end of the seventeenth century the red wines of Bordeaux have been much darker in color than Burgundies. Before then they resembled an *oeil de perdrix* (partridge's eye) because of their paleness and orangish-pink hue.

26. This claim is probably unfair, and in any case should be carefully checked.

27. Cross-ownership between Burgundy and Champagne is not uncom-

mon, however. La Maison Bouchard Père et Fils of Beaune and le Domaine William Fèvre of Chablis are now owned by Joseph Henriot, the largest landowner in Burgundy, with 177 hectares; and the Burgundian houses of LVMH and Bernard Arnault own several estates in Champagne and several châteaus in Bordeaux, among them Yquem and Cheval-Blanc. Château Rouget in Pomerol is an exception: for several years now it has been owned by Jean-Pierre Labruyère, a native of the Saône-et-Loire and a grower at Moulin-à-Vent, where he is head of the local producers' association. Note, too, the recent purchase of Domaine René Engel by François Pinault of Chateau Latour.

28. These and other oppositions were intelligently and humorously treated by *Le Monde* in a series of articles that appeared during the summer of 1999. The ones I have mentioned, taken from the 23 July issue, led my editor at Hachette, Louis Audibert, to commission the present work.

CHAPTER 2. MARKETS AND CONSUMERS

1. Quoted by Kauffmann, *Voyage à Bordeaux,* 93.

2. Dion, "Querelle des anciens et modernes sur les facteurs de la qualité du vin," 431. The Richelieu referred to here is the cardinal's grandnephew, Marshal Louis de Richelieu (1696–1788), the governor of Guyenne.

3. Lanversin, "Lettre d'un vigneron iconoclaste." This article is all the more paradoxical as it is mainly devoted to those stages in the making of wine that are "decisive" in determining its quality.

4. Gaston Roupnel, with his customary lyricism, used a similar expression in his preface to Camille Rodier's 1949 work *Le Clos de Vougeot:* "All around us there are only noble vineyards, predestined places, slopes beloved of the gods."

5. *Giscours Réalités* (July 1984).

6. Quoted as an epigraph to Boidron and Lemay, *Bordeaux et ses vins.*

7. Diodorus Siculus, *Bibliotheca Historica,* 5:26.

8. Dion, *Histoire de la vigne et du vin en France,* 104.

9. Ibid., 105.

10. Ibid., 107–16. See also Lachiver, *Vins, vignes, vignerons,* 33–35, which contests Dion's interpretation of the historical evidence only with regard to the *allobrogica* grape.

11. Dion, *Histoire de la vigne et du vin en France,* 121. See also Berthault, *Aux origines du vignoble bordelais,* a remarkable work that relies on recent archaeological discoveries in and around Bordeaux.

12. Berthault, *Aux origines du vignoble bordelais,* 43–54.

13. Ibid., 55–69.

14. Ibid., 65.

15. Belonging to this group are cabernet sauvignon, cabernet franc, merlot, petit verdot, Carmenère, and sauvignon, which is to say all the present-day grape varieties of Bordeaux and the Loire; see Lachiver, *Vins, vignes, vignerons,* 36–37. Lachiver also points out that cabernet was formerly called *vidure* in Bordeaux, a word that may have come from the Gascon *bit duro* (hard vine) on account of the hardness of its wood at the time of pruning, but perhaps also, for all we know, from *biturica* ("of the Bituriges," attested in Columella). If the modern French words *biture* (a booze-up or bender) and *se biturer* (to get drunk) derive from the same source, it would be a pleasing paradox, so contrary is this way of behaving to the modern Bordelais ethic of wine; but these pieces of slang belong either to the language of seafaring (*bit[t]ure* is supposed by some to refer to the chain of a ship's anchor) or, more plausibly, to the Franco-Norman dialect of the sixteenth century, in which *béture* (derived from Middle French *boiture* [drink] and *boire* [to drink]) signifies drinking to excess. See Garrier, *Histoire sociale et culturelle du vin,* 661–62.

16. See Vallery-Radot, *Vigne et vin, composantes d'une civilisation,* 6. The relief depicting the amorous adventures of grape pickers cannot be considered decisive, so common is this theme in Roman painting and sculpture.

17. See Gauthier and Joly, "Vignoble et viticulture dans le centre-est de la Gaule au 1er siècle apr. J.-C." This well-documented article proves the antiquity of viticulture, but not its extent.

18. Dion, *Histoire de la vigne et du vin en France,* 137.

19. Quoted in ibid., 139–47.

20. Ibid., 144. André Noblet, formerly the cellar master at the Domaine de la Romanée-Conti, was familiar with the method of provining since, in spite of the phylloxera, the owners of this prestigious estate continued to cultivate "old French vines," ungrafted onto American stocks, and treated the roots with injections of carbon sulfide until the Second World War (see Garrier, *Phylloxera*). In 1943, faced with dwindling supplies of wine, the owners decided to pull them out and to replant grafted vines. Noblet remembered the extraordinary intertwining of wood in the soil. Contrary to Marcel Lachiver's view (*Vins, vignes, vignerons,* 41), the rotting of the wood in the soil does not solve the problem, since provining never ceases. The technique employed at Areni, in Armenia, which consists of layering the original vine stock without totally burying it,

gives surprising results: enormous stocks that run for several dozen meters in a straight line, sending down roots every meter or so that then emerge from the ground to form hoops. These perfectly healthy vines, laden with grapes, cannot be dated with precision but are probably more than a hundred years old.

21. Roupnel, *Histoire de la campagne française,* 239–40; Pitte, *Histoire du paysage français,* 1: 17.

22. Dion, *Histoire de la vigne et du vin en France,* 150–51.

23. Ibid., 171.

24. Ibid., 175.

25. Ibid., 175–76.

26. Ibid., 180.

27. See Rodier, *Le Clos de Vougeot;* Lebeau, *Essai sur les vignes de Cîteaux;* Bazin, *Le Clos de Vougeot;* and Sivignon, *Cîteaux.*

28. The use of enclosure in this region for the purpose of protecting vines against stray cattle goes back to the Law of the Burgundians, promulgated in 501–2. See Dubreucq, "La vigne et la viticulture dans la loi des Burgondes."

29. Gadille, *Le vignoble de Bourgogne,* 157.

30. Ibid., 351–54.

31. See Beck, "Les clos du prince."

32. Enjalbert, *Histoire de la vigne et du vin,* 67–68.

33. Several hundred varieties of grapes, with multiple names and varying from one region to another, have been catalogued by Pierre Rézeau in his remarkable *Dictionnaire des noms de cépages en France.*

34. See Dion, *Histoire de la vigne et du vin en France,* 297. Rolande Gadille finds little to recommend this hypothesis; see *Le vignoble de Bourgogne,* 156–57.

35. Quoted in Dion, *Histoire de la vigne et du vin en France,* 293, and Garrier, *Histoire sociale et culturelle du vin,* 61–62.

36. See Tchernia and Brun, *Le vin romain antique.*

37. Dion, *Histoire de la vigne et du vin en France,* 47.

38. Quoted by Andrieu, *Le livre d'or du bourgogne,* 30.

39. Enjalbert, *Histoire de la vigne et du vin,* 65.

40. Ménard, "Le vin de Chablis dans la littérature médiévale."

41. Quoted by Guyotjeannin, *Salimbene de Adam,* 284–85. I am indebted to Isabelle Rousseau for calling my attention to this text.

42. See Dion, *Histoire de la vigne et du vin en France,* 365–98; Enjalbert, *Histoire de la vigne et du vin,* 40–42; Roudié, *Le vignoble bordelais,* 24–27; and Garrier, *Histoire sociale et culturelle du vin,* 63–65.

43. Dion, *Histoire de la vigne et du vin en France,* 381.

44. Ibid., 370.

45. Roudié, *Le vignoble bordelais,* 27.

46. Dion, *Histoire de la vigne et du vin en France,* 388–89.

47. Enjalbert, *Histoire de la vigne et du vin,* 44.

48. Butel and Poussou, *La vie quotidienne à Bordeaux au XVIIIe siècle,* 46.

49. Dion, *Histoire de la vigne et du vin en France,* 392–93.

50. Ibid., 398.

51. On the whole question of the establishment of foreign merchant dynasties at Bordeaux, see Butel, *Les dynasties bordelaises de Colbert à Chaban.*

52. Enjalbert, *Histoire de la vigne et du vin,* 85.

53. Butel, *Les dynasties bordelaises de Colbert à Chaban,* 28–29.

54. Ibid., 39–46.

55. See Barton and Petit-Castelli, *La saga des Barton,* and Pijassou, *Un grand vignoble de qualité,* 502–16.

56. Hermann Cruse, the son of a pastor in Holstein, a German duchy then attached to the Danish crown, came to Bordeaux in 1819.

57. Quoted by Clive Coates, *Grands Vins: The Finest Châteaux of Bordeaux and Their Wines* (Berkeley and Los Angeles: University of California Press, 1995), 310.

58. See Pijassou, *Un grand vignoble de qualité,* 339–40. Taverns such as the Royal Oake served meals on china with silverware, at individual tables covered with tablecloths, and wines in fine glasses, which, after the invention by George Ravenscroft in 1675 of lead oxide flux, were made from crystal. The French institution of the *restaurant* owes much to the English tavern. See Pitte, "Les espaces de la bonne chère à Paris à la fin du XVIIIe siècle."

59. Locke was a great connoisseur of fine wines, and his account of his travels in France between 1675 and 1679 constitutes an invaluable description of viticulture in the kingdom during this period. He mentions, for example, the relationship between the eminent quality of the wines of Haut-Brion and the gravelly soil of the district. See Unwin, "The Viticultural Geography of France in the 17th Century According to John Locke."

60. Saint-Évremond's tastes must therefore have been eclectic, for we know that during his exile in London he was an effective propagandist on behalf of the sparkling wine of Champagne.

61. Butel and Poussou, *La vie quotidienne à Bordeaux au XVIIIe siècle,* 51.

62. In large part thanks to René Pijassou's monumental and learned work on the Médoc, *Un grand vignoble de qualité.*

63. See Enjalbert, *Histoire de la vigne et du vin,* 66.

64. Quoted by Bazin, *La Romanée-Conti,* 32.

65. The episode of Fagon's prescription is analyzed with great erudition and subtlety by Bazin, in ibid., 30–35.

66. At the monastery of Cîteaux in the Middle Ages, the monks' wine was cut with 20 percent water, a practice that the Franciscan Salimbene de Adam, who traveled through Burgundy in 1248, described as typical of the age: only the English, he said, drank their wine pure—proof of a yet poorly concealed "barbarism" (see Richard, "Le vignoble et les vins de Bourgogne au Moyen Âge," 17). Of course, it depends which class of the English population he was talking about. Wine is seldom diluted today, except by priests during mass, in which the water mixed with wine in the chalice not only symbolizes the mixture of blood and water that spurted from Jesus' side on the cross after his death and the spear thrust of the Roman soldier, but also perpetuates an ancient custom. On the practice of diluting wine with water in the seventeenth and eighteenth centuries, and exceptions to it, see Gillet, *Par mets et par vins,* 174–76.

67. Bossuet wrote to his nephew on 31 March 1697, "If you are well, we are well also, thanks to oysters in the shell, Volnay, and [Saint-]Laurent" (*Correspondance,* 8: 211). I owe this quotation to Damien Blanchard. Saint-Laurent was a wine from Provence. Today one would not serve a Volnay with raw oysters. Other times, other tastes!

68. Quoted by Rodier, *Le vin de Bourgogne,* 151.

69. See Bazin, *La Romanée-Conti,* 35–41.

70. Abbé Claude Arnoux observed in 1728 that unlike the wines of Beaune, less pronounced in color, lighter, and meant to be drunk younger, those of Nuits attained their full quality only after five years. See ibid., 31.

71. Enjalbert, *Histoire de la vigne et du vin,* 68.

72. Bazin, *La Romanée-Conti,* 31.

73. See Gadille, *Le vignoble de Bourgogne,* 354–58, which relies in part on the work of Gaston Roupnel.

74. See Olney, *Romanée-Conti;* also Bazin, *La Romanée-Conti,* 128–48.

75. From the Picardy seigneury of Conty, whose name was borne by the cadet branch of the Condé family.

76. In 1760, as today, this *climat* was closed only to the south and the east.

The actual contract of sale described it as "une pièce de terre en vigne appelée la Vigne de la Romanée, close de murs du midy et de l'orient."

77. See Olney, *Romanée-Conti,* 33–34, and Bazin, *Romanée-Conti,* 133. Such legends are frequently encountered for many wines, spirits, and gastronomic products (Dom Pérignon and champagne, Napoleon III and Marie Harel's Camembert, Louis XVI and the foie gras of Strasbourg, and so on): unto those that have more shall be given. Despite their exaggerations, some of these stories nonetheless have an element of truth to them.

78. Olney, *Romanée-Conti,* 33.

79. In 1793 the harvest was 5 1/2 casks, or 1,254 liters, a yield of 7 hectoliters per hectare.

80. See Grivot, *Le commerce des vins de Bourgogne,* and Bazin, *Histoire du vin de Bourgogne,* 33–34.

81. See the section "Where Are They Consumed?" in chapter 4.

82. Enjalbert, *Histoire de la vigne et du vin,* 127; Bazin, *Chambertin,* 69.

83. Quoted by Bazin, *Montrachet,* 25.

84. Quoted by Gadille, *Le vignoble de Bourgogne,* 432–33. This practice has several features in common, even if it differs in other respects, with the custom in Bordeaux of distinguishing first and second wines. The practice no longer exists in Burgundy, at least not officially, but it survives (and even shows signs of gaining strength) in Bordeaux.

85. Enjalbert, *Histoire de la vigne et du vin,* 110–11.

86. Abric, "Stratégie d'achat des vins."

87. Enjalbert, *Histoire de la vigne et du vin,* 110.

88. Pijassou, *Un grand vignoble de qualité,* 373 ff. It was a little later that the *grands crus* of Lafite, Margaux, and Latour came to be clearly distinguished from one another, having only recently joined Château Haut-Brion in what would subsequently be the family of the *premiers grands crus classés* of the Graves and the Médoc, a classification not enlarged until 1973 with the promotion of Mouton.

89. Gamay and aligoté can, if cultivated to an exacting standard, yield charming and even elegant wines. The aligoté from the village of Bouzeron in the Côte Chalonnaise, for example, today rightly enjoys its own *appellation d'origine contrôlée* (AOC). The enthusiasm of Aubert de Villaine, co-manager of the Domaine de la Romanée-Conti, who owns and lives on an estate there, no doubt had something to do with this.

90. With regard to Burgundy, see Abric, "Stratégie d'achat des vins." (This well-documented article does not clearly say what the Beaune merchants did with the red and white Côtes de Rhône wines that they bought in abundant quantities in the nineteenth century. Plainly it was a matter of different estates acting in concert, which leaves the door open to all manner of conjecture. Françoise Grivot, herself the daughter of a Beaune merchant, is scarcely more explicit on this point [*Le commerce des vins de Bourgogne,* 66]. Why not admit that the practice of blending used to be very common, and this at a time when no law prohibited it? I shall return to the reasons for this awkward silence later.) With regard to Bordeaux, see Pijassou, *Un grand vignoble de qualité,* 497, 500.

91. Butel and Poussou, *La vie quotidienne à Bordeaux au XVIIIe siècle,* 45–46.

92. Enjalbert, *Histoire de la vigne et du vin,* 126.

93. Quoted by Gadille, *Le vignoble de Bourgogne,* 422. (The original manuscript by Abbé Tainturier, conserved in the municipal library of Dijon, was recently published with notes and commentary by Loïc Abric.) Until the Second World War, in Burgundy it was customary to co-plant up to 10 percent chardonnay in red wine vineyards to give a "ripe" acidity to the wine.

94. See Gadille, *Le vignoble de Bourgogne,* 425–27. The discussion of the timing of harvests borrows from Laurent, *Les vignerons de la Côte d'Or au XIXe siècle,* 108–68.

95. Pijassou, *Un grand vignoble de qualité,* 493–99.

96. Ibid., 492.

97. For the most part, wines in Bordeaux were matured in cask, as they have been in Rioja and Barolo until recently. Latour was traditionally given a year more than Lafite: five years rather than four.

98. Pitte, "Origine et géographie des formes de bouteilles de vin en France."

99. Roudié, "Le vignoble au présent," 206.

100. Garrier, *Histoire sociale et culturelle du vin,* 159.

101. Quoted by Bazin, *Chambertin,* 72.

CHAPTER 3. THE PHYSICAL ENVIRONMENT

1. See Pidoux, "Champlitte, une 'petite Bourgogne.'"

2. The percentage assigned to the properties of the Champagne region by

the INAO reflects the purchase price for grapes paid to growers by merchant houses and the cooperatives.

3. The standards for per-hectare yield are determined in accordance with the Plafond Limité de Classement (PLC).

4. Ángel A. Gargiulo, an Argentine agronomist, is persuaded that the opposite is true, but his claims are scarcely credible. His wines, obtained from hybrids with yields of two hundred hectoliters per hectare and even more, are quite high in alcohol, but they have not been the object of blind tasting comparisons. See Gargiulo, "Quality and Quantity."

5. Bettane and Desseauve, *Classement des meilleures vins de France 2003.*

6. Ibid.

7. This is also true of the wines of certain second-tier appellations in the Côte d'Or (Chorey-lès-Beaune, Ladoix, and Monthélie, for example, to mention only the Hautes-Côtes-de-Nuits and the Hautes-Côtes-de-Beaune).

8. Bettane and Desseauve, *Classement des meilleures vins de France 2003.*

9. See Gadille, *Le vignoble de Bourgogne.* This success was due in large part to the canon Félix Kir, who popularized the eponymous aperitif that mixes crème de cassis with aligoté; see chapter 2 and Bazin and Mignotte, *Pour le meilleur et pour le kir.*

10. See Legouy, "La renaissance du vignoble des Hautes-Côtes de Beaune et des Hautes-Côtes de Nuits," as well as Legouy's thesis of the same title.

11. From Hudelot's annual letter to clients and selected members of the trade ("Lettre annuelle du Château de Villars-Fontaine—Domaine de Montmain," 14 November 2003).

12. Prieur, "Vendanges précoces."

13. In Champagne the geographical complementarity is perfect. It is hardly an exaggeration to say that the Côte des Blancs produces grapes, the chalky plain produces sugar beets, and that by mixing the two Rheims and Épernay make champagne.

14. This quip is attributed by some to Gnafron, in rejoinder to Guignol (see Basse, *Le Rhône, la Saône et le Beaujolais*), by others to Léon Daudet (Garrier, *L'étonnante histoire du beaujolais nouveau,* 126).

15. See Duboeuf and Elwing, *Beaujolais, vin du citoyen,* and Garrier, *L'étonnante histoire du beaujolais nouveau.*

16. In his 2001 guide Robert Parker marvels at the 1997 Morgon: "Apart from magnificent and explosive scents of spice and black and red cherry that

literally shoot out from the glass, this wine exhibits a dense, meaty, moderately full-bodied and ample character, as well as a rich texture." Parker also sings the praises of the 1997 table wine, downgraded by some as being too atypical; in his view, it sets "a standard for Beaujolais." See Parker, *Guide Parker des vins de France,* 982.

17. To increase its color and help it keep longer, a part of the must used to be concentrated by boiling, or even roasting in the oven. See Baudel, *Le vin de Cahors,* 121–26.

18. Bettane and Desseauve, *Classement des meilleures vins de France 2003.*

19. See Pomerol, ed., *Terroirs et vins de France,* 186–87 and 228–29.

20. Thus the price of the 1999 Monbazillac Cuvée Madame from Château Tirecul la Gravière.

21. See Strang, *Vins du Sud-Ouest,* 162–65. This work is an excellent synthesis, lively and reliable, on the recent turn to quality, indeed excellence, in wine production in the southwest.

22. Flacelière, "Il faut découvrir les vins de Fronton."

23. The rehabilitation of tannat as a prestigious grape variety is due in part to Alain Brumont, owner of Châteaux Montus and Bouscassé in the Madiran appellation.

24. The same argument is employed in an entirely different context by Augustin Berque, who seeks to explain why mountains in Japan are largely uncultivated. Initially the reasons for this were associated with religious belief. In the plains, by contrast, improved techniques of irrigation led to the development of rice farming. With rising levels of investment there, particularly as a consequence of increased control over water supply, farmers in the mountains found it harder and harder to compete. Nonetheless, wine-producing properties yield a return on investment much more quickly than rice fields, especially in the case of vineyards devoted to making fine wines. See Berque, *Le sens de l'espace au Japon,* 68.

25. Fernand Pouillon, in his novel *Les pierres sauvages* (1964), marvelously describes the masterpieces that the Cistercian monks of the Abbaye du Thoronet managed to create from a type of stone that is notoriously hard to work.

26. Gadille, *Le vignoble de Bourgogne,* 466–67.

27. Ibid., 9.

28. Ibid., 303.

29. Quoted by Feuillat, "La recherche scientifique est-elle susceptible de faire progresser notre compréhension de l'influence du terroir sur la typicité des vins de chardonnay et de pinot noir?" 14.

30. Quoted by Ginestet, *Thomas Jefferson à Bordeaux,* 125.

31. See Ménard, "Le vin de Chablis dans la littérature médiévale."

32. Enjalbert, *Les pays aquitains, le modelé et les sols.*

33. Pijassou, *Discours lors de la cérémonie de remise des insignes de chevalier de l'ordre national du Mérite.*

34. This is a stone cast in the direction of Roger Dion.

35. Pijassou, *Un grand vignoble de qualité,* 1096–97.

36. The new generation of viticultural geographers in Bordeaux takes this line. See, for example, the harsh criticism of Roger Dion meted out by Réjalot, "Le modèle viti-vinicole bordelais dans sa filière (1980–2003)," 19.

37. Pijassou, *Un grand vignoble de qualité,* xvi.

38. Enjalbert, *Histoire de la vigne et du vin,* 191.

39. See Didier Ters, "Le retour à la terre," *Sud-Ouest* (21 January 2003). Olivier is an old property, of course, and it is quite possible that this land was under vine in the nineteenth century, prior to the phylloxera epidemic, or even earlier.

40. The great variability in volumes of hail produced in the Bordeaux region must nonetheless be noted. Philippe Roudié has shown that climatic and biological factors (parasite attacks in the latter case) are as influential as economic and political circumstances; see *Le vignoble bordelais,* 39.

41. These factors are analyzed by Gadille at various points in *Le vignoble de Bourgogne,* particularly in the first chapter of the third part.

42. See Ginestet, *Chablis,* 16–25. The legend of the discovery of the protective power of spraying (a drunken grower is said to have urinated on a vine one night in the spring, as a result of which the entire plant froze except the vine stock, whose buds were protected by an icy shell) is worth its weight in gold.

43. Pijassou, *Un grand vignoble de qualité,* 559–60.

44. Gadille, *Le vignoble de Bourgogne,* 347.

45. Ibid., 402–5; Pijassou, *Un grand vignoble de qualité,* 535.

46. Gadille, *Le vignoble de Bourgogne,* 393.

47. Olney, *Romanée-Conti,* 82–83.

48. Quoted in ibid.

49. See Renvoisé, *Le monde du vin,* 213. The author argues that the grant-

ing of the appellation *premier cru* to certain slopes was justified neither by the properties of the physical landscape nor by tradition, and that one may truly speak in this connection of insider trading. Renvoisé's book is no less refreshing than Pierre-Marie Doutrelant's *Les bons vins et les autres* was twenty years earlier.

50. Much more debatable has been the practice in Champagne of spreading manure from factories that process household waste. Excessive use of this fertilizer has had harmful consequences for yields, for the soils in this region now contain a non-negligible proportion of plastic debris, including blue and black garbage bags and bottle caps, which take a long time to degrade. The ultimate effect of such petrochemical products on the vines and on the taste of their grapes cannot be predicted, but this practice amounts to playing the sorcerer's apprentice—and provides evidence of the short-sighted economic, ecological, and oenological policies that for too long have prevailed in the vineyards of Champagne.

51. Pijassou, *Un grand vignoble de qualité,* 556–58.

52. See Enjalbert, *Les grands vins de Saint-Émilion, Pomerol et Fronsac* (plate XLII).

53. Ibid., 171 ff.

54. Pétrus fetches about €1,000 for each of the 35,000 bottles produced annually.

55. Enjalbert, *Les grands vins de Saint-Émilion, Pomerol et Fronsac* (plate LIX).

56. Ginestet, *Pomerol,* 146–47.

57. This is roughly equal to the area of the Romanée-Conti appellation in Burgundy.

58. Baby, "L'étalon de Saint-Émilion," 54. It is sometimes forgotten, however, how much gravel there is at Cheval-Blanc, and even more so in Figeac, where the proportion of cabernet franc and indeed cabernet sauvignon is relatively high.

59. Pomerol, ed., *Terroirs et vins de France,* 242.

60. Ginestet, *Barsac Sauternes,* 187. Until the major renovations carried out by Romain-Bertrand de Lur-Saluces in the nineteenth century, drainage was accomplished at Yquem by burying bundles of cut branches.

61. Such surprises sometimes occur in Burgundy. Thus, at Chorey-lès-Beaune, Domaine Daniel Largeot sells its village Aloxe-Corton at a slightly

higher price than its Beaune *premier cru* Les Grèves. This is a bit unfair, but it is a residual legacy of the historical disregard of wines from Beaune by the trade, which had hardly any respect for them. Indeed, when AOC classifications were being drawn up in the 1930s, merchants refused to propose Beaune wines vineyards for *grand cru* status on the pretext that customers placed greater confidence in the name of their house than in the origin of the wines.

62. Clos de Vougeot is on the order of ten to fifteen times less expensive, selling in the range of €50–80.

63. Château Latour goes for €150–400 a bottle, depending on the vintage.

64. Gadille, *Le vignoble de Bourgogne,* 342.

65. Rabaudy, "Sociando-mallet vainqueur de 132 châteaux."

66. Quoted in Cottereau, "Côtes de Castillon," 22.

67. In this connection it needs to be recognized that while Mouton Cadet is not cheap, it probably represents the top end of generic Bordeaux production, and that it gives evidence of genuine talent in the art of blending, on which Baron Philippe de Rothschild, S.A., congratulates itself by putting the words "L'Art de l'Assemblage" on the back label. This brand provides the reassurance sought by a bourgeois clientele that likes to drink a little table wine or to offer such wine to guests, while hesitating to venture into the unknown. Currently some sixteen million bottles of Mouton Cadet are sold each year throughout the world. See Réjalot, "Marques ou châteaux," 104.

68. The 1855 classification was established by the Bordeaux chamber of commerce for the purpose of showcasing the leading vineyards of the Gironde at the Universal Exposition of that year in Paris. This list was limited exclusively to the red wines of the Médoc, with the exception of Château Haut-Brion, and to the sweet white wines of Sauternes and Barsac. It has been revised only once, in 1973, when Château Mouton Rothschild was elevated from the first rank of the *deuxième crus* to the category of *premiers.* Occasionally the classification is contested, but no one has really wanted to overturn it. The ranking of dry white wines goes back to 1959 and that of Saint-Émilion to 1955. The latter has periodically been revised (most recently in 1996), a most welcome thing.

69. From the 1823 edition of Locke's *Observations,* quoted by Unwin, "The Viticultural Geography of France in the 17th Century According to John Locke," 404.

70. Thomas Jefferson, "Notes of a Tour into the Southern Parts of France

&c.," in Julian P. Boyd, ed., *Papers of Thomas Jefferson,* vol. 11 (Princeton, N.J.: Princeton University Press, 1955), 417; quoted by Ginestet, *Thomas Jefferson à Bordeaux et dans quelques autres vignes d'Europe,* 126. The passage from Locke has obviously been interpreted in Bordeaux as if it accounted for an incontestable reality; see, for example, Enjalbert, *Histoire de la vigne et du vin,* 98. René Pijassou, in a private communication to the author dated 13 March 2001, regretted that Tim Unwin, in his fine article on Locke, had "forgotten to emphasize that famous remark that underlies the notion of high-quality *terroir,* 'only a ditch between': only a simple ditch separated [Monsieur Pontac's] vineyard of Haut-Brion from the nearest vineyards, whose wine was incomparably less good. It is a pity that [Unwin] did not stress this first known affirmation of the notion that a particular wine-producing property may produce better wines than neighboring properties, even those closest to it, separated by 'only a ditch between.'" The real pity is that Pijassou neglected the words "the merchants assured me." This is something more than a mere detail incidental to the point Locke was making; it carries the same weight as Jefferson's "It is pretended that . . ."

71. Feuillat, "Ultimes mystères du terroir bourguignon," 77.

72. Quoted by Légasse, "Y a-t-il encore du raisin dans le vin français?" 31.

73. See Pitte, "Cultures régionales, culture universelle."

74. Girard, *Les origines de la culture,* 195.

75. See Roudié, "'Bordeaux,' un modèle pour la viti-viniculture mondiale," 410–13.

76. With regard to problems of drainage, Gérard Seguin, a professor at the Institut d'Oenologie de Bordeaux and the author of scholarly works and innumerable technical reports, is a leading specialist.

77. See Bourguignon, *Le sol, la terre et les champs,* and Joly, *Le vin du ciel à terre.*

78. Vineyards there used to be full of snails. All medieval Burgundian churches are decorated with sculptures of vines covered with snails. A glimpse of this region may be had in the heart of Paris on the porch of the Hôtel de Cluny.

79. See Bazin, *Le vin bio, mythe ou réalité?* 71–73.

80. Ibid., 150.

81. See Sadrin and Sadrin, *Mersault,* 80–83; also Bazin, *Histoire du vin de Bourgogne,* 69.

82. Clones are available from nurseries, which have played a large role in the homogenization of the world's vineyards.

83. Quoted in Ducasse, *Rencontres savoreuses,* 216.

84. Blight was rampant in the 1970s and up until 1985. The use of potash was encouraged by a government viticulture official, André Vedel, who recommended the staggering proportion of 2,400 kilograms (more than five thousand pounds) per hectare; see Renvoisé, *Le monde du vin,* 222. The potash mines may have been shut down in Alsace, but they could have been reopened in the vineyards of Burgundy. It needs also to be kept in mind that its effects are not transient, since potash remains in the soil for a very long time.

85. By contrast, consider the apocalyptic landscape of vineyards in Champagne that have been "enriched" with fertilizer made from urban waste (see note 50). See also Renvoisé, *Le monde du vin,* 96–97.

86. See Gaudillère, "La grande rue." It is true that La Grande Rue is a narrow strip of land wedged between La Tâche and Romanée-Conti, and that its absence from the *grand cru* classification of 1936 was simply due to the fact that Henri Lamarche did not think it wise to press the matter at a time when sales of wine had fallen off dramatically.

87. Beeston, *Mes hommes du vin,* 185.

88. See Rigaux, *Ode aux grands vins de Bourgogne,* 116–17; also Burtschy and Jayer, *Gault-Millau* 356 (September 2002).

89. See Renvoisé, *Le monde du vin,* 205.

90. See Tupinier, "Rendements et qualités."

91. Ducasse, *Rencontres savoreuses,* 205–23.

92. See Peynaud, *Le goût du vin,* 195–202, as well as the collection of interviews published as *Oenologue dans le siècle,* which contains a list of Peynaud's 289 publications up through 1995. See also Roudié, "'Bordeaux,' un modèle pour la viti-viniculture mondiale."

93. See Peynaud, *Oenologue dans le siècle,* 78.

94. Jonathan Nossiter's 2004 film *Mondovino* takes a very dim view of Rolland, one of the world's leading wine consultants; but if Rolland has a great many clients, it is because they value his advice. No one has forced them to hire him.

95. See Puisais et al., *Précis d'initiation à la dégustation;* Léglise, *Une initiation à la dégustation des grands vins;* and Peynaud, *Le goût du vin.*

96. Chauvet, *Le vin en question.*

97. Cryoextraction—the use of freezing temperatures to eliminate some of the water contained in the must for the purpose of concentrating it—is accomplished altogether naturally by winter in parts of the world (Germany, the United States, and Canada) where ice wines are made.

98. Bettane, "Éloge de l'industrie."

99. From a television show on Baron Philippe de Rothschild hosted by Jean Lacouture and aired 23 September 1983 on FR3 (later to become France 3).

100. A fine description of this practice can be found in the chapter devoted by Fiona Beeston to Jacky Confuron in *Mes hommes du vin,* 183–91; see also Bardet, "Les érotomanes du vin."

101. Trampling grapes at the age of seventeen, as the author of the present volume did by way of initiation into the world of wine, bears some resemblance to Obélix's immersion when he was little in the pot containing a magic potion.

102. The former capacity was definitively fixed in 1884 by the chamber of commerce of Bordeaux; see Roudié, *Vignobles et vignerons du Bordelais (1850–1980),* 104. Beaujolais traditionally stands apart from the rest of Burgundy, with casks of 216 liters.

103. This was the 2003 price for casks made by François de Saint-Romain in the Côte d'Or, owner of one of the best cooperages in France.

104. See Boidron and Lamay, *Bordeaux et ses vins,* 2288; see also Latrive, "Malesan, appellation d'origine marketing."

105. See Réjalot, "Le modèle viti-vinicole bordelais dans sa filière (1980–2003)," 117–19. In Castel's new cellar (Lestac is an anagram of Castel) at Blanquefort, fifty thousand American oak barrels can be stored.

106. See, for example, the brief and harsh indictment by Hugh Johnson, "Parkérisés!"

107. From an interview with François Simon, "Le bon vin selon Robert Parker," *Le Figaro* (8 October 1998), 13.

108. Like every influential institution, the *Guide Parker* is the object of scathing attacks and even grave suspicions regarding its integrity; on the recent investigation into Parker's dealings in Bordeaux and the controversy surrounding it, see McCoy, *The Emperor of Wine,* 286–88, 292–93.

109. In certain domaines the casks are traditionally brought out into the courtyard in the middle of the winter. At the Domaine de la Romanée-Conti, André Noblet used to open the cellar windows on a very cold day. All filtering, no matter how delicate it may be, impoverishes the wine to some extent. In

some cases it produces wines of perfect clarity and brilliance that are nonetheless totally thinned out. There is no longer any risk in shipping them, of course, but what a waste!

110. The volume edited by Jacky Rigaux and Christian Bon, *Les nouveaux vignerons,* while it pays far more attention to viticulturalists from Burgundy (twenty-two) than from Bordeaux (two) and other regions, nonetheless brings together fascinating accounts of the efforts to improve quality being made by a certain number of growers today who seek to give the fullest possible expression to the riches of their natural environment. Of particular interest is the article by Aubert de Villaine on the work being done at Domaine de la Romanée-Conti. I hasten to add that holding such a view of a book subtitled "The Awakening of the *Terroirs*" in no way contradicts the argument of my 1997 article "Pour en finir avec le pseudo-terroir," in which I criticized the idea that the landscape in its physical aspect suffices by itself to explain the excellence of a particular region's wines.

111. Quoted by Ducasse, *Rencontres savoreuses,* 234.

112. See, for example, Waldin, "Life Is Sweet in Bordeaux." This vitriolic article appeared on the eve of Vinexpo 2001 and demonstrates, if any further proof is needed, how demanding the market of Anglo-Saxon connoisseurs has become.

113. "André Ostertag, vigneron en Alsace," *Gault-Millau* (September 1995), 30.

114. A reverse osmosis system, for example, costs between €50,000 and €100,000, if not a bit more. Some "over-the-row" tractors cost much more.

115. Quoted by Néauport, *Réflexions d'un amateur de vin,* 7. [A *muid* was a measure of liquid capacity, on the Paris market equal to about 270 liters, or roughly 64 gallons; many regional variants existed. —Trans.]

116. Quoted by Ginestet, *Thomas Jefferson à Bordeaux,* 34.

117. Quoted by Guy Trocque in his review of Lynch, *Mes aventures dans le vignoble de France,* published in *Historiens-Géographes* 387 (July 2004): 487.

118. Flaubert, *Dictionnaire des idées reçues,* 82.

119. Grivot, *Le commerce des vins de Bourgogne,* 61–66.

120. Despite weak competition from cooperatives and *récoltants-manipulants* (growers who make wine from their own grapes), this is still largely the case in Champagne.

121. Grivot, *Le commerce des vins de Bourgogne,* 65.

122. Gadille, *Le vignoble de Bourgogne,* 460.

123. In the early 1930s, Pierre Scize recounted the scenes that could be observed in autumn in the small train stations of the Côte d'Or: "The air was saturated with the smell of grapes. Step up, ladies and gentlemen. Examine the labels on the cars. Here is the harvest from the Hérault and the one from the Gard, which come in search of their letters of nobility under the presses of the Côte"; see Scize, "Le vin de Bourgogne," 13. The paradox is that this trade was thriving at a time of falling demand for wine. But it should not come as a surprise. Today growers in Languedoc still foresee no drop in their production of grapes for table wine, despite a shrinking market. In time-honored French fashion, they lobby for government subsidies.

124. At the end of his career Gâcon was actually selling wine from the Midi, only now unblended, in Burgundy-style bottles with a flowery label bearing the legend "Cuvée du Père Jules."

125. George, *La région du bas-Rhône,* 437.

126. Quoted by Lutin, *Châteauneuf-du-Pape,* 13–14.

127. See Robert Sabatier, *Les vins du Rhône et de la Méditerannée* (Paris: Montalba, 1978), quoted by Orizet and Orizet, *Les cent plus beaux textes sur le vin,* 114.

128. Curnonsky, "De la Bourgogne gastronomique."

129. See Pijassou, *Un grand vignoble de qualité,* 590–94 and 818–31, and Roudié, *Vignobles et vignerons du Bordelais (1850–1980),* 207–9 and 373–78.

130. See Butel, *Les dynasties bordelaises de Colbert à Chaban,* 287.

131. Quoted by Unwin, "The Viticultural Geography of France in the 17th Century According to John Locke," 407.

132. Pijassou, *Un grand vignoble de qualité,* 591.

133. These blendings, if they were not carried out on the Chartrons quays, took place in the warehouses of English importers in London and Bristol, whence the expression *travail à l'anglaise.*

134. Pijassou, *Un grand vignoble de qualité,* 820.

135. Curnonsky, "L'Aquitaine gastronomique," 28.

136. Roupnel, *Nono,* 288–89.

137. Roudié, *Vignobles et vignerons du Bordelais (1850–1980),* 207.

138. Curnonsky, "L'Aquitaine gastronomique," 28.

139. Still today, the French themselves are not averse to having it both ways. The Alsatians finally won permission to keep the name *tokay* for one of their most delicious grape varieties, thus named more than three centuries ago after the great Hungarian wine. It would be difficult today for a producer to

call his wine Médauc in order to improve sales, as was done in 1905 (see Pijassou, *Un grand vignoble de qualité,* 820); but what is one to say when a merchant sells a thin generic Bordeaux under a perfectly legal label bearing the name of an imaginary château registered as a commercial trademark and depicted with striking realism? It must be recognized that some of these wines, though their quality in relation to price may be disputed, are nonetheless excellent. In order to make the wine sold under the name Michel Lynch, for example, a good Bordeaux brand marketed without the benefit of a fake château, only four samples were approved for blending out of sixty *cuvées* that were tasted one day in winter 2001–02 (personal communication dated 31 January 2002 from Jean-Michel Cazes). Michel Bettane, somewhat provocatively, has boasted of the merits of these brand-name wines, so long as they are well made and cheap (less than €4–5 per bottle). This second condition is far from being met in every case, however; see Bettane, "Éloge de l'industrie."

> 140. Vous êtes par trop rigolos
> Australiens immenses!
> Mettez-vous bien dans vos ciboulots
> Où règnent les démences
>
> Qu'il n'est d'autre vin bourguignon
> —Croyez-en un ivrogne—
> Que celui que nous bourgognons
> Aux coteaux de Bourgogne. . . .
>
> Vous planteriez, ô Melbournois!
> Sur vos coteaux barbares,
> Les plus fins de nos ceps gaulois,
> Nos pinots les plus rares,
>
> En vain! Car à ces gaillards-là,
> À ces vrais gentilshommes,
> Il faut ce terroir de gala,
> Dont, Dieu merci! nous sommes.

From a poem entitled "Bourgogne d'Australie," in Ponchon, *La muse au cabaret,* 84–87.

141. See the account in Butel, *Les dynasties bordelaises de Colbert à Chaban,* 84–87.

142. See the article in *Le Figaro* (18–19 May 2002), 19.

143. Garrier, *Histoire sociale et culturelle du vin,* 415–16; also Doutrelant, *Les bons vins et les autres,* 73–78.

144. This light color is considered acceptable for wines made from the pinot grape only in Champagne (sparkling pink wines such as the rosé champagne of Laurent Perrier and the still pink wines from Les Riceys, Bouzy, and Cumières in cool years) and in Alsace.

145. Doutrelant, *Les bons vins et les autres,* 14. This delightful book, first published in 1976, caused much gnashing of teeth; see Pijassou, *Un grand vignoble de qualité,* 1099.

146. See Cherruau, "Un grand cru du Médoc est soupçonné de tromperie sur la qualité." This article was followed by an interview with Jean-Michel Fernandez, the cellar master at the time. His answers shed a great deal of light on the realities of high-end viticulture:

> My concern was to make the best wine possible as far as blending is concerned. When I came I found vats of wine from young Giscours vines, not even worthy of the property of La Hourringue, on the other side of the road, which is only a Haut-Médoc but which has parcels of old vines that are thirty years old and that are marvelous. In the interest of Giscours's second wine, we used a vat of Haut-Médoc to improve the Margaux. Before doing this, since it's illegal, I spoke about it with Éric Albada-Jelgersma. I explained to him that, in the interest of quality, many people did this. It still meant having two AOCs in the same cellar. He replied, "Well, fine, go ahead." But I do not have the right to say that I acted under influence or under constraint.

This way of implicating the owner, a Dutch billionaire, and, incidentally, the entire profession, is a constant in all cases of fraud: "Everyone does it, as you know perfectly well!"

147. See Fischler, *Du vin,* 107–33. This chapter is entitled "Scandal at Giscours, or the Anatomy of a Media 'Bubble.'"

148. This makes Bordeaux by far the foremost AOC region in France. National production of wines of this category averages some twenty-five million hectoliters annually. This and all the figures that follow are taken from official INAO statistics.

149. Given the scale of foreign competition today, French wines will be able to hold their own on the world market only if they are sufficiently original, and therefore concentrated, while at the same time preserving their subtlety. Doing this is a challenge at sixty hectoliters per hectare, an average figure that conceals much higher yields in the generic appellations.

150. At Lafayette Gourmet in Paris in 2004, for example, Romanée-Conti 1997 sold for €3,812 a bottle, and the 1999 for €4,570 a bottle.

151. Anecdote related by Ginestet, *Pomerol,* 44.

152. See the article in *Le Figaro Entreprises* (18 June 2001), 12.

153. This is the official figure of the Société d'aménagement foncier et d'établissement rural (SAFER).

154. It must be kept in mind that Burgundy *grand cru* wines have no fixed price. In 1996, a Methuselah (about six liters) of 1990 Romanée-Conti sold at Sotheby's in London for the equivalent of about €25,000.

155. See Rousseau, "S'offrir un vignoble," and Bratberg, "Les fortunes du Bordelais flambent." The largest fortunes in the department of the Gironde are associated with wine. According to the December 2000 issue of *Capital,* Éric de Rothschild headed the list at €464 million, with Philippine de Rothschild next at €401 million. Domaine de la Romanée-Conti, in the Côte d'Or, placed fifth with an estimated value of €53 million, and Faiveley sixth with €48 million.

156. This is understandable, considering the price paid to growers by merchants for a kilogram of grapes, €4.25 in 2003. At twelve thousand kilos per hectare, this yields a gross revenue of €51,000 per hectare. Some consumers may view the quality-price relation of champagne unfavorably, considering that for €15–20 a bottle still wines can be had that are more exciting, but in the light of these figures one sees why growers and merchants have no interest in upsetting the status quo. Hence the large sums that they profitably invest in real estate and advertising aimed at persuading people that no party is complete without champagne, the symbol of "luxury, relaxation, and pleasure" (as one slogan has it).

CHAPTER 4. INCOMPARABLE WINES

1. Quoted in Larmat, *Atlas de la France vinicole,* n.p.

2. A charming poem by Brigitte Level likening Pommard to Pomerol appeared in the 20 May 1974 issue of *La journée viticole,* later quoted by Orizet and Orizet, *Les cent plus beaux textes sur le vin,* 85–86. Here is an extract:

> Goût de truffe et goût de cerise,
> De cassis et de venaisons,
> En chaque verre qui nous grise
> Nous goûtons les quatre saisons. . . .
> Les dégustant l'on s'émerveille;
> Chacun se voudrait rossignol
> Pour chanter, Pommard, tes merveilles,
> Et tes délices, Pomerol!

[Flavor of truffle and cherry,
Of cassis and of venison,
In each intoxicating glass
We taste the four seasons. . . .
Tasting them fills us with wonder;
If only we were nightingales,
Singing of your marvels, Pommard,
And Pomerol, of your delights!]

3. Fanet, *Les terroirs du vin,* 48–49.

4. Ibid., 44–46.

5. See Pijassou, *Un grand vignoble de qualité,* 554. By contrast, a few of these grapes still remain in Musigny, the great red wine appellation of Burgundy, where chardonnay is allowed to be planted in up to 10 percent of the total area. Only the Champagne region survives today as a conservatory of ancient varieties: blanc de blancs (made from grapes grown on the Côte des Blancs south of Épernay), blanc de rouges (Montagne de Reims), and blends of wines from white and red grapes.

6. These were probably Syrah. This may be why for a long time no one found the idea of blending wines from Bordeaux with ones from Hermitage at all shocking.

7. See Pijassou, *Un grand vignoble de qualité,* 553–54; also Roudié, *Vignobles et vignerons du Bordelais (1850–1980),* 96–100.

8. Its counterpart in Alsace is known as Edelzwicker.

9. Bazin, *Le Clos de Vougeot,* 183.

10. Quoted in Pijassou, *Un grand vignoble de qualité,* 553.

11. Ambrosi et al., *Guide des cépages,* 86. These grape varieties bore different names in the Middle Ages.

12. See Fanet, *Les terroirs du vin,* 94–97.

13. Ibid., 95.

14. Enjalbert, *Les grands vins de Saint-Émilion, Pomerol et Fronsac,* 514–15.

15. See Dion, *Histoire de la vigne et du vin en France,* 285–300. Rolande Gadille disputes the direct role of the duke in the selection and baptism of pinot claimed by Roger Dion; see *Le vignoble de Bourgogne,* 156–67. Henri Enjalbert, caught once again in flagrante delicto with Bordelais chauvinism, claims that Dion extrapolated from the text of 1395 and that we do not know which noble grapes were cultivated in the late fourteenth century; see *Les grands vins de Saint-Émilion, Pomerol et Fronsac,* 309. This amounts to disregarding the many

other texts mentioned by Dion that clearly mention the excellence of pinot at this time. The best proof of it is the shipment to Bruges at the beginning of 1375 of six *queues* and one *poinçon* (about twenty-five hectoliters) of *"vin de pinot vermeil"* that the duke made in anticipation of his upcoming stay in the city. It is plain that the selection of fine plants occurred much earlier in Burgundy than in Bordeaux, and just as plain that this does not in any way diminish the excellence of the wines of Bordeaux from the end of the seventeenth century onward. Here we have a fine example of the convergence of critical animus against Roger Dion, whose bold hypotheses and utter outspokenness upset viticultural geographers in his own time, and continue to do so today.

16. Dion, *Histoire de la vigne et du vin en France,* 297.

17. Quoted by Bréjoux, *Les vins de Bourgogne,* 34. This work contains long excerpts from the charter of Philip the Bold.

18. Ibid., 298.

19. Dion, *Histoire de la vigne et du vin en France,* 298–99.

20. The admirable riesling planted on both sides of the Rhine in France and Germany is also an austere grape, producing a wine noted for its mineral elements and straightforward character. In the past some Catholic Alsatian growers used not to cultivate riesling, considering it "Protestant." I owe this detail to Gérard Boesch, a winemaker in Westhalten.

21. I thank Jean-Louis Tissier for the opportunity to taste the exotic Burgundy made from this grape, which reminds one a bit of the mondeuse of Savoy and even syrah.

22. Réjalot, "Le modèle viti-vinicole bordelais dans sa filière (1980–2003)," 254.

23. The best work on this succession of families remains Butel, *Les dynasties bordelaises de Colbert à Chaban.*

24. In this regard see the interesting catalogue accompanying the 1998 "Châteaux Bordeaux" exposition at the Centre Georges-Pompidou in Paris, edited by Jean Dethier.

25. In a pair of superb articles Philippe Roudié has analyzed the process by which the majority of wine-producing estates in Bordeaux were named "châteaus" in the nineteenth century, even when they contained no building that from near or far resembled a castle. Relying on a fascinating series of maps, he also explains the origin and distribution of the names of these manor houses. See Roudié, "Vous avez dit 'château'?" and "'Bel Air' ou 'Bellevue,' 'Latour' ou 'Beauséjour'?"

26. From an article in the May–June 2002 issue of *Senso,* quoted by Patrice de Beer, "Des odeurs dans tous les sens," *Le Monde* (13 July 2002), 11. I have no explanation for the image Veilletet gives of Yquem, apart perhaps from the autumnal mists of the Garonne Valley, which in that season may seem to resemble somewhat the Valois district north of Paris. [The songs and legends of this part of the Île-de-France, where Nerval spent his childhood, form the subject of part of *Les filles du feu* (1854).—Trans.] The other likenesses asserted by Veilletet are scarcely less tenuous: the Moueix family, which owns Château Pétrus and other properties in Pomerol, is originally from Corrèze; the château and park at Malle have the look of a Venetian villa in the Brenta Valley; and the facade of the cellars at Cos d'Estournel (there is no true château) is crowned by three Chinese-style turrets, and the main gate is adorned with coelacanths from the palace of the sultan of Zanzibar.

27. See Conan, "Micro-cuvées, macro-excellence"; also Flacelière, "Vins de garage." Prices for such wines are beginning to come down, however; see Panos Kakaviatos, "Garage Wines Face Troubled Times," *Decanter* (1 July 2005).

28. La Mondotte, for example, is a collection of plots that the commission had refused to include within the area of Château Canon-La-Gaffelière, a *grand cru* that sells for between €50 and €100 per bottle. The owner, Stephan von Neipperg, wagered that from this depreciated land he could bring forth a wine clearly superior to the *grand cru.* He would appear to have won his bet, if the taste of the wine's buyers can be trusted.

29. This prestigious and extensive domaine in the Côte de Beaune plays an essential role in determining the price of wines in Burgundy. Each year's production may be tasted very shortly after vinification, on the third Sunday in November of every year, when it is offered at auction for the benefit of the hospital in Beaune. The prices realized are based on the qualities of the vintage, and the region as a whole generally follows this indicator; see Moine, *Un quart de siècle de ventes de vins aux Hospices de Beaune.* It should be pointed out that the largest local merchants (such as Jacques Boisseaux, the managing director of Patriarche) are the first to bid, hoping to inflate the valuation of the vintage by removing lots early in the afternoon. It would be unfair, nonetheless, not to recognize their genuine affection for this unusual and distinctively Burgundian charitable institution. In 2000, the 140th wine sale took in a total of €5.3 million for 727 casks (each 228 liters). The average price was €9,331 per cask for white wines, €6,851 for reds, with top prices of €24,100 for a Batard-Montrachet,

cuvée Dames de Flandres, and €15,279 for a Mazis-Chambertin, *cuvée* Madeleine Collignon.

It should be noted, too, that the vineyard of the Hospices de Beaune is the only ecclesiastical domaine to have survived the French Revolution. The rest were confiscated by the state and sold off; some remained intact for a time under a single owner, as in the case of Clos de Vougeot until 1889. The other great domaines have been dismantled.

30. The contrast in size between properties in the two regions has consequences for their electoral geography. The villages of the "noble" wine area of the Côte d'Or, dominated by owner-growers, tend to vote for the right, while those of the Médoc, where farmworkers are a majority, vote for the left (even though the workers are well paid). By contrast, the city of Bordeaux votes for the right, whereas Dijon has recently tilted to the left.

31. Beeston, *Mes hommes du vin,* 167.

32. Some retailers apply this principle as well. I have myself been firmly advised by the sommelier of a famous restaurant in Burgundy against ordering a certain Comtes Lafon *premier cru* Meursault, though it appeared on the wine list, on the grounds that it was a very particular wine and not necessarily to everyone's taste. The reality is that such precious and very expensive bottles are reserved for the most important customers. "You see," he explained by way of further excuse, "we can only get one case a year." I did not have the presence of mind to save face by ordering a Bordeaux.

33. On this point the principal wine guides in France and abroad are in agreement.

34. By contrast, brands with flowery names are apt to both attract and delude poorly informed buyers. One trading house in Burgundy markets 135 brands; see *La Revue du Vin de France* (May 2001), 24.

35. The leading exponent of this practice is a large merchant in the Jura. It is instructive to look at the back of Cocks's and Féret's guide to the wines of Bordeaux to see which brands are flooding the large retail outlets. Most of them come from merchant houses that also own one or several excellent classed vineyards. In 2003, for example, in a widely placed advertisement, the owners of William Pitters, Bernard Magrez and his son Philippe, identified themselves as "owners of prestigious vineyards," and boasted, "The passion of our *grands crus* has inspired our Malesan." On Malesan, now marketed by the Castel Group, see Réjalot, "Le modèle viti-vinicole bordelais dans sa filière (1980–

2003)," 45, 80. The same practice is followed, of course, in the worlds of high fashion and gastronomy, whose profitability depends on lines of ready-to-wear clothes, accessories, and perfumes in the one case, and on the food-processing industry in the other.

36. See, for example, the report entitled "À vos caddies," *Gault-Millau* (September 2002), 162–74.

37. Quoted by Mathieu, "Beaune."

38. See the interview with Henri Tricot in *Le Quotidien de Paris* (29 November 1982).

39. "The New Burgundy," *Wine Tidings* 226 (2002): 6. Henri Jayer famously remarked in the late 1970s that whereas 80 percent of Burgundy was good at the outset, only 20 percent was good once the wine was bottled. Today 80 percent is good in bottle. This—as Clive Coates points out, emphasizing the importance of cellar work—is the real revolution.

40. The variability of wine from one year to another is a French—and, by extension, Western European—peculiarity that Anglo-Saxons have difficulty understanding. Jeffrey Wilkinson, president of Southcorp, the leading Australian wine producer (with 7,500 hectares and producing more than 200 million bottles per year), was quoted at Vinexpo 2003 as saying, "I respect the traditions of Bordeaux, but we have a very different approach to marketing. We do not change prices with each vintage. Our customers want prices to stay the same. They don't understand why we should be more expensive one year than another." See *Libération* (26 June 2003), 19.

41. Generally speaking, people from Bordeaux do not like being taken for southerners, for fear of being confused with characters out of Pagnol. As Paul Berthelot put it, "Mysticism . . . is foreign to the Bordelais, and the petulance of the southerner is obnoxious to him. He dreads nothing so much as being introduced as someone born and bred in the Midi. An uneducated accent in others amuses him; before long, it will be the monopoly of Toulouse and Marseilles" (*Herlot de Grandières, le roi des vignerons*, 87). Berthelot, himself from Bordeaux, went on to gently poke fun at his native city: "It is difficult for people in Bordeaux to accept that talent may not be [exercised only in] the family vineyard or [in] practicing an honorable trade. Art, poetry, letters, science should, in the eyes of certain Bordelais, be the prerogative of wealthy amateurs. The poet venerated by the city has always been Ausonius, not so much because he was tutor to the emperor and a provincial governor as because he owned a vine-

yard." Berthelot was also a great judge of wines; see Curnonsky, "L'Aquitaine gastronomique," 27.

42. In the case of the best *grand cru* vineyards, it is the owners who take the initiative by adroitly distributing the newly bottled vintage, in several phases, among their regular brokers, who generally do not question the offer. These rituals are well described by Ginestet, *Les Chartrons.*

43. In Rodier, *Le Clos de Vougeot,* 12.

44. See Laleuf, "Vin et sagesse chez Colette."

45. Quoted by Andrieu, *Le livre d'or du bourgogne,* 69.

46. See Demossier, *Hommes et vins.*

47. Ducasse, *Rencontres savoreuses,* 206.

48. J'suis l'négociant Yves Thomas
Le spécialiste du vin, pas du jaja.
Y a pas d'soleil sous la terre,
Drôl' de croisière.
Jamais j'm'ennuie, j'ai dans la tête
Le nom des vins que j'me répète. [Etc.]

49. The capital and the sales of Baron Philippe de Rothschild S.A. are seven to eight times greater than those of Moillard, but this is obviously not the only reason for the contrast between the two events.

50. On Anglomania in Bordeaux, see Butel, *Les dynasties bordelaises de Colbert à Chaban,* 20–24.

51. See Beeston, *Mes hommes du vin,* 100.

52. See, for example, Mauriac's treatment of Bordeaux in *Préséances;* also Doutrelant, "Snob comme le Médoc," in *Les bons vins et les autres,* 17–25, and Ginestet, *La bouillie bordelaise.*

53. Kauffmann, *Voyage à Bordeaux,* 129.

54. The family is not exclusively based in the Médoc, however; Éric de Rothschild has established himself at Château Rieussec in the Sauternais district and at Château l'Évangile in Pomerol.

55. The provincial atmosphere of Dijon in the 1930s is affectionately sketched by M. F. K. Fisher in *Long Ago in France.*

56. See Cobbold, "Vin des villes, vin des champs."

57. See Bériac, "Bordeaux le nez en l'air."

58. See Maby, "Paysage et imaginaire," and Pigeat, *Les paysages de la vigne.*

59. Jacques Néauport, who divides the French into two categories (pro-

Bordeaux and pro-Burgundy/Côtes-du-Rhône), argues that the whole north of France has now been conquered by the wines of the ancient province of Guyenne; see *Les tribulations d'un amateur de vin*, 11.

60. Roger Dion points out that in the Walloon region of Belgium a party where guests enjoy a bit of wine is still called a "réunion de Bourgogne." See *Histoire de la vigne et du vin en France*, 299.

61. Kauffmann, *Le Bordeaux retrouvé*, 124–26.

62. Quoted without source by Andrieu, *Le livre d'or du bourgogne*, 27. *Se non è vero, è bene trovato!*

63. See Aldred, "À la recherche du pain perdu," 48–49.

64. See Pitte, "Les espaces de la bonne chère à Paris à la fin du XVIIIe siècle."

65. See Garrier, *Histoire sociale et culturelle du vin*, 141–42.

66. See Aron, *Le mangeur du XIXe siècle*, 139–48.

67. Ibid., 144.

68. See the special issue ("La Gastronomie") of *Le Crapouillot* (July 1932), 29.

69. See Hulot, "Les caves de la République: La cave du Sénat."

70. See Hulot, "Les caves de la République: Le Quai d'Orsay."

71. See Mantoux, "Les caves de la République: Trésors cachés de la Mairie de Paris."

72. See Jégu, "Les caves de prestige: L'hôtel Le Bristol à Paris."

73. This usage does not seem to be very old. It is mentioned in the current edition of Larousse, but not in the 1874 edition of Littré.

74. *Burgundy* might describe a certain color of Kiwi shoe polish, for example. The Québecois seem to be totally unaware of the French usage of *bordeaux* in this context. I owe this information to Luc Bureau.

75. See Roudié, "'Bordeaux,' un modèle pour la viti-viniculture mondiale," 404.

76. See Bazin, *Paul Masson, le Français qui mit en bouteilles l'or de la Californie*.

77. See Huetz de Lemps, *Vignobles et vins d'Espagne*, 280.

78. See Enjalbert, *Un vignoble de qualité en Languedoc*. Mas de Daumas Gassac is indisputably an excellent *terroir*. The combination of a great deal of vine-growing and winemaking expertise with an equal amount of willingness to learn from experience explains Aimé Guibert's success. When the California winemaker Robert Mondavi sought to establish himself on another slope of Aniane covered with low trees and shrubs, Guibert led the virtuous ecological

campaign against the foreign invader, who stood accused of endangering the beautiful "natural" vegetation and of posing a threat to the *"grand cru."* On this affair, see Jones, "'Power in Place.'"

79. This quite acceptable wine is actually imported to France by CEF Anju Enterprises in Paris.

80. See Claisse, "L'oenologue des antipodes."

81. See Pitte, "Origine et géographie des formes de bouteilles de vin en France." In Burgundy, the *bourguignonne* consisted of a cylindrical section 14 to 15 centimeters long (5½ to 6 inches), with shoulders sloping at an angle of 140 or 150 degrees. In Bordeaux, the *bordelaise* extended 18 to 20 centimeters (7 to 8 inches) from the bottom to the base of the neck, the shoulders forming an angle of 110 to 120 degrees with the body of the bottle. No one knows why this latter bottle was called *frontignane;* see Roudié, "La mystérieuse bordelaise." It seems not to have any relation to the wine-producing town of Frontignan in Languedoc.

82. The bottles dating from 1787 that belonged to Thomas Jefferson, some of which are still in circulation, had a severely truncated upstanding conical shape with very sloping shoulders. But the *frontignane* or *bordelaise* bottle did not come into general use until the latter part of the nineteenth century. Curiously, Château Haut-Brion continues to put its wines in an old-style bottle, a slightly truncated cone with sloping shoulders.

83. Quoted by Cavignac, "Le vin dans les caves et les chais des négociants bordelais au XIXe siècle," 113.

84. See ibid., 115–16.

85. Sur le flacon qu'il tient toujours horizontal,
   Il présente aussitôt un flacon de cristal;
   L'oeil attentif, fixé sur le brilliant liquide,
   Sa main le fait couler tant qu'il paraît limpide.
   Si, de tartre ou de lie, un atome apparaît,
   Il s'arrète . . . le fond ne vaut pas un regret.
   C'est ainsi que toujours transparente et vermeille,
   La liqueur doit sortir d'une vieille bouteille.

From a poem originally published in 1849, "Les grands vins de Bordeaux," quoted in ibid., 114.

86. By the late nineteenth century it became possible to produce much finer glassware from crystal or lead than from ordinary glass. When the glass or crystal is thick, glasses can be fashioned only in the form of a wide-mouthed

cup or goblet. By tapering and blowing a bubble that is then cut off at the top, one obtains the tulip shape that is indispensable for appreciating the aromas of wines.

87. Grimod de la Reynière, *Manuel des amphytrions,* 228–29.

88. I am indebted for this information to M. Bachy, former head of Saint-Gobain, S.A.

89. I owe these details to M. Lo Cicero of GAI S.p.A, which manufactures bottling equipment near Alba in Piedmont, Italy. I thank Gianpaolo Dogliani for giving me a basic introduction to the technical aspects of bottling.

90. For the moment, no Alsatian viticulturalist seems to have followed suit.

91. Creignou, "Épaule à la bordelaise," 61.

92. Just the same, there are many horizontal labels in Bordeaux, among them that of Haut-Brion, which is well suited to the exceptional shape of the bottle.

93. See *Mouton Rothschild.* Contributions were solicited from all the great contemporary painters by Baron Philippe, and later by his daughter Philippine. In 1993, a problem arose: Balthus had drawn a little girl in what certain American guardians of public virtue judged to be a lascivious position. Bottles meant for export to the United States therefore carried expurgated labels without the drawing.

94. See Lampre, *Bordeaux par ses étiquettes,* and Bazin, *L'étiquette du vin en Bourgogne et Beaujolais.*

95. See Farnoux-Reynaud, *Vins de Bordeaux, vins de châteaux,* 138.

96. See, for example, the painting *The Marriage at Cana* (1563) by Veronese in the Louvre.

97. See *Le déjeuner d'huîtres* (1734) in the Musée Condée de Chantilly, and similar paintings by de Troy in the Musée Carnavalet in Paris.

98. Tempting though it is to suppose, the word "cup" [*coupe* in French] has nothing to do with the practice of diluting wine [*coupage*]. The Latin word from which it derives, *cupa,* denoted a large wooden vessel.

99. Diodorus Siculus, *Bibliotheca Historica,* 5.25–27.

100. Quoted by Querre, *Éloge de Michel de Montaigne prononcé à l'Académie des Gastronomes,* 18.

101. The addition of ice to wine goes back to remotest antiquity (see Planhol, *L'eau et neige*). Today this practice is condemned by all connoisseurs, but it has been replaced in the United States and certain Mediterranean countries by the refrigeration of white and rosé wines to very low temperatures. In Paris,

light red wines are increasingly served chilled or iced in the summer, with very harmful consequences for the wine's bouquet.

102. Thus the slogan of the Austrian glassmaker Georg Riedel, "To each wine its glass." See the article in the 21 November 2001 edition of *Le Monde*.

103. *Vins et vignobles de France*, 73.

104. This "ISO glass," as it is called after the name of its sponsoring body, the International Standards Organization, has been mandated by the INAO in France. See This, *Molecular Gastronomy*, 251–53.

105. Renvoisé, *Le monde du vin*, 221.

106. Juppé, "Le vin, la chance de Bordeaux," 34.

107. Michel de Montaigne, *Essays*, II: 2; see *The Complete Essays of Montaigne*, trans. Donald M. Frame (Stanford, Calif.: Stanford University Press, 1958), 248; quoted by Querre, *Éloge de Michel de Montaigne prononcé à l'Académie des Gastronomes*, 15.

108. In certain social circles in England wine is drunk after the meal, in sensible quantities, accompanied by cheeses.

109. Quoted by Farnoux-Reynaud, *Vins de Bordeaux, vins de châteaux*, 132.

110. Ibid., 131.

111. The irreplaceable Bernard Ginestet has written a moving account of these gatherings, *La mémoire des Oenarques*.

112. Thus the expression "Il a une trogne d'ivrogne" refers to someone who looks as though he has had too much to drink.—Trans.

113. Et puis que l'on s'étonne
     Qu'un fils de vigneron
     Vienne au monde environ
     Dix mois après l'automne!

Quoted by Royer, *Les vignerons*, 241.

114. These were probably *climats* of Pommard. There is one today called La Refène.

115. Ce joyeux enfant de septembre,
     Frère jumeau de nos raisins,
     Va faire plus loin que la Sambre
     Bien vendre et bien payer nos vins.
     En la Micande, en la Rufaine,
     Au rouge bord dites sans fin:
     Vive le Roi, vive la Reine,
     Vive Monseigneur le Dauphin! . . .

Sans parler ici du champagne
Prenne qui voudra pour sa part
La beaune, le nuits, le chassagne.
Pour moi, je m'en tiens au pommard.
De ce nectar bouteille pleine
Pour vos glous-glous dites sans fin:
Vive le Roi, vive la Reine,
Vive Monseigneur le Dauphin!

Quoted by Royer, *Les vignerons,* 243–44.

116. I thank Xavier de Planhol for drawing my attention to this difference in a private communication dated 19 February 2001.

117. Probably equal proportions of green beans and butter!

118. The absence of dessert may seem surprising. Cheese, though never mentioned on these menus, was always served as a matter of course.

119. This type of menu is common at banquets in Burgundy. In the course of the final dinner of the Rencontres Internationales Jules-Guyot, held on 20 March 1998 in Beaune, three large appetizers preceded a beef bourguignon, cheeses, and desserts. Six different wines were served apart from the crémant. At a wedding dinner in Chorey-lès-Beaune, held on 28 August 2004, two appetizers followed by a *trou bourguignon* of marc preceded the main course, cheeses, a layer cake, and an immense buffet of desserts. Seven wines were served.

120. In the old days it was three o'clock in the morning. See Cadilhac, "À la gloire du vin," 89.

121. Menu published in *Paris Match.*

122. See Berchoux, *La gastronomie.*

123. There were 250 exhibitors and 80,000 visitors the first year the fair was held, and 900 exhibitors and 500,000 visitors four years later, in 1925.

124. This list is taken from the 1935 *Guide gastronomique de la France.*

125. Having gone to Paris after the war, Raymond Oliver, son of the great Louis, bought the Grand Véfour du Palais-Royal and showcased the cuisine of the southwest with dishes such as *lamproie à la bordelaise* and *foie gras de canard* together with the wines of Bordeaux and Armagnac. The Oliver family's restaurant in Langon is now owned by Claude Darroze, whose niece, Hélène, went to Paris in 1999 with the same purpose and equal passion, opening her own restaurant on the rue d'Assas in Saint-Germain-des-Prés.

126. Coulon, *Le cuisinier médoquin,* 28.

127. It had been preceded by the creation in 1922, by Count Jules Lafon, of

the Paulée de Meursault, a banquet at which each grower shared his wines, with a literary work being composed in honor of the event each year. Today La Paulée is associated with the annual Hospice de Beaune wine auction, held on the third Sunday of November, and the dinner of the Confrérie du Tastevin the night before. Together these three events constitute "Les Trois Glorieuses."

128. See Boitouzet, *Les Chevaliers du Tastevin,* and Berthier and Sweeney, *Les confréries en Bourgogne.*

129. See Ginestet and Prigent, *Essai esthétique sur la présence des confréries du vin en pays bordelais,* 25–31.

130. *La pôchouse,* a kind of *murette* or sauce made with white wine and cream in which various fish from the Saône River are cooked, is the specialty of Verdun-sur-le-Doubs.

131. Already in the fifth century, Sidonius Apollinaris described the Burgundians as reeking of butter and onion! See Chapelot and Fossier, *Le village et la maison au Moyen Âge,* 23.

132. See Farnoux-Reynaud, *Vins de Bordeaux, vins de châteaux,* 135–36.

133. S'appuyer une bécasse
Sans l'égayer d'un Corton
Autant ronger la carcasse
D'une volaille en carton.

Quoted by Andrieu, *Le livre d'or du bourgogne,* 69.

134. Noah, for example, an American hybrid white grape variety with a foxy taste that was introduced in France at the time of the phylloxera epidemic, has been outlawed since the 1950s on account of a toxic aldehyde found in wines made from it that causes mental disturbances.

135. See Peynaud, *Oenologue dans le siècle,* 69.

136. This comment was made by the geographer Marie-Françoise Courel, president of the École Pratique des Hautes Études in Paris, during the course of a dinner held on 14 February 2002 at which Bordeaux was served. It cannot be considered an innocent remark, coming from a specialist in satellite imagery.

137. I owe this strong maxim to M. ———, an educated connoisseur of great Bordeaux wines. I leave it to him to identify himself, if he dares!

138. Quoted by Andrieu, *Le livre d'or du bourgogne,* 17.

139. This claim occurs in a doctoral thesis defended by Arbinet in 1652; quoted in ibid., 34.

140. From Roupnel's preface to Rodier, *Le Clos de Vougeot,* 26.

141. Roald Dahl, *My Uncle Oswald* (New York: Knopf, 1980), 40; quoted by Bazin, *La Romanée-Conti,* 143.

142. Vincenot, "Propos d'amour," 183–84.

143. This name may come from the popular old expression that a good wine has "got love."

144. Qui dit un bon vigneron
     Semble dire un bon luron,
     Un joyeux, un bon vivant,
     Tour à tour buvant,
     Tour à tour aimant,
     Du vin au sexe passant,
     Et dévôt à saint Vinçant [*sic*].

"Le réveil bourguignon" (7 February 1891); quoted by Royer, *Les vignerons,* 179.

145. Quoted by Bazin, "Le bordeaux, un sujet interdit à table."

146. Clos-Jouve, *Le promeneur lettré et gastronome en Bourgogne, de Dijon à Lyon,* 47; Lelong, *Le pain, le vin et le fromage,* 117.

147. Bazin, *La Romanée-Conti,* 157. [The expression "Couvent des Oiseaux" refers to fashionable private schools, parochial or other, that offer girls from good families a strict education.—Trans.]

148. Chablis, je voudrais qu'en tes armes
     Une croix d'honneur figurât,
     Car grâce à tes divines larmes
     L'on voit des héros dans tes gars,
     Puis en temps de paix
     Le jus de tes ceps
     Infuse suprême vaillance
     À tes vignerons
     Au nez rouge et rond
     L'envie de repeupler la France!

Quoted by Ginestet, *Chablis,* 187.

149. From the French edition, quoted in "Du côté de chez Inoué," *Le Nouvel Observateur* (26 February–6 March 1991).

150. In northern Europe, by contrast, many people are in the habit of drinking a great deal on an empty stomach, furtively on Saturday nights, in order to forget everything—even, the next morning, the fact that they had been drinking the night before.

151. Benjamin, *Le vin, lumière du coeur,* 56.

152. Juppé, "Le vin, la chance de Bordeaux."

153. In this same interview, Juppé confessed that he would bring with him to a desert island several cases of Bordeaux and one bottle of Romanée-Conti!

154. Yet in Burgundy full-bodied wines are said to have chewiness (*mâche*), whereas in Bordeaux they are said to have vigor (*sève*); see Bréjoux, *Les vins de Bourgogne,* 173.

155. Farnoux-Reynaud, *Vins de Bordeaux, vins de châteaux,* 33–34, 41.

156. Ibid., 41.

157. Farnoux-Reynaud, "Le vin de Bordeaux," 9.

158. See, in this connection, Rémy, *Mes grands bordeaux.* In his life as a diplomat, Pierre-Jean Rémy (since 1988 a member of the Académie Française) seems to have drunk only Bordeaux. They are in any case the only wines that left him with memories, particularly the ten cases that were given to him on the occasion of his fiftieth birthday by his former lovers. Can one imagine a similar book of reminiscence entitled *Mes grands bourgognes?* No, that would ring false.

159. Ibid., 10.

160. Quoted by Bardet, "Les érotomanes du vin," 44. This article, published in a popular magazine by a female author, is one of the most erotic pieces about wine to have appeared in recent years.

161. Curnonsky, "L'Aquitaine gastronomique," 28.

162. Malagar, the family estate in the Premières Côtes de Bordeaux, was the setting for Mauriac's novel *La chair et le sang* (1919), among other works.—Trans.

163. See Jouanna and Villard, eds., *Vin et santé en Grèce ancienne.*

164. See Perdue, *Le paradoxe français.*

165. See Maury, *Soignez-vous par le vin;* also Ky et al., *Les vertus thérapeutiques du bordeaux.* The latter work is more detailed in its medical aspect, but talks only in a very general way about oenological matters. One learns, in particular, that the wines of Bordeaux can be used for therapeutic purposes in baths, through intravenous injection, or in the form of rectal suppositories, but that they are still administered orally in most cases; see page 241. Nothing comparable has yet been written by physicians or friends of Burgundy.

166. Juppé, "Le vin, la chance de Bordeaux," 34.

167. Quoted by Montandon, "Les fantastiques bouteilles d'un buveur enthousiaste," 62–63.

168. See Schwartz, *Le vin et sa musique.*

169. Cohen, "Le vin français inspire ma musique."

170. See Rothschild, *Le culte de vin.* In this regard one should note the regrettable absence of a true national museum of wine in France. Interesting regional museums do exist, such as the one at Beaune established through the efforts of Georges-Henri Rivière and Roger Duchet, a former mayor of Beaune. Nor does there exist a major museum of food, cooking, and gastronomy.

171. The photographic album by Biéville and Godeaut, *Châteaux, demeures de charme dans le vignoble bordelais,* gives a superb glimpse of these collections.

172. See my earlier discussion in chapter 2 of the BIVB advertising campaign, "Land blessed by the gods."

173. See *Réforme* 2910 (18–24 January 2001), 12; and *Réforme* 2912 (1–7 February 2001), 6.

174. René Pijassou wrote me a stern letter on 13 March 2001. "The analysis . . . is complete nonsense," he said, adding that when he mentioned the offending article to two managing directors of *premiers grands crus classés* in the Médoc, "They roared with laughter. What a fine response, don't you think?" Michel Réjalot, who was then preparing his doctoral thesis, which addresses this question in both a very detailed and biased way, wrote me on 23 March 2001: "My sense of the matter is so different from yours that I am liable to quickly lose my temper and argue in a way that might seem to you quite 'aggressive.'" No, not at all—these fits of anger are extremely revealing.

175. See Espagne, *Bordeaux-Baltique,* and Réjalot, "Le modèle viti-vinicole bordelais dans sa filière (1980–2003)," 262–63. Réjalot develops a long and remarkable argument in this connection, but while he discusses the leading firms and major figures of the wine trade, he does not say a word about wine and drinking habits, which is a pity.

176. See Butel, *Les dynasties bordelaises de Colbert à Chaban,* 45.

177. Ibid., 73.

178. See Roudié, "Le vignoble au présent," 197–202.

179. It is true that evening dress is required at the dinners of the Confrérie des Chevaliers du Tastevin, but this is obviously a way of impressing foreign guests while at the same time cleverly disarming them by means of ceremonies that have an entirely different tone.

180. Dumay, *Guide du vin,* 192.

181. See Réjalot, "Le modèle viti-vinicole bordelais dans sa filière (1980–2003)," 338–42. The author's conviction that the Bordeaux château is

descended from the Roman villa, a profoundly Latin and Catholic structure, is therefore contradicted by his own showing that the frequent changes of ownership in the Bordelais are a product of Protestant culture. In most cases Protestant influence has prevailed over Catholic tradition, and it is rather hard to understand why pointing out this fact annoys Michel Réjalot, since it harms neither the identity nor the prosperity of the Bordeaux region, nor the happiness of living on the banks of its two rivers or between them.

182. Ibid., 259.

183. Doutrelant, *Les bons vins et les autres,* 15.

184. This point was made by Jacques Schneider in an interview with Guillemette de Sarigné in the 16 December 2000 issue of *Le Figaro Madame.*

185. From Musset's *La coupe et les lèvres;* quoted by Bernet, *Anthologie des poètes du vin,* 97.

186. Some of these publications have now begun to appear in French as well.

187. By way of example, a bottle of Château Branaire purchased in 1995 for 115 francs (€17.55) was worth €50 in 2001—an average annual increase in value of 18.9 percent. See Bogaty, "Le vin, un placement de connoisseurs," 95.

188. Quoted by Capatti and Montanari, *La cuisine italienne,* 192.

189. Originally published in English in 1958, simultaneously with the Danish edition, as one of five tales in *Anecdotes of Destiny.*—Trans.

190. See Roudié, "'Bel Air' ou 'Bellevue,' 'Latour' ou 'Beauséjour'?" 72.

191. Though these links may now seem merely a piece of folklore, one would be wrong to neglect them or to treat them with cool detachment, as Michel Réjalot does; see "Le modèle viti-vinicole bordelais dans sa filière (1980–2003)," 28.

192. See Dion, *Histoire de la vigne et du vin en France,* 291–94.

193. Quoted by Andrieu, *Le livre d'or du bourgogne,* 21.

194. Quoted in ibid., 23.

195. Quoted in ibid., 27.

196. See Holt, "Wine, Community and Reformation in Sixteenth-Century Burgundy." I thank Denis Crouzet for having drawn my attention to this article.

197. See ibid., 86.

198. See ibid., 91.

199. Pirotte, *Autres arpents,* 31. I am indebted to Jean-Louis Tissier for this reference.

200. See Bazin and Mignotte, *Pour le meilleur et pour le kir.*

201. Quoted by Clos-Jouve, *Le promeneur lettré et gastronome en Bourgogne, de Dijon à Lyon,* 29.

202. See *La Saint-Vincent tournante,* 14–16.

203. The French word *spirituels* here also carries the sense of "witty."—Trans.

204. Krau, *Le vin dans la Bible.* The sermon concluded with a courageous recognition of the dangers that threatened Europe on the eve of the Second World War. Later made canon of Dijon, Édouard Krau died in 1954, a few days before the feast of Saint Vincent.

CONCLUSION

1. See Millau, "Les olympiades du vin." The only bias in the tasting was that no Bordeaux *premier grand cru classé* was chosen for consideration. In the view of Christian Millau and Jo Gryn, "this decision was the most honest one possible, with respect to the foreign competitors."

2. Millau's remark, published in a magazine that depends in large measure on advertising, is evidence also of an outspokenness that is much to be praised. The same thing may be said about *La Revue du Vin de France.*

3. See Cobbold, *Les plus grands crus du monde.*

BIBLIOGRAPHY

Abric, Loïc. "Stratégie d'achat des vins de la vallée du Rhône par les négociants beaunois." *Annales de Bourgogne* 73 (2001): 253–60.

Alaux, Jean-Pierre, and Noël Balen. *Cauchemar dans les Côtes de Nuits.* Paris: Fayard, 2004.

Aldred, Jonathan. "À la recherche du pain perdu." *Emmanuel College Magazine* (Cambridge) 82 (1999–2000): 44–52.

Ambrosi, Hans, et al. *Guide des cépages.* Paris: Éditions Eugen Ulmer, 1997. Original German edition, 1994.

Andrieu, Pierre. *Le livre d'or du bourgogne.* Paris: Rôtisserie de la reine Pédauque, n.d.

Aron, Jean-Paul. *Le mangeur du XIXe siècle.* Lausanne: Ex Libris, 1974.

Atlas de Cîteaux (1680–1730). Précy-sous-Thil: Éditions de l'Armonçon, 1998.

Baby, Nicolas. "L'étalon de Saint-Émilion." *L'Amateur de Bordeaux* 71 (December 2000): 52–55.

Bardet, Marie. "Les érotomanes du vin." *Gault-Millau* 356 (September 2002): 42–48.

Barton, Anthony, and Claude Petit-Castelli. *La saga des Barton.* Levallois: Manya, 1991.

Basse, Martin. *Le Rhône, la Saône et le Beaujolais.* Lyon: Consortium générale de publicité de Lyon, n.d.

Baudel, José. *Le vin de Cahors.* Parnac: Les Côtes d'Olt, 1987.

Bazin, Jean-François. "Le vignoble des Hautes-Côtes de Nuits et de Beaune: Histoire d'une renaissance." *Les Cahiers de Vergy* 6 (1973).

———. *Le Clos de Vougeot.* Paris: Jacques Legrand, 1987.

———. *Montrachet.* Paris: Jacques Legrand, 1988.

———. *Chambertin: La Côte de Nuits de Dijon à Chambolle-Musigny.* Paris: Jacques Legrand, 1991.

———. "Le bordeaux, un sujet interdit à table." *L'Amateur de Bordeaux: Spécial Bordeaux Bourgogne* 34 (March 1992): 68–75.

———. *La Romanée-Conti: La Côtes de Nuits de Vosne-Romanée à Corgoloin.* Bassillac: Jacques Legrand, 1994.

———. *Histoire du vin de Bourgogne.* Paris: Éditions Jean-Paul Gisserot, 2002.

———. *Paul Masson, le Français qui mit en bouteilles l'or de la Californie.* Saint-Cyr-sur-Loire: Alain Suton, 2002.

———. *Le vin bio, mythe ou réalité?* Paris: Hachette, 2003.

———. *L'étiquette du vin en Bourgogne et Beaujolais: Histoire et illustration.* Mâcon: JPM Éditions, 2003.

Bazin, Jean-François, and Alain Mignotte. *Pour le meilleur et pour le kir: Le roman d'un mot-culte.* Mâcon: JPM, 2002.

Beauroy, Jacques. "Les facteurs historiques du développement du vin de qualité en Bordelais aux XVIIe et XVIIIe siècles." *Études Champenoises* 6 (1988): 111–20.

Beck, Patrice. "Les clos du prince: Recherches sur les établissements viti-vinicoles ducaux." *Annales de Bourgogne* 73 (2001): 103–16.

Beer, Patrice de. "Des odeurs dans tous les sens." *Le Monde* (13 July 2002): 11.

Beeston, Fiona. *Mes hommes du vin.* Paris: Plon, 1989.

Benjamin, René. *Le vin, lumière du coeur.* Paris: Les Amis de l'Originale, 1948.

Berchoux, Joseph. *La gastronomie ou l'homme des champs à table.* Reprint of 1801 edition, with preface by Jean-Robert Pitte. Grenoble: Glénat, 1989.

Bériac, Jean-Pierre. "Bordeaux le nez en l'air." *L'Amateur de Bordeaux* 58 (March 1998): 60–68.

Bernet, Henri. *Anthologie des poètes du vin.* Lyon: IAC Éditions, 1944.

Berque, Augustin. *Le sens de l'espace au Japon: Vivre, penser, bâtir.* Paris: Éditions Arguments, 2004.

Berthault, Frédéric. *Aux origines du vignoble bordelais: Il y a 2000 ans, le vin à Bordeaux.* Bordeaux: Féret, 2000.

Berthelot, Paul. *Herlot de Grandières, le roi des vignerons: Moeurs bordelaises.* Paris: Jules Tallandier, 1929.

Berthier, Marie-Thérèse, and John-Thomas Sweeney. *Les confréries en Bourgogne: Histoire-Vins-Gastronomie.* Besançon: La Manufacture, 1992.

Bettane, Michel. "Éloge de l'industrie." *La Revue du Vin de France* (December 2001–January 2002): 84.

———. "Vin de nez, vin de niais." *La Revue du Vin de France* (May 2002): 68.

Bettane, Michel, and Thierry Desseauve. *Classement des meilleures vins de France 2003.* Paris: Éditions de la Revue du Vin de France, 2002.

Biéville, Diane de, and Jean-Pierre Godeaut. *Châteaux, demeures de charme dans le vignoble bordelais.* Bordeaux: Aubéron, 1994.

Bogaty, Thierry. "Le vin, un placement de connoisseurs." *Le Nouvel Économiste* (26 July 2001): 94–99.

Boidron, Bruno, and Marc-Henry Lemay. *Bordeaux: Vins et négoce.* Bordeaux: Féret, 2000.

———. *Bordeaux et ses vins.* Bordeaux: Féret, 2001.

Boitouzet, Lucien. *Les Chevaliers du Tastevin: Histoire de la confrérie.* Nuits-Saint-Georges: Société bourguignonne de propagande et éditions, 1984.

Bourguignon, Claude. *Le sol, la terre et les champs.* Paris: Sang de la Terre, 1989.

Bratberg, Jean-Moïse. "Les fortunes du Bordelais flambent." *Capital* (December 2000): 98–99.

Bréjoux, Pierre. *Les vins de Bourgogne.* Paris: L. Larmat, 1967.

Brillat-Savarin, Jean-Anthelme. *The Physiology of Taste, or, Meditations on Transcendental Gastronomy.* Trans. M. F. K. Fisher. New York: Heritage Press, 1949. First published in Paris, 2 vols., in 1825.

Burtschy, Bernard, and Henri Jayer. *Gault-Millau* 356 (September 2002): 52–53.

Butel, Paul. *Les dynasties bordelaises de Colbert à Chaban.* Paris: Perrin, 1991.

Butel, Paul, and Jean-Pierre Poussou. *La vie quotidienne à Bordeaux au XVIIIe siècle.* Paris: Hachette, 1980.

Cadilhac, Paul-Émile. "À la gloire du vin: Fêtes en Bourgogne." *Cuisine et vins de France* (3 March 1948): 87–90.

Capatti, Alberto, and Massimo Montanari. *La cuisine italienne: Histoire d'une culture.* Paris: Seuil, 2002.

Cavignac, Jean. "Le vin dans les caves et les chais des négociants bordelais au XIXe siècle." In *Les boissons: Production et consommation aux XIXe et XXe siècles: Actes du 106e Congrès national des sociétés savantes. Perpignan, 1981, Histoire moderne et contemporaine,* 1: 103–20. Paris: CTHS, 1984.

Cerveau, Marie-Pierre. "Le commerce des vins de Bourgogne: Étude géographique." Ph.D. diss., Université de Paris–Sorbonne (Paris IV), 1996.

——. "Les égarements de la région viticole bourguignonne ou les tribulations d'un bateau ivre." *Annales de géographie* 614/615 (July–October 2000): 444–58.

Chapelot, Jean, and Robert Fossier. *Le village et la maison au moyen âge.* Paris: Hachette, 1980.

Chapuis, Claude. *Corton.* Bassillac: Jacques Legrand, 1992.

Chapuis, Louis. *Vigneron en Bourgogne.* Paris: Robert Laffont, 1980.

Chauvet, Jules. *Le vin en question.* Paris: Jean-Paul Rocher, 1998.

Cherruau, Pierre. "Un grand cru du Médoc est soupçonné de tromperie sur la qualité." *Le Monde* (2 June 1998): 8.

Claisse, Guy. *Entre-Deux-Mers.* Paris: Jacques Legrand, 1991.

——. "L'oenologue des antipodes." *L'Amateur de Bordeaux* 66 (1999): 38–40.

Claval, Paul. *Atlas et géographie de la Haute-Bourgogne et de la Franche-Comté.* Paris: Flammarion, 1978.

Clos-Jouve, Henri. *Le promeneur lettré et gastronome en Bourgogne, de Dijon à Lyon.* Paris: Amiot-Dumont, 1951.

Coates, Clive. *Grands Vins: The Finest Châteaux of Bordeaux and Their Wines.* Berkeley and Los Angeles: University of California Press, 1995.

Cobbold, David. *Les plus grands crus du monde.* Paris: Hatier, 1996.

——. "Vin des villes, vin des champs." *L'Amateur de Bordeaux* 58 (March 1998): 70–73.

Cohen, Leonard. "Le vin français inspire ma musique." *Le Figaro Magazine* (29 September 2001): 91.

Conan, Éric. "Micro-cuvées, macro-excellence." *L'Express* (16 March 2000): 30–32.

Contour, Alfred. *Le cuisinier bourguignon.* Beaune: Lambert, 1896.

Cottereau, Jean. "Côtes de Castillon: Oublier Saint-Émilion." *L'Amateur de Bordeaux* 34 (March 1992): 18–25.

Coulon, Christian. *Le cuisinier médoquin.* Bordeaux: Confluences, 2000.

Coulon, Marcel. *Toute la muse de Ponchon.* Paris: Éditions de la Tournelle-Laboratoires pharmaceutiques Corbière, 1938.

Courrian, Philippe, and Michel Creignou. *Vigneron du Médoc.* Paris: Payot et Rivages, 1996.

Creignou, Michel. "Épaule à la bordelaise." *L'Amateur de Bordeaux* 66 (December 1999): 60–61.

Curnonsky. "L'Aquitaine gastronomique." *Le Crapouillot* (July 1932): 25–28.

———. "De la Bourgogne gastronomique." *Cuisines et vins de France* 3 (March 1948): 71.

Demossier, Marion. *Hommes et vins: Une anthropologie du vignoble bourguignon.* Dijon: Éditions Universitaires de Dijon, 1999.

Dethier, Jean, ed. *Châteaux Bordeaux.* Paris: Centre Georges-Pompidou, 1988.

Dinesen, Isak. *Anecdotes of Destiny.* London: M. Joseph, 1958.

Dion, Roger. "Querelle des anciens et modernes sur les facteurs de la qualité du vin." *Annales de Géographie* 61 (November–December 1952). Reprinted in Dion, *Le paysage et la vigne,* 205–26.

———. *Histoire de la vigne et du vin en France des origines au XIXe siècle.* Paris: Flammarion, 1977; first published privately in 1959.

———. *Le paysage et la vigne: Essais de géographie historique.* Paris: Payot, 1990.

Doutrelant, Pierre-Marie. *Les bons vins et les autres.* Paris: Seuil, 1984.

Duboeuf, Georges, and Henri Elwing. *Beaujolais, vin du citoyen.* Paris: J.-C. Lattès, 1989.

Dubreucq, Alain. "La vigne et la viticulture dans la loi des Burgondes." In "Vins, vignes et vignerons en Bourgogne du Moyen Âge à l'époque contemporaine," special issue of *Annales de Bourgogne* 73 (2001): 39–55.

Ducasse, Alain. *Rencontres savoureuses.* Paris: Plon, 1999.

Dumay, Raymond. *Guide du vin.* Paris: Livre de Poche, 1971.

Enjalbert, Henri. *Les pays aquitains, le modelé et les sols.* Bordeaux: Bière, 1960.

———. *Histoire de la vigne et du vin: L'avènement de la qualité.* Paris: Bordas, 1975.

———. *Les grands vins de Saint-Émilion, Pomerol et Fronsac.* Paris: Bardi, 1983.

———. *Un vignoble de qualité en Languedoc: Mas de Daumas Gassac.* Clermont l'Hérault: Imprimerie Chalaguier, 1985.

Espagne, Michel. *Bordeaux-Baltique: La présence culturelle allemande à Bordeaux aux XVIIIe et XIXe siècles.* Paris: CNRS Éditions, 1991.

Fanet, Jacques. *Les terroirs du vin.* Paris: Hachette, 2001.

Farnoux-Reynaud, Lucien. "Le vin de Bordeaux." *Le Crapouillot* (August 1931): 9–12.

———. *Vins de Bordeaux, vins de châteaux.* Lyon and Paris: IAC, 1950.

Feuillat, Michel. "Ultimes mystères du terroir bourguignon." *L'Amateur de Bordeaux* 34 (March 1992): 76–77.

———. "La recherche scientifique est-elle susceptible de faire progresser notre compréhension de l'influence du terroir sur la typicité des vins de chardonnay et de pinot noir?" In *Les Terroirs du chardonnay et du pinot noir: Rencontres internationales Jules-Gayot,* 13–16. Beaune: Institut Jules Guyot, 1998.

Fischler, Claude. *Du vin.* Paris: Odile Jacob, 1999.

Fisher, M. F. K. *Long Ago in France: The Years in Dijon.* New York: Prentice Hall Press, 1991.

Flacelière, Christian. "Vins de garage: La F1 de la vigne." *Le Figaro* (2–3 September 2000).

———. "Il faut découvrir les vins de Fronton." *Le Figaro Magazine* (29 March 2003): 97.

Flaubert, Gustave. *Dictionnaire des idées reçues.* Paris: Mille et une nuits, 1994; first published in 1911.

Gadille, Rolande. *Le vignoble de Bourgogne: Fondements physiques et humains d'une viticulture de haute qualité.* Paris: Les Belles Lettres, 1967.

Gargiulo, Ángel A. "Quality and Quantity: Are They Comparable?" *Journal of Wine Research* 3 (1991): 161–81.

Garrier, Gilbert. *Phylloxera: Une guerre de trente ans, 1870–1900.* Paris: Albin Michel, 1989.

———. *Histoire sociale et culturelle du vin.* Paris: Larousse-Bordas, 1998.

———. *L'étonnante histoire du beaujolais nouveau.* Paris: Larousse, 2002.

Gaudillère, Thierry. "La grande rue: Naissance d'un grand cru." *Bourgogne Aujourd'hui* 5 (August–September 1995): 37.

Gauthier, Émile, and Martine Joly. "Vignoble et viticulture dans le centre-est de la Gaule au 1er siècle apr. J.-C." In *Actualité de la recherche en histoire et archéologie agraires: Actes du colloque international AGER V, sept. 2000,* 191–208. Besançon: Presses Universitaires Franc-Comtoises, 2003.

George, Pierre. *La région du bas-Rhône.* Paris: J.-B. Ballière, 1935.

Gilbank, Gérald-Jack. *Les vignobles de qualité du sud-est du Bassin parisien, évolution économique et sociale: Chablis, Pouilly-sur-Loire, Sancerre, Quincy, Reuilly, Menetou-Salon, Irancy, Saint-Bris.* Privately published in Paris, 1981.

Gillet, Philippe. *Par mets et par vins: Voyages et gastronomie en Europe (16e–18e siècle).* Paris: Payot, 1985.

Ginestet, Bernard. *La bouillie bordelaise.* Paris: Flammarion, 1975.

———. *Pauillac.* Paris: Jacques Legrand et Nathan, 1983.

———. *Côtes de Bourg.* Paris: Jacques Legrand et Nathan, 1984.

———. *Margaux.* Paris: Jacques Legrand et Nathan, 1984.

———. *Saint-Julien.* Paris: Jacques Legrand et Nathan, 1984.

————. *Saint-Estèphe.* Paris: Jacques Legrand et Nathan, 1985.

————. *Chablis.* Paris: Jacques Legrand et Nathan, 1986.

————. *Barsac Sauternes.* Paris: Jacques Legrand et Nathan, 1987.

————. *Bordeaux supérieur.* Paris: Jacques Legrand et Nathan, 1988.

————. *Médoc.* Paris: Jacques Legrand, 1989.

————. *Côtes de Blaye.* Paris: Jacques Legrand, 1990.

————. *Les Chartrons: Édouard Minton, courtier bordelais.* Paris: Acropole, 1991.

————. *Fronsac, Canon-Fronsac.* Bassillac: Jacques Legrand, 1994.

————. *Thomas Jefferson à Bordeaux et dans quelques autres vignes d'Europe.* Bordeaux: Mollat, 1996.

————. *Pomerol.* Bassillac: Jacques Legrand, 1996.

————. *La mémoire des Oenarques.* Bordeaux: Mollat, 1998.

Ginestet, Bernard, and Claude Prigent. *Essai esthétique sur la présence des confréries du vin en pays bordelais à la fin du IIe millénaire.* Bordeaux: Arts Graphiques d'Aquitaine, 1993.

Girard, René. *Les origines de la culture.* Paris: Desclée de Brouwer, 2004.

Grimod de la Reynière, Balthazar. *Manuel des amphytrions.* Paris: A.-M. Métailié, 1983. First published in 1808.

Grivot, Françoise. *Le commerce des vins de Bourgogne.* Paris: Sabri, 1964.

Guichard, François. "Le dit et le non-dit du langage des étiquettes." *Annales de géographie* 614/615 (July–October 2000): 364–80.

Guide gastronomique de la France. Paris: EDNA Nicoll, 1935.

Guyotjeannin, Olivier. *Salimbene de Adam: Un chroniqueur franciscain.* Tournai: Brepols, 1995.

Haziot, David. *Le vin de la liberté.* Paris: Robert Laffont, 2000.

Higounet, Charles, ed. *La seigneurie et le vignoble de Château Latour: Histoire d'un grand cru du Médoc (XIVe–XXe siècle).* 2 vols. Bordeaux: Fédération historique du Sud-Ouest, 1974.

Hinnewinkel, Jean-Claude. "Appellations et terroirs en Bordelais." *Travaux du Laboratoire de géographie physique appliquée* 17 (February 1999): 9–24.

Holt, Mark P. "Wine, Community and Reformation in Sixteenth-Century Burgundy." *Past & Present* 138 (February 1993): 58–93

Huetz de Lemps, Alain. *Vignobles et vins d'Espagne.* Bordeaux: Presses Universitaires de Bordeaux, 1993.

Huetz de Lemps, Christian. *Géographie du commerce de Bordeaux à la fin du règne de Louis XIV.* Paris: Mouton, 1975.

Hulot, Mathilde. "Les caves de la République: La cave du Sénat." *La Revue du Vin de France* (December 2000–January 2001): 26–29.

———. "Les caves de la République. Le Quai d'Orsay: Sa cave somptueuse est la plus belle ambassade." *La Revue du Vin de France* (December 2000–January 2001): 44–47.

Jégu, Pierrick. "Les caves de prestige: L'hôtel Le Bristol à Paris." *La Revue du Vin de France* (May 2001): 112–15.

Johnson, Hugh. *The Story of Wine.* London: Mitchell Beazley, 1989.

———. "Parkérisés!" *Slow* (October–November 1999): 14–15.

Joly, Nicolas. *Le vin du ciel à terre: La viticulture en biodynamie.* Paris: Sang de la Terre, 2003.

Jones, Alun. "'Power in Place': Viticultural Spatialities of Globalization and Community Empowerment in the Languedoc." *Transactions of the Institute of British Geographers* 3 (September 2003): 367–82.

Jouanna, Jacques, and Laurence Villard, eds. *Vin et santé en Grèce ancienne.* Supplement to *Bulletin de correspondance hellénique* 40 (2002).

Juppé, Alain. "Le vin, la chance de Bordeaux." Interview by Michel Guillard in *L'Amateur de Bordeaux* 58 (March 1998): 34–37.

Kaikō, Takeshi. *Romanée-Conti 1935.* Arles: Philippe Picquier, 1993.

Kakaviatos, Panos. "Garage Wines Face Troubled Times." *Decanter* (1 July 2005).

Kauffmann, Jean-Paul. *Le Bordeaux retrouvé.* Privately printed and circulated, 1989.

———. *Voyage à Bordeaux.* Paris: Caisse des dépôts et consignations, 1989.

Krau, Édouard. *Le vin dans la Bible: Sermon prononcé en l'église de Vosne-Romanée le 28 janvier 1939 à l'occasion de la fête de Saint Vincent.* Dijon: L. Venot, 1939.

Ky, Tran, François Drouard, and Jean-Michel Guilbert. *Les vertus thérapeutiques du bordeaux: Histoire naturelle et culturelle, diététiques, biologie.* Paris: Artulen, 1991.

Lachiver, Marcel. *Vins, vignes, vignerons: Histoire du vignoble français.* Paris: Fayard, 1988.

Laleuf, Geneviève. "Vin et sagesse chez Colette." In *Les Boissons: Production et consommation aux XIXe et XXe siècles. Actes du 106e Congrès national des sociétés savantes, Perpignan 1981, Histoire moderne et contemporaine,* 1: 213–32. Paris: CTHS Éditions, 1984.

Lampre, Caroline. *Bordeaux par ses étiquettes.* Paris: Herscher, 2000.

Lanversin, Jacques de. "Lettre d'un vigneron iconoclaste." *La Revue du Vin de France* (November 1993): 8.

Laplanche, Jean. "Oui, nous sommes des culs-terreux: Entretien avec Jean-Paul Kauffmann." Special Bordeaux-Burgundy issue of *L'Amateur de Bordeaux* (March 1992): 42–52.

Larmat, Louis. *Atlas de la France vinicole: Les vins de Bordeaux.* Paris: Louis Larmat, 1949.

Latrive, Florent. "Malesan, appellation d'origine marketing: Un bordeaux fabriqué 'pour plaire au plus grand nombre.'" *Libération* (2 June 2002): 24–25.

Laurent, Robert. *Les vignerons de la Côte d'Or au XIXe siècle.* 2 vols. Paris: Les Belles Lettres, 1958.

Lawton, Hugues, and Jean Miailhe. *Conversations et souvenirs autour du vin de Bordeaux.* Bordeaux: Confluences, 1999.

Lebeau, Frère Marcel. *Essai sur les vignes de Cîteaux des origines à 1789.* Dijon: Centre Régional de Documentation Pédagogique, 1986.

Légasse, Périco. "Y a-t-il encore du raisin dans le vin français?" *Marianne* (22–28 June 1998): 30–33.

Léglise, Max. *Une initiation à la dégustation des grands vins.* 2nd ed. Marseille: Jeanne Laffite, 1984.

Legouy, François. "La renaissance du vignoble des Hautes-Côtes de Beaune et des Hautes-Côtes de Nuits." *Annales de géographie* 614/615 (July–October 2000): 459–72.

———. "La renaissance du vignoble des Hautes-Côtes de Beaune et des Hautes-Côtes de Nuits." Ph.D. diss., Université de Paris–Sorbonne (Paris IV), 2002.

Lelong, Maurice. *Le pain, le vin et le fromage.* Les Hautes Plaines de Mane: Robert Morel, 1972.

Lichine, Alexis. *Encyclopédie des vins et des alcools de tous les pays.* Paris: Robert Laffont, 1998.

Luginbuhl, Yves. "La 'montagne' un paysage de liberté pour le vignoble de Bourgogne." *L'Espace Géographique* 1 (1984): 13–22.

Lur-Saluces, Alexandre de. *La Morale d'Yquem: Entretien avec Jean-Paul Kauffmann.* Paris: Grasset, and Bordeaux: Mollat, 1999.

Lutin, Aude. *Châteauneuf-du-Pape: Son terroir, sa dégustation.* Paris: Flammarion, 2001.

Lynch, Kermit. *Mes aventures dans le vignoble de France: Un américain sachant cracher.* Paris: Jacques Legrand, 1990.

Maby, Jacques. "Paysage et imaginaire: L'exploitation de nouvelles valeurs ajoutées dans les terroirs viticoles." *Annales de Géographie* 624 (2002): 198–211.

Mantoux, Thierry. "Les caves de la République: Trésors cachés de la Mairie de Paris." *La Revue du Vin de France* (February 2001): 198–211.

Mathieu, Gilles. "Beaune: 2,000 vignerons inquiets pour leur avenir." *Le Bien Public* (5 July 2002): 5.

Mauriac, François. *Préséances.* Paris: Flammarion, 1962.

Maury, E. A. *Soignez-vous par le vin.* Paris: Jean-Pierre Delarge, 1974.

McCoy, Elin. *The Emperor of Wine: The Rise of Robert M. Parker, Jr. and the Reign of American Taste.* New York: Ecco, 2005.

Ménard, Philippe. "Le vin de Chablis dans la littérature médiévale." In *L'histoire littéraire: Ses méthodes et ses résultats. Mélanges offertes à Madeleine Berthaud,* ed. Luc Fraisse, 405–14. Geneva: Droz, 2001.

Millau, Christian. "Les olympiades du vin." *Gault-Millau* 214 (February 1987): 68–75.

Moine, Henri. *Un quart de siècle de ventes de vins aux Hospices de Beaune.* Péronnas: Éditions de la Tour Gile, 1997.

Montandon, Alain. "Les fantastiques bouteilles d'un buveur enthousiaste: Hoffmann et le vin." In *La correspondance du vin,* 51–70. Paris: Guitardes, 1981.

Mouton Rothschild: L'art et l'étiquette. Privately published by Baron Philippe de Rothschild S.A., 1995.

Néauport, Jacques. *Réflexions d'un amateur de vin.* Paris: Jean-Paul Rocher, 1996.

———. *Les tribulations d'un amateur de vin.* Lormont: La Presqu'île, 1998.

Olney, Richard. *Yquem.* Paris: Flammarion, 1985.

———. *Romanée-Conti.* Paris: Flammarion, 1991.

Orizet, Louis, and Jean Orizet. *Les cent plus beaux textes sur le vin.* Paris: Le Cherche Midi, 1984.

Parker, Robert. *Guide Parker des vins de France.* Paris: Solar, 2001.

Perdue, Lewis. *Le paradoxe français.* Avignon: Barthélemy, 1995.

Peynaud, Émile. *Le goût du vin.* Paris: Dunod, 1980.

———. *Oenologue dans le siècle: Entretiens avec Michel Guillard.* Paris: La Table Ronde, 1995.

———. *Le vin et les jours.* 2nd ed. Paris: Payot, 1996.

Pidoux, Jean-Pierre. "Champlitte, une 'petite Bourgogne.'" *Viti* (February 1992): 18–19.

Pigeat, Jean-Paul. *Les paysages de la vigne.* Paris: Solar, 2000.

Pijassou, René. *Un grand vignoble de qualité: Le Médoc.* 2 vols. Paris: Tallandier, 1980.

———. *Discours lors de la cérémonie de remise des insignes de chevalier de l'ordre national du Mérite.* Université de Bordeaux–III, 20 May 1988.

———. "Le Clos de Vougeot dans les années 1860–1872." In *Des vignobles et des vins à travers le monde: Hommage à Alain Huetz de Lemps,* ed. Claude Le Gars and Philippe Roudié, 265–92. Bordeaux: Presses Universitaires de Bordeaux, 1996.

Pirotte, Jean-Claude. *Autres arpents.* Paris: La Table Ronde, 2000.

Pitte, Jean-Robert. *Histoire du paysage français.* 2 vols. Paris: Tallandier, 1983; one-volume edition, 2001.

———. "Un géographe du vouloir humain." Preface to Roger Dion, *Le paysage et la vigne.* Paris: Payot, 1990.

———. "Cultures régionales, culture universelle." *Géographie et Cultures* 14 (Summer 1995): 3–8.

———. "Pour en finir avec le pseudo-terroir: Les vrais facteurs de la qualité du vin." In *Pratiques anciennes et genèse paysages: Mélanges de géographie historique à la mémoire du Professeur Jean Peltre,* ed. André Humbert, 195–212. Nancy: Centre d'études et de recherche sur les paysages, University of Nancy II, 1997.

———. "Origine et géographie des formes de bouteilles de vin en France." In *Mondes contemporains. Les entreprises et leurs réseaux: Hommes, capitaux, techniques et pouvoirs, XIXe–XXe siècle. Mélanges en l'honneur de François Caron,* ed. Michèle Merger and Dominique Barjot, 793–807. Paris: Presses de l'Université de Paris–Sorbonne, 1998.

———. "À propos du terroir." *Annales de géographie* 605 (January–February 1999): 86–89.

———. "La nouvelle planète des vins." *Annales de géographie* 614/615 (July–October 2000): 340–44.

———. "Le vin de Bordeaux est-il protestant?" *L'Amateur de Bordeaux* 71 (December 2000): 44–50.

———. "Les espaces de la bonne chère à Paris à la fin du XVIIIe siècle." In *Place, Culture, and Identity: Essays in Historical Geography in Honor of Alan R. H. Baker,* ed. Iain S. Black and Robin A. Butlin, 132–42. Québec: Presses de l'Université Laval, 2001.

———. *French Gastronomy: History and Geography of a Passion.* Trans. Jody Gladding. New York: Columbia University Press, 2002.

Planhol, Xavier de. *L'eau de neige. Le tiède et le frais: Histoire et géographie des boissons fraîches.* Paris: Fayard, 1995.

Pomerol, Charles, ed. *Terroirs et vins de France: Itinéraires oenologiques et géologiques.* Orléans: Éditions du BRGM, and Paris: Total, 1984.

Ponchon, Raoul. *La muse au cabaret.* Paris: Charpentier, 1920.

———. *La muse gaillarde.* Paris: Fasquelle, n.d.

Prieur, Martin. "Vendanges précoces: Alerte en Bourgogne." *Énergies* 3 (February 2004): 12–14.

Puisais, Jacques, et al. *Précis d'initiation à la dégustation.* Paris: Institut Technique du Vin, 1969.

Querre, Daniel. *Éloge de Michel de Montaigne prononcé à l'Académie des Gastronomes* (9 May 1966). Privately printed in Mâcon, 1967.

Rabaudy, Nicolas de. "Sociando-mallet vainqueur de 132 châteaux." *Le Figaro* (22 December 1999): 19.

Réjalot, Michel. "Bordeaux-Champagne: Propriété ou négoce." *Annales de Géographie* 614/615 (July–October 2000): 426–43.

———. "Marques ou châteaux: Quel négoce à Bordeaux dans les années 2000?" *Sud-Ouest Européen* 14 (2002): 99–110.

———. "Le modèle viti-vinicole bordelais dans sa filière (1980–2003): Un idéal français dans la tourmente." Ph.D. diss., Université de Bordeaux III, 2003.

Rémy, Pierre-Jean. *Mes grands bordeaux.* Paris: Albin Michel, 1997.

Renvoisé, Guy. *Le monde du vin: Art ou bluff.* 2nd ed. Rodez: Éditions du Rouergue, 1996.

Rézeau, Pierre. *Le dictionnaire des noms de cépages en France: Histoire et étymologie.* Paris: CNRS Éditions, 1997.

Richard, Jean. "Aspects historiques de l'évolution du vignoble bourguignon." In *Géographie historiques des vignobles,* ed. Alain Huetz de Lemps, 1: 187–96. Bordeaux: CNRS Éditions, 1978.

———. "Le vignoble et les vins de Bourgogne au Moyen Âge: Un état de la recherche." *Annales de Bourgogne* 73 (2001): 9–117.

Rigaux, Jacky. *Ode aux grands vins de Bourgogne: Henri Jayer, vigneron à Vosne-Romanée.* Précy-sur-Thil: Éditions de l'Armançon, 1997.

Rigaux, Jacky, and Christian Bon, eds. *Les nouveaux vignerons: Le réveil des terroirs.* N.p.: Éditions de Bourgogne, 2002.

Rodier, Camille. *Le vin de Bourgogne.* Dijon: Damidot, 1920.

———. *Le Clos de Vougeot.* Dijon: L. Venot, 1949.

Rothschild, Edmond de. *Le culte de vin.* Paris: Gallimard, 1997.

Roudié, Philippe. *Le vignoble bordelais.* Toulouse: Privat, 1973.

———. "La mystérieuse bordelaise." *L'Amateur de Bordeaux* (August 1984): 9–11.

———. *Vignobles et vignerons du bordelais (1850–1980).* 2nd ed. Bordeaux: Presses Universitaires de Bordeaux, 1994.

———. "Le vignoble au présent." In *Bordeaux, vignoble millénaire,* ed. Gérard Aubin et al., 163–208. Bordeaux: L'Horizon Chimérique, 1996.

———. "'Bordeaux,' un modèle pour la viti-viniculture mondiale." *Cahiers d'Outre-Mer* 50 (October–December 1997): 403–22.

———. "Vous avez dit 'château'? Essai sur le succès sémantique d'un modèle viticole venu du Bordelais." *Annales de Géographie* 614/615 (July–October 2000): 415–25.

———. "'Bel Air' ou 'Bellevue,' 'Latour' ou 'Beauséjour'? Quels noms pour les 'châteaux' du Bordelais et de Bergeracois?" In *Le vin à travers les âges: Produit de qualité, agent économique,* ed. Centre d'Études et de Recherches Institutionnelles Régionales, 61–78. Bordeaux: Féret, 2001.

Roupnel, Gaston. *Nono.* Paris: Plon, 1910.

———. *Histoire de la campagne française.* Paris: Grasset, 1932.

Rousseau, Hervé. "S'offrir un vignoble." *Le Figaro Patrimoine* (8 June 2001): 26–27.

Royer, Claude. *Les vignerons: Usages et mentalités des pays de vignobles.* Paris: Berger-Levrault, 1980.

Sadrin, Paul, and Anny Sadrin. *Mersault.* Bassillac: Jacques Legrand, 1994.

La Saint-Vincent tournante. Nuits-Saint-Georges: Éditions du Tastevin, 1999.

Salomon, Jean-Noël. "L''effet terroir': Facteurs naturels et vin." *Travaux du Laboratoire de géographie physique appliquée* 17 (February 1999): 25–35.

Schirmer, Raphaël. "Le regard des géographes français sur la vigne et le vin." *Annales de Géographie* 614/615 (July–October 2000): 345–63.

Schwartz, Ylan. *Le vin et sa musique: Harmonies bordelaises.* Bordeaux: Art et Arts, 1998.

Scize, Pierre. "Le vin de Bourgogne." *Le Crapouillot* (August 1931): 13–17.

Sivignon, Josette. *Cîteaux, nature sauvage, nature maîtrisée.* Nuits-Saint-Georges: Musée Municipal, 1998.

Sollers, Philippe. "Je suis né dans le vin." In *La correspondance du vin,* 199–209. Paris: Guitardes, 1981.

Strang, Paul. *Vins du Sud-Ouest.* Rodez: Éditions du Rouergue, 1997.

Tainturier, Abbé. *Remarques sur la culture des vignes de Beaune et lieux circon-voisins.* Ed. Loïc Abric. Précy-sous-Thil: Éditions de l'Armançon, 2000; first published in 1763.

Tchernia, André, and Jean-Pierre Brun. *Le vin romain antique.* Grenoble: Glénat, 1999.

Ters, Didier. *Haut-Médoc.* Paris: Jacques Legrand, 1987.

———. *Moulis Listrac.* Paris: Jacques Legrand, 1987.

———. "Le retour à la terre." *Sud-Ouest* (21 January 2003).

This, Hervé. *Molecular Gastronomy: Exploring the Science of Flavor.* Trans. M. B. DeBevoise. New York: Columbia University Press, 2006.

Tupinier, Christophe. "Rendements et qualités: À l'épreuve du temps." *Bourgogne aujourd'hui* 33 (April–May 2000): 52–55.

Unwin, Tim. *Wine and the Vine: A Historical Geography of Viticulture and the Wine Trade.* London: Routledge, 1991.

———. "The Viticultural Geography of France in the 17th Century According to John Locke." *Annales de Géographie* 614/615 (July–October 2000): 395–414.

Vallery-Radot, Maurice. *Vigne et vin, composantes d'une civilisation.* Paris: Office Internationale de la Vigne et du Vin, 1989.

Vincenot, Henri. "Propos d'amour." In *La correspondance du vin,* 178–84. Paris: Guitardes, 1981.

Vins et vignobles de France. Paris: Larousse, 2001.

Waldin, Monty. "Life Is Sweet in Bordeaux: It's Time We Stopped Swallowing the Hype of These Over-sugared Wines." *Harper's* (8 June 2001): 16.

Weber, Charles, and Jean-Paul Griffoulière. *Guide officiel du Bordelais bon chic: 1er traité d'ethnographie mondaine.* Versailles: PMO Éditions, 1987.

Whalen, Philip. *Gaston Roupnel: Âme paysanne et sciences humaines.* Dijon: Éditions Universitaires de Dijon, 2001.

INDEX

Text:	11/15 Granjon
Display:	Trade Gothic
Compositor:	BookMatters
Printer and Binder:	Thomson-Shore, Inc.